By Bruce Catton

Waiting for the Morning Train

Prefaces to History

Grant Takes Command

The Centennial History of the Civil War
Coming Fury
Terrible Swift Sword
Never Call Retreat

Grant Moves South

American Heritage Picture History of the Civil War (narrative)

America Goes to War

This Hallowed Ground

Banners at Shenandoah (juvenile)

U.S. Grant and the American Military Tradition

The Army of the Potomac: A Trilogy
Mr. Lincoln's Army
Glory Road
A Stillness at Appomattox

The War Lords of Washington

WAITING FOR THE MORNING TRAIN

BRUCE CATTON

Waiting for the Morning Train

AN AMERICAN BOYHOOD

☆

1972

DOUBLEDAY & COMPANY, INC.

GARDEN CITY, NEW YORK

ISBN: 0–385–07460–3
Library of Congress Catalog Card Number 72–76134
First Edition after a Limited Edition of 250 Copies

To George R. Catton

CONTENTS

ILLUSTRATIONS

The Publisher wishes to thank Mary Dawn Earley of American Heritage for her help in gathering and editing the photographs.

WAITING FOR THE MORNING TRAIN

CHAPTER ONE

View from the Frontier

First there was the ice; two miles high, hundreds of miles wide and many centuries deep. It came down from the darkness at the top of the world, and it hung down over the eaves, and our Michigan country lay along the line of the overhang. To be sure, all of the ice was gone. It had melted, they said, ten thousand years ago; but they also pointed out that ten thousand years amounted to no more than a flick of the second hand on the geologic time clock. It was recent; this was the frontier, where you could stand in the present and look out into the past, and when you looked you now and then got an eerie sense that the world had not yet been completed. What had been might be again. There was a hint, at times, when the dead winter wind blew at midnight, that the age of ice might some day return, sliding down the country like a felt eraser over a grade school blackboard, rubbing out all of the sums and sentences that had been so carefully written down; leaving, barely legible, a mocking *quod erat demonstrandum.*

Now and then it was a little confusing. The contrast between the old and the new was too great. There was nothing for the mind to get hold of; what probably had been was hardly more real than what possibly might yet be. We lived less than three hundred miles from Detroit, which seemed to be a door looking into the future, showing unimaginable things; and three hundred miles in the other direction, off into the desolate north country, lay the bleak spine of the upper peninsula of Michigan, a reef of the oldest rocks on earth—pre-Cambrian rocks, laid down before there were any living creatures to be fossilized, rocks dead since the hour of creation. There was no way to comprehend that reef. The geologists said that it was two billion years old, or perhaps three billion—a measure of the age of the earth—and there is no way to digest any such figures. The mind cannot grasp a time span like that. The scientist's book is as far beyond our comprehension as the book of Genesis, which simply asserts that the entire job was done in six days, with a seventh day for rest. Take it either way you please, you wind up with something you have to accept on faith. Real understanding is impossible.

In any case, the north country is very old. It is also very empty. Take a two-hundred-mile tape measure, long enough to span the lower peninsula of Michigan from east to west, and move it northward, broadside on; once you pass Lake Superior your tape strikes nothing at all except primitive wilderness, clusters of stubby firs, tamarack bogs and barren tundra, with the left-over fragments of the old age of ice lying beyond. Take the tape on to the North Pole and go down the far side of the globe; you will be deep in Siberia before you strike anything more than a trading post or a mining camp, or—visible symbol of the age of fear—an outpost of national defense.

It was and is all empty, a land that could not be lived in except by a few understanding stone age tribes, and across its emptiness lies the gray shadow of a profound unease. The ice age, if it comes back, will come from up here; and if that, after all, is a thin chance, a crippling wisdom has reached us in this century; the Enemy may some day come down from the north, aiming at Detroit and Chicago and everything they stand for, including ourselves, bringing fire instead of cold. That is why I can look out of the window in the room where I write and see unobtrusive white domes on the skyline—radar domes, scanning the north country with unsleeping attention. To be sure, we do not give them much thought. Life in Michigan north of the industrial zone is easy and pleasant, with fish to be caught and clear lakes for swimming, lonely streams for canoes and the big lake itself for larger craft; here it is possible to escape from the steamy, overcrowded, overactive middle west and get back to something we knew long ago, when it was good enough just to breathe the clean air and feel sunlight and wind on your shoulders. But the white domes are there, and it is not quite possible to forget what they stand for. This is the frontier, a place for looking before and after, where we try to think what we shall do with the future only to discover that we are conditioned by what we have already done with the past. The frontier! Three quarters of a century have passed since we announced that America's last frontier was gone forever. We were wrong. In spite of ourselves we have moved on into an undiscovered world. We shall always have a frontier, because we are not facing a finite North American continent whose menaces and surprises must some day all be tabulated; we are facing an infinite universe, and the last challenge has yet to be formulated. Possibly we shall encounter it tomorrow morning.

It may be that the Indians knew something.

One of the odd things about this Michigan frontier is that it contained a people who may have been the first metal-users on earth; or, if not the first, among the first, isolated here thousands of miles from anything that would later be described as civilization. In the land on and near the base of the Keweenaw peninsula, which juts out into the cold surf along the southern shore of Lake Superior, there lived a people who made things out of copper—axes, chisels, knives, spear-points, ornaments of all kinds. They started doing this possibly seven thousand years ago—an immensely long time, as human history is measured: before Abraham tended his flocks near Ur of the Chaldees, indeed before Ur so much as existed—and doing it they stood at the very threshold of technological development.

It was fairly simple. They were primitive forest people who had stumbled into an area where there were lumps of pure copper waiting to be picked up and used—not copper ore, but virgin copper, in shining big nuggets. To them, a lump of copper was no doubt just another stone with pleasing characteristics. It could be hammered and ground into shape with less effort, and to far better effect, than the bits of taconite, flint, quartzite and slate they had been using, and the tools and weapons made of it were far more effective than the stone implements they already had. As they went on using it they began to learn things about copper. They found that most of it was embedded in hard quartz; and sooner or later they learned how to extract these lumps of pure metal so that they could take them home and make things out of them. (Dig away the earth and expose the ledge that contains these copper nuggets; build a hot fire on it, then pour cold water on the heated rock so that it cracks. Once it cracks the copper can be gouged out with wooden spuds and stone hammers.) They also learned how to treat the copper so that it would not become brittle under all the hammering and grinding—heat it, plunge it in water, work on it some more, repeat the heat-and-water treatment; these Indians had evolved what a later generation of metallurgists could call annealing.

While they did all of this the earth beneath their feet was still taking shape. The level of what would be known as the Great Lakes (still fresh from the glaciers, in those days) rose and fell in centuries-long rhythm. Some of the copper culture sites went two hundred feet under water, then emerged long after with their charred fire-pits and abandoned stone hammers to draw the attention of prospectors, land-lookers and scientists. The land itself rose, ten feet or more in the course of a century, for generation after generation; there is a theory that the resilient earth was slowly springing back into shape once the over-whelming weight of the ice sheet was removed. As the earth rose it cut off the old outlet of the Great Lakes, at North Bay in Ontario; now the current of the lakes moved down through Lake Erie and broke a way across the Niagara escarpment. And while all of these changes were taking place, the Indians who made things out of copper continued to ply their trade. They had copper mines, and coppersmiths, and some sort of export trade in the finished product, at a time when all the rest of the New World and most of the Old lived deep in the age of chipped flint and polished stone. Clearly these people were right on the edge of entering the age of metals.

It was no long distance away from them. To the extraction of pure metal from conglomerate ores was only one more step; from smelting to casting was only one step beyond that; these steps taken, the Indians would have been well on their way, and what they could do with one metal could presently have been done with another. (Bear in mind that these people were living squarely on top of one of the richest deposits of iron ore on earth.) They had the mental capacity to figure out and to take these steps. No one who has examined the mathematics, the astronomy and the intricate, labyrinthine structures of abstract thought that came later in Central America and Mexico can doubt that the American red man was perfectly well qualified for any sort of advance he might care to make.

The trouble with that kind of advance is that there is no end to it. Development becomes compulsive. It is never possible to call a halt. Once you take the first step you have committed yourself to take the last, some day, even if the last step goes straight off the edge of a precipice. It is fairly easy for man to assert his mastery over his earthly environment, but once he has asserted that mastery he has to go on exercising it no matter where the exercise takes him. The age of applied technology has one terrible aspect—each new technique has to be exploited to its absolute limit, until man becomes the victim of his own skills. The conquest of nature cannot end in a negotiated peace. Invent a simple device like the automobile, to get you from here to there more quickly than you could go without it; before long you are in bondage to it, so that you build your cities and shape your countryside and reorder your entire life in the light of what will be good for the machine instead of what will be good for you. Detroit has shown us how that works.

In any case, these copper-country Indians never took that next step. With one foot on the threshold they paused, then turned away; guided by simple inertia or by an uncanny prescience, whichever you prefer. The use of copper declined, then finally ceased altogether, as the bits of virgin metal became harder to find. The Indians made certain inventions—birchbark canoes, frail craft indeed for the stormy lakes, but so well conceived that when the white man arrived he went on using them for centuries, and still duplicates the flawless pattern in aluminum; and snow-shoes, ingenious devices of rawhide thongs strung on frames of birch and ash, enabling men to travel across country in the drifted wintertime. But with things like these the Indians stopped. They remained in the stone age, with its simplicities, its limited horizons and its strange, chilling mythology, which lay between an uneasy belief in magic and a groping faith (half dark suspicion and half desperate hope) that there are un-seen powers all about, to be fled from or to be appealed to de-pending on the whim of the moment. They took the world as they found it. In the north country they remained hunters and fishermen, now and then trading furs for corn with the tribes farther south; in the lower peninsula, where soil and climate were a bit more favorable, they took to part-time farming, and in winter the men went off on hunting expeditions, and in the spring they tapped the maple trees and made sugar. Life went on without very much change, and the pines and the hardwood forests lay across the lake country like a cool twilight, lived in but not exactly used.

Then at last the men who could use this country began to appear; Frenchmen, who filtered in here about the time when the English were looking at Virginia and Massachusetts. They hoisted the fleur de lys on the ground overlooking the rapids of the St. Marys River while the Sun King was advancing his realm toward bankruptcy by building the palace at Versailles, and they ventured along the shingle and sand of the endless beaches and into the shallow inlets that opened the way into the unknown back country. They were eternally inquisitive, looking for furs to ornament robes and make hats for courtiers, for waterways leading to China (they thought briefly they had found one, when they got to Green Bay on the western side of Lake Michigan; then they thought it lay beyond the next height of land), and as a matter of fact they were looking for something they could not have defined, because this new world promised more than it had yet delivered.

The first of them apparently was a man known as Etienne Brulé, a lieutenant of Samuel de Champlain, and he got up to the Straits of Mackinac and the St. Marys River country before any European ever stepped on Plymouth Rock. He was looking for furs, for new country, for experiences he could not have had in Europe; he found what he sought, he paid for it, and probably it was all worth it. He lived with the Indians in nameless wigwam-towns along Lake Superior, and sometimes he got on well with his hosts and sometimes he waged a one-man war against them. No one is quite sure just what became of him; the legend is that he was killed in some campfire row, and that the Indians who killed him admired his daring so much that they cut out his heart and ate it, hoping to acquire some of his virtues. His story flickers out inconclusively, somewhere between the forest and the biggest of the lakes, and if he was the first European to lose himself and to die of it in the great north country he was far from being the last. One of the things the New World offered to the questing European was a chance to go off into nowhere and disappear, and at one time or another a good many white men have taken advantage of it.

At times it seems as if the country itself resisted the European invasion more effectively than the Indians did, although the Indians were far from passive. Men disappeared in the long forests, and all anyone ever knew about them was that they were gone. There was Father René Menard, for instance, a priest who established a mission on Keweenaw Bay in the year 1660;

he set out one winter's day on a trip into the trackless interior, and that was the last of him, and whether he was killed by suspicious savages or simply by winter starvation is not known. There was also the ship *Griffin,* built a few years after Father Menard's disappearance by the explorer La Salle, who brought shipwrights and sailors to the upper Niagara River, who put together and launched a stout little square-rigger and sailed all the way to Green Bay. He loaded it with furs, enough to finance an ambitious venture into the Mississippi country if he could just get the cargo back to Montreal, and sent it off toward the lower lakes. The *Griffin* never got there, and to this day no one knows what happened to it except that it sailed off into the storms and slipped over the edge of the world—first in a long succession of ships to be lost with all hands on the Great Lakes.

Whether or not they survived to tell about it, the French filtered more and more deeply into the back country; and if some of them had their troubles with the Indians some of them got the Indians to help them. Father Marquette, the saint-like little Jesuit who went the length of Lake Michigan and down into the Illinois country for the greater glory of God, had Indian helpers, and when he fell mortally ill on his way back toward Michilimackinac, where Lake Michigan meets Lake Huron, it was his Indian helpers who made his last moments easy, buried him on a sandy promontory, put up a cross to mark his grave, and then slipped away northward to bear news of his passing. Later on they returned to collect his bones and take them back to the straits for Christian burial. (The towns of Ludington and Frankfort today have heated argument about the site of his death. One marker identifies the place at the entrance to the Ludington harbor and another marker makes similar identification at the entrance to the Frankfort harbor, and learned expositions support each claim.) Obviously, not all of the Indians were hostile; in a noncommittal way, some of them were quite friendly.

These Michigan Indians after all were not exactly like the tribes farther east. They lacked the incredible, breath-taking ferocity of the Iroquois, for instance; and although as primitive men they carried their passions near the surface, and were fully capable of putting captured enemies into the fire if the mood possessed them, they never quite made a hideous ritual out of it in the Iroquois manner, deriving ecstasies from the infliction of pain and going to fantastic lengths to prolong the victims' suffering so that the general orgy that followed the final gasp might have maximum dimensions. They were tough enough, to be sure. The Chippewas actually muscled the Sioux tribes out of the western Lake Superior country, and under the Ottawa chief Pontiac various associated tribes nearly drove the British out of the whole Great Lakes area, destroying the forts at St. Joseph and Michilimackinac and laying a long siege to the fort at Detroit. Later on, when the Americans fought the British for possession of the lakes country, the Indians fought effectively on the British side, overwhelming the outpost at Chicago and slaughtering its garrison, and committing a famous massacre of prisoners along the River Raisin, in southeastern Michigan. Anyone who fought these Indians knew that he had been in a war.

Yet the memory of terror, the ever-present dread of the sudden blow in the darkness—the blend of fear and hatred that led otherwise well-intentioned Christian men to believe that the God of love would be pleased if all Indians were exterminated outright—never became part of the Michigan heritage. The American settlers dispossessed the tribesman as completely here as anywhere else, but they did not slaughter him while they were doing it. They did not have to; they were not afraid of him, and if the red man was there to be trodden on he did not have to be kicked first.

Probably there were two reasons for this. To begin with, white settlement came mostly after the Indians' power had been broken. There were few white man's towns or farms until Pontiac and the baleful Chief Tecumseh had been beaten, and hardly any of the men who made productive clearings in the wilderness ever had to worry about people who might come at them out of the woods with scalping knives and fire arrows. The long haunted years known to the settlers in Massachusetts and Virginia were not duplicated here. The wars were over.

Even more important was the fact that here the white man reduced the Indian to impotence simply by touching him. The newcomers corrupted him, not by intent but just by living beside him. Indian society began to come unraveled not long after Étienne Brulé went to whatever fate he finally got, and it kept on unraveling until it fell completely apart. Exposure to the complexities of European civilization was too much for it. The red man had to adjust every aspect of his life to a scale of values he could neither understand nor control, and it was too much for him. He could not make the adjustment, and he could not conceivably keep from trying to make it.

This was so because the white men offered, for a price, material goods which the Indian had to have—things like knives and hatchets made of steel in place of implements of chipped stone; brass kettles in place of birchbark buckets; needles and fishhooks and awls made of metal instead of splintered bone; woolen cloth for blankets and clothing instead of crudely dressed skins or mats woven of pounded bark fibers; guns and bullets and gunpowder to replace bows and arrows. Along with these riches, offering life a dimension primitive man had not dreamed of before, there were brandy and rum, strengthened by abominable additives until they almost reached the level of outright poison, which passed into common speech under the accurately descriptive name of firewater. No power on earth could keep the Indian from trying to get these things once he got acquainted with them, and he was willing to pay any price that might be demanded.

The demanded price, of course, consisted of furs. The Indian set out to get the furs, and that was what turned his life upside down. He became a hired hand for the invaders, and so passed from his own society into theirs, before he knew that anything was happening to him; he was the market for the factories of England and France, and at the same time he was the source of supply for an industry that reached from the uncombed trader at Michilimackinac to the richest shops in London and Paris, with a vast network of warehouses and middlemen and cargo vessels lying between. Stone age man abruptly found himself part of an infinitely complex society which he could not hope to comprehend. What men made or bought and sold on the far side of an ocean he had never seen laid down the conditions of his existence. Over many centuries he had adjusted himself to the mysterious wilderness where he lived, and suddenly the ways of life and the habits of mind that came out of that adjustment meant nothing at all. Without wanting it to happen he had become part of a culture which had no more than a temporary marginal place for men like him, and there was no way on earth for him to get out of it.

For several generations the process was gradual, almost imperceptible, and it was fairly painless. The seasons came and went as they always had, the canoe brigades came and went with dripping paddles and red-sashed voyageurs, and the Indian went up the rivers and into the forests to exercise his skills, so on the surface nothing much had changed; yet there was some premonition of disaster, or men like Pontiac and Tecumseh could never have persuaded the tribes to take to the warpath. The warpath was followed and it led to utter defeat, and shortly after this several things happened, the sum of them meaning outright catastrophe. The Michigan country became trapped out, so that the furs that were the price of life became harder and harder to get. At the same time the fashions that dictated the scope and speed of the fur trade began to change. At the moment when beaver and marten pelts became ruinously scarce they became worth less and less, and the Indian was pauperized through no fault of his own. When white men took the trouble to offer advice they told the Indian that he must take up the white man's way—that is, he must work for wages at whatever

jobs might be available, or he must become a farmer and produce crops for a market which was erratic and as mysterious as
the market for furs.

Not many jobs were available at that moment in the land of
the Great Lakes, and there was little in the red man's background
to fit him for any of them. He could become a hanger-on around
the docks of the new seaports, helping to load cordwood on
steamboats, or he could do odd jobs here and there—for a store-
keeper, perhaps, or a mill-owner, or someone similar—but such
work was scanty and seasonal and there was nothing in the
Indian's frame of reference to give it any meaning. Farming
was not much better. The Indian knew how to cultivate the
garden plot that provided him with corn and beans and squash
to supplement his diet of fish and game, but raising crops for
the market was something else again. Most of the country he
was supposed to farm was covered with trees, and when the trees
were removed it developed that this timber country offered some
of the poorest farming land in North America, as white farmers
learned to their cost a little later.

So there was little for the Indian to do except go to seed,
which mostly he did with bewildered resignation. He had solved
the problem of life in the wilderness, which is to say that he
had worked out a culture that enabled him to keep his self-respect
and put him in rough harmony with the world he lived in. Now
life presented him with problems that were not only beyond
solution; they were problems he could not even understand.

At this point the white man stepped up the pace. What he
proposed to conquer was not the Indian but the wilderness. He
was attacking the earth itself, and his only real concern with
the Indian was to keep him from being an obstacle. To be sure,
by the second decade of the nineteenth century the Indian in
the Michigan country was dying on the vine, but the Americans
who had designs on the land had intricate laws concerning the
land and its use and these laws required the composition and
registration of numerous pieces of paper. Land titles, in short,

had to be cleared. The Indian had never heard of such things, but according to the white man's law the red man held the title to all of this land and he had to be persuaded to surrender it. And in the years just before and shortly after 1820 a man named Lewis Cass took care of that.

Cass was one of the notables of the early middle west. He was governor of Michigan territory in the days before statehood. Later he became a member of the United States Senate, still later he was an unsuccessful Presidential candidate against Zachary Taylor, and he served finally as Secretary of State in the cabinet of James Buchanan, eyeing with stony disapproval the convolutions of Buchanan's course at the time when the rising issue of slavery was being so clumsily evaded; resigning, at last, a few months before the Buchanan administration ingloriously ceased to be. One of Cass's minor misfortunes was that the art of photography did not develop until he was well on in years; the portrait by which he is remembered was taken when he was old, and it shows an unhappy face with sagging cheeks and eye pouches and a twisted mouth, the eyes having the look of a man who finds the world gone out of proper alignment. In his younger days he had a quality which the photographer came along too late to catch.

Anyway, in 1820 Cass led a small flotilla of canoes up from Detroit, cruising along the western shore of Lake Huron, going on up the St. Marys River as far as the rapids, portaging over the height of land to Lake Superior, following the dangerous south shore all the way to the western tip of the lake, going overland by difficult portages to the headwaters of the Mississippi, descending that stream to the outpost of Prairie du Chien and coming back across what is now Wisconsin to Green Bay. After a brief pause there for reorganization Cass went down Lake Michigan to Chicago, then an inconsiderable military station and trading post, from which point he made his way cross-country to Detroit, while the flotilla went up along the east shore of the lake to Mackinac and came down Lake Huron by the same route it had used on the way out. All in all, Cass and his men had made quite a trip—four thousand miles or more, up and back, one of the great feats of exploration in American history, done competently and without fanfare under conditions of hardship and peril.

Hardship and peril in full measure, certainly. Traveling the Great Lakes by birch-bark canoe was risky business. The canoes that carried men and supplies were exceedingly frail and would inevitably be twisted into fragments if they were caught in rough water. Inasmuch as the lakes can be as vicious as the North Atlantic when the winds come up, this meant that the expedition had to stay close to the shore all the way, running into the beach and hauling the canoes up beyond reach of the surf whenever the breezes stiffened. To make a traverse across the mouth of an open place like Saginaw Bay, or to cruise along the pictured rocks in Lake Superior with no shelving beach anywhere near, was to risk the lives of every man in the party. Repeatedly they had to camp for two or three days at a time waiting for better weather. Every mile of the way Cass and his men had to carry the certain knowledge that in case of disaster there was no help anywhere within reach. They were on their own.

But there seem to have been compensations: chiefly, a sense of wonder, because this unstained new country spoke a compelling language of its own, which could neither be wholly understood nor in any way ignored. It spoke of darkness and remembered ice, of everlasting winter and a malignant frozen hostility; yet it suggested that winter might not be the last word after all. Here and there, in the configuration of the silent land rising above the blue water, the long bluffs crowned with green unbroken forest, there was the voice of a different spirit.

Go up along the eastern side of Lake Michigan, steer northeast when the land bends away at Point Betsie, and you come before long to Sleeping Bear Point—an incredible flat-topped sand dune rising five hundred feet above the level of the lake and going north for two miles or more. It looks out over the dark water and the islands that lie just offshore, and in the late afternoon the sunlight strikes it and the golden sand turns white, with a pink overlay when the light is just so, and little cloud shadows slide along its face, blue-gray as evening sets in. Sleeping Bear looks eternal, although it is not; this lake took its present shape no more than two or three thousand years ago, and Sleeping Bear is slowly drifting off to the east as the wind shifts its grains of sand, swirling them up one side and dropping them on the other; in a few centuries it will be very different, if indeed it is there at all. Yet if this is a reminder that this part of the earth is still being remodeled it is also a hint that the spirit back of the remodeling may be worth knowing. In the way this shining dune looks west toward the storms and the sunsets there is a profound serenity, an unworried affirmation that comes from seeing beyond time and mischance. A woman I know says that to look at the Sleeping Bear late in the day is to feel the same emotion that comes when you listen to Beethoven's Emperor Concerto, and she is entirely right. The message is the same. The only trouble is that you have to compose a planet, or great music, to say it persuasively. Maybe man—some men, anyway—was made in the image of God, after all.

The men of the Cass expedition, of course, were no mystics, but hardheads who had gone out to count and measure, and to those tasks they devoted themselves. Even so, young Henry Rowe Schoolcraft seems to have been touched. Schoolcraft went along as a mineralogist, tapping stones with a hammer and collecting fragments for the Secretary of War, and when he wrote his famous narrative telling what had been seen and done he was wholly matter-of-fact; too much so, for he had an epic to write and he composed a War Department report. Yet he seems to have been smitten, somewhere along the way, by a deep feeling for the Indians who lived in this land, and later on he became an Indian agent, established himself at Sault Ste. Marie, and spent most of his time collecting Indian legends and the word-of-mouth tales that passed for Indian history. He got a huge tangle of them, and the poet Longfellow eventually read what Schoolcraft wrote down and out of it made the poem *Hiawatha*. This may have been no favor for generations of school children, who had to read it when they would have preferred to be doing something else, but in a way it was one of the by-products of the Odyssey of Lewis Cass.

The men Cass led never lost sight of the fact that their trip into this unknown country would eventually be the means of its transformation. Sooner or later these men in their canoes were going to pull many men after them, and they were well aware of it. The wilderness was to be conquered; this particular bit of earth, craggy and hungry as it might seem, was about to be re-shaped, and when the budding scientists in the party made their notes about soils and rocks and plants and temperatures they were thinking of people who some day would come here to make homes. These later-comers would need to know how to use this country.

That was where the emphasis lay. This country was going to be used; and if this was the case it was above all things necessary to know about the Indians. Were the British authorities in west-ern Canada in fact inciting them to resist the venturesome Amer-icans—present at that time mostly as fur traders—and if so how could this be stopped? How many military posts, situated pre-cisely where, would be needed to control the red man and thwart the scheming Briton? Finally, how much effort would it take to induce the red man to surrender the title to his homeland?

That the Indian's way of life was doomed had been recognized from the start. President James Monroe had spoken on the sub-ject in a recent message to Congress.

"Independent savage communities," he said, "cannot long exist within the limits of a civilized population . . . To civilize them, and even to prevent their extinction, it seems to be in-dispensable that their independence as communities should cease and that the control of the United States over them should be complete and undisputed."

The Secretary of War, John C. Calhoun, who took a much more relaxed view of the proper scope of the authority of the Federal government in 1820 than he could take a few years later, had given Cass instructions stressing the importance of working on the Indians so that they would give up their lands to the whites. Calhoun pointed out that speedy settlement of the lower peninsula of Michigan was both inevitable and desirable, and he emphasized the obvious: "This can best be effected by an entire extinguishment of the Indian title."

Entire extinguishment was attained without delay. Cass had already persuaded the Indians to give up their claim to land around Saginaw Bay. On this trip westward he got title to land on the American side of the St. Marys rapids, and Fort Brady was before long built at Sault Ste. Marie; gifts, oratory, and a subtle reminder that the Americans held all of the high cards seemed to be all that was needed, and in the years that followed Cass's trip more cessions of title were painlessly negotiated. By 1840, or thereabouts, the Indians had given away the entire state of Michigan. Their independence as communities had ceased, as President Monroe said it should; the Indian's fate was settled, and the wilderness was doomed, windy pinewoods, veins of copper-bearing quartz, mountains of iron ore and all.

As far as the Indian was concerned the process was relatively humane. A few red men were transplanted bodily to new reservations in the unsettled west, but mostly the Michigan Indians stayed where they were, groping helplessly to grasp the white man's way, losing their old culture and finding the new culture hard to assimilate. There were schools and missions, here and there, to help them, and annual payments from the Federal government, and by and large the business was done without the ugly brutality that was observed in so many other parts of America. After all, these had mostly been friendly Indians.

To be sure, they paid a price. There is a story, probably apoch-ryphal but significant none the less, about a United States Sena-tor who was running for re-election a few years ago. According to this story, the Senator got to a small north country town one evening to make a campaign speech, and just before he was led into the hall where the speech was to be delivered the local party chairman gave him a briefing about the issues that were on peo-ple's minds locally.

"You'll notice, at the back of the hall, quite a few Indians," he said. "It would be helpful if somewhere in your speech you could say that you are fully aware of their problem and that you will do your best to solve it."

The Senator promised that he would do this. Then—moved by simple curiosity—he asked: "By the way, what is their problem?"

The local man looked at him wide-eyed.

"What's their problem?" he repeated. "God damn it, they're *Indians!*"

Yet the Indian was incidental. It was the earth and the fullness thereof that mattered. It passed into American hands just as the tools to exploit it were being perfected—the tools and the driving urge to use them—and the men who held the tools moved in as if they had to get the job finished before nightfall. They suc-ceeded (at any rate, recognizable nightfall has not yet come) and in about a century the job was done. The trees had gone to build homes for half of America, the copper had gone to serve the new age of electricity, and if the iron lasted longer it had been moved south by millions of tons, in a progress as inexorable as the Sleeping Bear's ponderous drift to the eastward, to make railroads and machinery and skyscrapers and weapons; and the land was left bruised and scarred, with the radar domes to indi-cate that the age of applied technologies advances by geometrical progression.

So we live as the Indians of Lewis Cass's time lived, between cultures, compelled to readjust ourselves to forces that will not wait for us. There is no twentieth-century culture; the twentieth century is simply a time of transition, and the noise of things collapsing is so loud that we are taking the prodigious step from the nineteenth century to the twenty-first without a moment of calm in which we can see where we are going. Between nineteenth century and twenty-first there is a gulf as vast as the one the stone-age Indians had to cross. What's our problem? We're Indians.

CHAPTER TWO

Our Town

According to the Bible, a city that is set upon a hill cannot be hid. We used to repeat that text often, and I suppose we were a bit smug and self-righteous about it; our city was built upon a hill, and if it was visible to all men it had been meant from the first to be a sign and a symbol of a better way of life, an outpost of the New Jerusalem sited in backwoods vacancy to show people the way they ought to go. To be sure, it was not exactly a city. It was in fact the tiniest of country villages, containing probably no more than three hundred and fifty inhabitants, and it has grown no larger to this day. And the hill on which it was built was not really much of a hill. It was a small flat plateau rising less than two hundred feet above the surrounding country, with a placid lake to the north, a narrow valley containing an insignificant creek to the east, and gentle slopes coming up from a broad river valley to the west and south. It was not impressive to look at, although it commanded some pleasant views and it was high enough to get a cooling breeze on all but the hottest summer days.

The name of this town was Benzonia, and when we tried to tell strangers about it we usually had trouble because most people refused to believe that there was any such word. Like the town itself, the name had been self-consciously contrived. The story we were always told—and as far as I know it was perfectly true—had it that this name was a Greek-Latin hybrid put together by learned men who wanted a word that would mean "good air." That was fair enough. The air was good there, and there was no harm in saying so. But most people seemed to think that the word was a corruption of something the Pottawattomi Indians or the French traders had left behind them. When Americans founded towns here they usually gave them plain names, like Thompsonville, or Arcadia, or Empire.

Names had a way of getting twisted out of shape. The most striking example in the entire state, probably, was a rocky islet in northern Lake Michigan which the French had named Île aux Galets; after a couple of decades of American occupation it became Skillagalee, and it has remained that way ever since. The river that flowed past our town on the south and west the French had named La Rivière aux Bec Scies, in honor of the sawbill duck, or merganser, which was plentiful there in the early days. But forty miles up country the river came out of a pleasant little lake which had been named Betsey's Lake by its first white settler, Betsey of course being his wife. So it was Betsey's River at one end, and Aux Bec Scies at the other, and before many years Betsey won out, even though somebody did change the spelling of her name. It is the Betsie River today, and the original mergansers are long gone and long forgotten. Something like that might have happened to Benzonia.

The town had been founded as an act of faith. In a two-hundred-mile radius it was probably the only town that had not been established by men who wanted to cash in on the lumber boom. All around the state the little settlements were springing up, and the reason for their existence was always the same—cut the pine trees down, float the logs down the rivers, put a sawmill at the river mouth to turn the logs into boards, load the boards on schooners or sway-backed steamboats, ship them off to Chicago or to Buffalo, and keep it up as long as the timber lasted. Once the trees are gone, dismantle the mills and move on, and if some of the people cannot get away they may stay on and try hardscrabble farming among the stumps. Life in lumber towns had an active present but no future to speak of. The lumber town was much like the mining camp. It was not going anywhere.

But our town was different. It was put there by men who believed that there was going to be a future, and who built for it. When they looked about them they saw people instead of trees; what was going on, as far as they were concerned, was not so much the reduction of pine logs to sawn timber as the foundation of a human society. They believed in the competence and benevolent intent of Divine Providence, and with certain reservations they had faith in the men through whom the purpose of Providence was to be worked out. We were all put on earth to serve that purpose; therefore it was all-important to show everyone what that purpose was and how it could best be served. People had to be educated. They needed a light for their feet, and the light could come only from a Christian education. Benzonia was founded by people who thought that the fringe of a boundless forest was just the place to start a college. A college town it was, from the beginning, laid out and built at a time when the entire county in which it was situated contained no more than five hundred inhabitants.

This happened in 1858, and the nation was unconsciously nerving itself for the first of the prodigious shocks the next hundred years were to bring, the American Civil War. The founding fathers were men from Oberlin College. They brought with them Oberlin's characteristic discontent with the things that are and its impassioned belief in the things that some day will be. They also had another trait instilled at Oberlin—a conviction that faith without works is of small account. Their faith was in the revealed religion as expounded by the Congregational Church, although they suspected that the revelation might be modified here and there by godly men who took prayerful thought, and by this faith they wholeheartedly lived.

So they founded the town of Benzonia, shaving the hilltop of its surviving trees and making a plat of streets and building lots. It took time to do all of this, but in five years a good start had been made, the clearing was dotted with new homes, and in 1863 the new college opened its doors and went into operation: Grand Traverse College, newest and tiniest of the educational institutions of a struggling new state.

To say that Grand Traverse College opened its doors is to speak figuratively, for at that moment the college had no doors. It had no building of any kind, had in fact nothing but high hopes and pious determination, and its first classes were held in the living room of somebody's home, with the students boarding around in the homes of other villagers. There were thirteen students when the college went into operation, and the entire community was responsible for them. Under the articles drawn up by the associated settlers, the town was to be "a temperance, anti-slavery, educational Christian community"; the college was to be open "to both sexes, without distinction of color," and the townspeople were pledged to give all possible help to students who had no money and needed to support themselves by manual labor. Each settler was bound to give the college a fourth of his land to provide an endowment fund.

Thus the assets of the college were small, because the cash value of cut-over timber land in that part of Michigan just then was not large. If this college was to accomplish anything at all the faith of the men who founded it had to be translated somehow into works. Much would depend on the spirit that moved in the breasts of the men who had brought town and college into being.

These men were intensely logical. They believed in the perfectibility of human society, and a man who held that belief must of course do what he could to bring perfection about. It was not enough to exhort people to lead a better life; you had to lead a better life yourself, and do it in such a way that all men would see it. If society was to lift itself by its bootstraps, your place to begin was with your own bootstraps. Life in a community dedicated to this belief is apt to be rather special, and it was so in our town. Growing up in Benzonia was just a bit like growing up with the Twelve Apostles for next-door neighbors. You never could forget what you were here for.

In a way this was uncomfortable. To meet the nagging problems of this world while you are thinking about the requirements of the next one does not always come easily; nor does constant preoccupation with such matters make you popular with your neighbors. Benzonia was not well liked by the rest of the county. We were suspected of thinking ourselves better than other folk, and of having standards that were too high for any earthly use, and probably there was something in the charge. I remember one time a baseball team from a nearby town came over to play our team. Our team was badly beaten, and afterward I watched a wagonload of out-of-town fans start off on the homeward trip. These people were jubilant, and a woman sitting beside the driver called out gaily: "We came here to see Benzony get trimmed, and by Jolly they *did* get trimmed." This was bad to hear. There was malice in it; furthermore, the woman had said "by Jolly," which was simply a thin disguise for "by Golly." No one knew just what "Golly" was a euphemism for, but it clearly was some sort of profanity, and no woman in Benzonia would have used the word. It appeared that the children of darkness had triumphed over the sons of light.

For our part, we returned the favor. We were, I suppose, annoyingly conscious that we were the sons of light, and now and then we were disturbed because the children of darkness seemed to be in the majority. I remember once when there was some sort of county election: local option, I suppose, in which the voters were asked to say whether the sale of alcoholic liquors should be prohibited. Benzonia supported the measure, but most of the rest of the county opposed it, and in the election Benzonia was roundly beaten. A few days afterward a citizen met my father on the street and asked him how he felt about the way the election had gone.

"I feel like Lazarus," said Father.

Like Lazarus?

"Like Lazarus," Father repeated. "According to the Bible, Lazarus was licked by dogs."

So much for the opposition.

So there was an especial flavor to life in our town, and it remained at full strength for generations. Probably this was inevitable, inasmuch as we felt that the eye of God was constantly upon us. The knowledge that the God of the Old Testament was watching every act and recording every word was sobering, and it could lead an impressionable child (or an impressionable adult, for that matter) to strange thoughts. A few of my own memories may as well be cited.

I had, for instance, read a scriptural text saying that a man who took the Lord's name in vain could not be held guiltless. This probably was the one unforgivable sin, hinted at elsewhere in the Bible, and when I heard a man say "God damn it!"—which could be heard, now and than, even in Benzonia—I suffered acutely. The blasphemer, as it seemed to me, was almost certainly condemning himself to hell, without hope of pardon, and it was not pleasant to think about this.

Yet life in our town was not altogether grim. The God whose unquestioned reality obsessed us had a softer aspect. He could be friendly and helpful, and no problem was too small to be taken to Him. Looked at largely, the promises outweighed the threats. The world around us might be hostile but we did not feel lost in it. The story was going to have a happy ending if we had the wit to reach out and grasp it. This was not just something we took on faith; in one way or another most of us had had experiences that seemed persuasive. In a wholly fantastic way I had had one myself, long before I was out of knee breeches, and as the years passed the memory of it first sustained me, then baffled me and finally faded out into a haunting daydream. (It occurs to me that a modern generation may need explanation of the expression "before I was out of knee breeches." Early in this century no boy put on long pants until he was fully adolescent. The change was one of the momentous tidemarks of life, and to say that a thing happened while the boy wore knee breeches was to say that it happened while he was still a child.)

What happened was that at the age of nine I got religion.

To be sure, I had been a true believer from the cradle. But no one inherited his faith, in our town; abundant testimony showed that God entered your heart only at your own express invitation. The experience was said to be unmistakable, and the true life of the spirit began then and then only. I had not been baptized as a baby, because my parents felt that this sacrament should not be celebrated until the child was old enough to know what was happening. At nine, then, I was ready to be saved.

I had been attending church and Sunday School regularly—everybody did, in our town—and I knew all the texts. I had also heard much about the wonderful peace and happiness that came into one's life when the first great religious experience was met and embraced. One gave up sin, which was easy to do when God was in your heart, and thenceforward one lived a good life without conscious effort. As it happened I had not been committing any sins, because some things are beyond the range of a small child, and my conscience was fairly clear; I had nothing to give up. However, I did have an abiding problem. It was my daily task to fill the woodbox by the kitchen stove and to keep it full, and although this was the mildest of chores it was a pesky nuisance; that woodbox always seemed to need filling when I most wanted to do something else, and the ancient Israelites who complained bitterly because they had to make bricks without straw were my blood brothers. As it happened, my impatience with this job of work came to a head just when the desire to be saved was overtaking me, and the two got linked together in my mind. It did seem that a boy in a state of grace would be able to do his work cheerfully and without repining. At last I did what the adults of that time and place did when the cares of this world looked too big: I took it to the Lord in prayer. One night I knelt by the bedside and invited the Living Presence to enter my soul, with a rider to the effect that I would like some help with the woodbox. (The ardent prayers of a devout nine-year-old must have long echoes somewhere.) Then, with a load off of my mind, I went to sleep.

What happened next was odd, although it did not seem odd to me at the time. I awoke, next morning, with a lightness of heart that I had not known before. Quite simply, I was totally happy. When I had dressed I went to the kitchen and found the woodbox empty, as I had known it would be. Off to the woodshed I hurried, to get a huge armload of split sticks and carry them to the box; then back to the wood shed for another load, until the hated box was full to the top. This was no abominable chore; if it was not exactly fun it was at least marvelously easy. During the rest of the day I kept checking on that box, and when I found the stock running low I trotted brightly off and got some more. Never was there such a filler of woodboxes.

During the next few days I told my parents that a great awakening had come to me. I did not mention the woodbox; that was a special arrangement that did not need to be talked about, and although I was deeply convinced that an unseen hand was helping me I did not want to describe it to anyone. In any case it was arranged that I should be baptized. Baptism took place in due time and I was admitted to membership in the church. I was perhaps a bit young for it, but as far as I could see I had had a religious experience as good as the best. I was saved, if I could just make it stick.

One more recollection, even though it does not concern me personally . . . Our minister was an entirely lovable little man named Harlow S. Mills. A widower, he lived with his widowed sister, Mrs. McConnaughey, who was as gentle and as lovable as he was; and I remember hearing her tell my mother about her experience with a thimble. She had been busy with her housework, one day, and had reached the point where she had to do some mending, and find her thimble she could not; she looked high and low, but it was nowhere. So, in desperation, she bowed her head and uttered a short prayer: Would the Lord please guide her to that thimble? Opening her eyes, she knew at once where to look—back of a curtain, on a window ledge in the dining room. She went and looked, and there of course was the thimble. She took it and got her mending done, duly grateful for the favor done by Omnipotence.

Well, that was part of the atmosphere of our town. We knew the Old Testament God, of course, and He could be stern; but at the same time we worshipped a homely friendly God, who could help a small boy fill the woodbox, and find a nice old lady's thimble for her—and, all in all, He was a nice sort of God to have.

It remains to be said that ecstasy is, of necessity, short of life. I suppose my time for floating through the air and making light of the chores of boyhood lasted, altogether, ten days or two weeks. Then the workaday world caught up with me. Life slipped back into its familiar groove, the woodbox became again what it had been before, and in short I returned to normal, although I struggled hard enough to keep that glowing, intimate contact with the infinite. The memory of it lasted for a long time. Even after I was a grown man I used to look back on that brief period and wonder idly: What in the world was going on then, anyway?

The Bible is fairly strong medicine for a small child, and it can touch off diverse chains of thought and emotion. It occurs to me that I ought to mention an event that took place in the same year that I got religion. Some six months before that glad occasion I crucified a doll.

The Easter season had recently passed, and of course we had been reading and hearing about the crucifixion. One day I was looking through the bookshelves in my father's study, and I came on somebody's commentary on the New Testament. Why I should take that book out and look through it I cannot say, but I did, and in the book I found a chapter on crucifixion—not *the* crucifixion, just crucifixion as practiced by the Romans in the old days. It was an oddly bloodless chapter, saying nothing about the sufferings of the condemned but going into a good deal of detail about the process by which they were executed, and it struck me as most interesting. I went out of doors, after a while, and in the barn I found a very old rag doll, long since abandoned. This seemed to be grist for my mill. I dug up a couple of laths, a hammer, and some shingle nails, made a cross, crucified this lopsided doll, and planted the burdened cross on a sandhill back of the barn. Then I went on about my business—back to fill the woodbox, as likely as not—in a that's-that frame of mind. The next time I went back of the barn, cross and doll had vanished. I never heard a word from my parents about it, although they must have known that I was responsible. I sometimes wonder what they said to each other about it.

You were apt to go from one extreme to the other, in a truly pious environment; which may be one reason why ministers' sons in that day were more or less expected to become loose livers when they grew up. There seemed to be such a lot to live up to, and there were times when the way of the transgressor looked attractive. If you could be damned eternally for swearing, why not go whole hog and indulge in more entertaining sins? According to small-town folklore a good many young men worked it out that way.

Yet it was not all burdensome. Literal acceptance of the Christian creed had compensations. A man knew where he stood. He had a perspective on life that unbelievers did not have. Turn faith into an unquestioned certainty and he could fill his woodbox without vain regrets; he lived, in fact, in a different sort of world, and he could go through life without worrying about the grisly shapes that might be hiding on the far side of the next hill. One night at prayer meeting one of our village elders was describing the deathbed of his good Uncle Frank, who had just closed out a well-spent life. In his final moment Uncle Frank turned to the elder and said: "Oh, if you could only see what I see . . . if you could only see what I see." Then he died, his face all aglow; and neither the elder who told the story nor the men who listened to him had a moment's doubt that Uncle Frank had been given a glimpse across the River Jordan, seeing on the farther shore a glory not to be described.

Unfortunately, to have advance knowledge about the next world does not necessarily fit one for the things that are going to happen in this one, and our community was never quite able to make a go of Grand Traverse College. Some progress was made, to be sure. A few years after instruction was first offered in someone's living room a two-story frame building was put up, containing a chapel, a study hall and several recitation rooms; but after no more than five years of use this building took fire one night and was utterly destroyed. In my boyhood there was a legend: some unregenerate students, it was said, had hidden in this building after dark, when it was untenanted, to indulge in the forbidden vice of smoking, and had clumsily set the place on fire. There was a moral lesson in this. We were against smoking, not so much because it was bad for the health as because it was morally wrong, and it seemed only natural that erring young men, guided into self-indulgence by the devil, should burn down a college. I do not know whether there was a shred of truth in this tale, but the college did have to start over again.

It did this by taking over a three-story frame building on the eastern edge of the campus. This building was known as East Hall, and for a couple of decades it was the entire college plant. To it, each year, came a handful of young people seeking an education; to them, each year, the college gave the best it had to offer, which obviously was not very good. The general level of instruction probably was about equal to that of an ordinary small-town high school. Year in and year out, the college had virtually no money at all, and the trustees and settlers had to scratch hard to keep the modest bills paid. The place was dreadfully isolated; I don't suppose there is a town between Canada and Mexico today that is as far away from everything as Benzonia was in the '70s and '80s. There was no railroad within many miles; in the long winters steamboat service on Lake Michigan was either non-existent or extremely erratic, and communication with the outer world depended entirely on a stagecoach line from Manistee, thirty miles to the south, to Traverse City, thirty-five miles to the northeast.

Hardly anyone beyond the range of that stagecoach had ever heard of Grand Traverse College. Most of the students left after a year or two and went off to become school teachers in western Michigan lumber towns, and in a way the college justified its existence by giving them all the training they ever got. But the output was thin and the outlook was dark. The good people who had founded the college tried hard but they did not have much to show for their efforts.

In the 1890s there was a bit of light. The Congregational Churches of western Michigan formally sponsored this college and pledged financial support. For some reason the name was changed, from Grand Traverse College to Benzonia College, a reasonable amount of money was made available, and there was an expansion program. East Hall was turned into a girls' dormitory and central dining place, with living quarters for the president and his family on the ground floor, and a new building was put up—a two-story frame oblong with a stubby bell-tower at one end, named Barber Hall in honor of one of the founding fathers. Barber Hall contained a study hall, four or five classrooms, a chapel, a diminutive library, and a room which passed as laboratory and museum for the physical sciences. This room was somewhat primitive; there was no running water, and there was no gas for Bunsen burners, but there was a zinc-topped table and there were shelves behind glass doors along one wall, containing instructive specimens. I can dimly remember seeing a row of rocks, representing Heaven knows what, and a glass jar full of alcohol containing a human fetus. There was also a skeleton in one corner. As a center for instruction in physics, chemistry and zoology it was grotesquely inadequate but it was more than the college had ever had to offer before, and for a brief time there was a general feeling that things at last were on their way.

It was natural for people to feel so. All across the middle west the story seemed to be the same. A college was founded in pioneer days, there was a hard struggle for survival during the early years, then as the country grew up all around there was money, and recognition, and a flood of students, and eventually the college was established solidly, able to hold its head up in any company. In the southern third of the lower peninsula it worked perfectly. There the land was part of the great middle west, like Ohio and Indiana, gently rolling, with good soil underfoot. It had trees, but they were an encumbrance rather than a source of wealth—hard woods, almost entirely, difficult to handle, worth next to nothing from the lumberman's viewpoint. They were simply removed in order that the land underneath them could be used, and once they were felled most of them were burned just to get them out of the way. The lower tiers of Michigan counties quickly became part of the rich central farm belt, settlers came in by the thousands, villages grew into little cities and as they grew established themselves firmly as market towns and modest cultural centers. The country was laced with railroads, the big cities like Chicago and Detroit were within easy reach, and the colleges that had been brought into being took root and prospered. There were Adrian, Alma, Hillsdale, Olivet, Kalamazoo, Hope, the state university at Ann Arbor, the agricultural college at East Lansing, and a number of state-supported normal colleges to train teachers. They grew up with a growing country.

But the country around Benzonia College never grew up. It passed from lusty adolescence to an uneasy senility. When the lumber was gone—and although everybody said that the supply was inexhaustible it was gone before most people realized it—there was nothing much to take its place. The soil that had supported the forest was too thin and sandy for good farming. There was a narrow belt along the west shore, running close to Lake Michigan through a dozen counties, where cherry and apple and peach orchards could do well, and some of the sand hills would grow potatoes nicely, although the latter fact did not help much because so many people raised potatoes that the bottom fell out of the market. So just when the college seemed to be establishing itself the conditions under which it could survive began to deteriorate. All up and down western Michigan the population started to decline. The towns and villages began to learn what boarded-up stores looked like, and the hills and broad valleys were dotted with abandoned farms whose owners had cut their losses and gone south, letting collapsing buildings and weedy fields go to the state by means of the next sheriff's sale.

So there was less money than before. There were fewer people to support a college, and despite those promising pledges they had less to support it with, and there were fewer young people to go to it if it stayed in operation. By the end of the 1890s the sands had run out. Benzonia College could exist no longer. The trustees met to consider the situation. They could tell a dead end when they saw one; they could also reflect on the fact that for all of the fine talk about a college this institution had never really offered anything much better than preparatory school training. The next step was inevitable: the college was voted out of existence, and in its place there was a preparatory school, Benzonia Academy, inheriting the two college buildings, such money as the college had, and its underpaid faculty. (Inheriting also, for what they might be worth, the hopes, the dreams and the selfless dedication that had underwritten thirty-odd years of failure.) This change from college to academy took place in the year 1900.

All of this was part of the background against which people who grew up in this town passed their childhood. Underlying everything was the basic American faith of the nineteenth century—that progress toward life's higher levels is not merely possible but is at all costs required of God-fearing men; not something taken for granted, but something to be worked for. It was known, to be sure, that there were men who did not fear God, but that did not matter; it was only necessary to keep their number from increasing, so that they could eventually be outnumbered, sunk by the weight of a believing majority—outvoted, so to speak, at some celestial polling place.

Yet this faith, vibrant and compelling as it was, was beginning to be tinged by the hard knowledge that fate was not always just. Like all other earthly endeavors, the struggle to build the new Jerusalem could end in flat failure. Eternal progress might be the law of life, but there undeniably were hollow places in the road. The town had been born because of the college, and now the college was gone, and the abundant prayers and hard work that had gone into its founding and support had perhaps been wasted. There was still the academy, to be sure, but when the trustees voted to make the change they were taking hold of the slippery end of the rope. A small seed of doubt had been planted, no larger than a grain of mustard seed but capable of growth. Maybe the ice really was going to come back, some day.

No matter. There was still the present, and the city that had been set upon a hill could not be hid. The scriptures told man to build after the pattern that had been shown him on the mount. If the first attempt had failed the pattern was still there, and what could not be done on a large scale could possibly be done on a small one. It would be tried, at any rate.

In a way the change from college to academy came at the right moment. As the population shrank and economic health declined, more and more young people had to go away because if they stayed at home they could not make a living. The industrial belt downstate offered jobs in factories and shops and drew many young men from the worked-out timber country; but it was already clear that the boy who hoped to rise in the world needed a college education. That people should rise in the world was fundamental in the divine scheme of things. (Progress implied a certain freedom from the grinding toil that kept a man from developing mind and spirit, and factory life early in this century looked like grinding toil incarnate.) If Benzonia could no longer give a young man a college education it could at least prepare him for college and plant in him the desire to go there. It was of course inconceivable that the land's natural resources should not be exploited to the fullest extent, but it was even worse to let human resources go undeveloped.

There was another imperative. The small-town high schools in the timber country were distressingly weak. (In that time and place a small town was really small; if it had as many as fifteen hundred inhabitants it was a city and to the best of its ability it conducted itself accordingly.) Typically, a dying small town had an undernourished high school and the merest handful of students, with three or four in a graduating class—all of them girls, often enough; there did not seem to be anything to hold the boys. The boys lounged about town for a good part of their teens, rootless and aimless, until they drifted off to Detroit or Flint or Jackson, and they never saw or heard anything to make them think there was anything better to do. People who were familiar with the scene revised the old saying: God made the country and man made the city, they said, but the devil himself made the small town. My father, who had taught school in lumber towns, used to remark that this was true and that he had seen more than enough of the devil's own handiwork. It was felt that Benzonia Academy might redeem some of these young men. It could point them in the right direction, and it could probably prepare them for college better than the ineffectual little high schools could do.

To an extent, this worked. In the few years of life that lay ahead of it—that academy lasted eighteen years, altogether—the school did get quite a number of young men from the withered villages, and a gratifying percentage went on to college. This brought problems, now and then. Parents of boys who had no desire to be educated, no regard for authority and no patience with any sort of discipline used to send them off to our academy in the despairing hope that it could "make something" out of them. In too many cases nothing at all could be made of them, and after a term or two they would be shipped back to their homes, presumably unredeemed. In the main, however, the institution did what it set out to do. It even drew some students from the big cities, where devout parents were beginning to suspect that the huge high schools eroded youthful innocence and put worldly standards in place of those laid down in the churches. First and last, the academy had a number of students from the suburbs of Chicago.

In any case, as the new century got under way this academy fell into its stride. It saw itself as a preparatory school, preparing young men and women for college or for life itself, and within reasonable limits it lived up to this vision. It must be understood that this academy in no faintest way resembled the great preparatory schools of the east. It had no money to speak of and scant prospect of getting any, its faculty was largely home-grown, and no one ever acquired any prestige by enrolling as a student. As I was entering my teens someone gave me various books written by one Ralph Henry Barbour, describing life at the New England prep schools, with lavish emphasis on football, baseball and a glamorous country-club existence, and it was clear to me that he was not talking about Benzonia Academy. At times I used to wish that our school could be bigger, richer, more distinguished, and above all things free of girls—our academy was co-educational, and Mr. Barbour's schools definitely were not. Matters became even worse when I read that English classic, *Tom Brown's School Days.* The effort to transpose Rugby into the minor key of Benzonia gave me mental indigestion. In the end I accepted the fact that we were not in the least like the eastern prep school or the English public school. We were just different, and there was no use pretending otherwise.

It did not matter much, because our town was offbeat from the beginning. Between them, the town and the school represented a cultural lag, although we had never heard of such a thing. Our life was adjusted to something that had been seen in the nation's youth, before the Civil War; I suppose one reason why that war has always seemed so real to me is that in a sense

I grew up before it happened. We were out of date without knowing it. The country was moving out from under us before we
realized that anything in particular had changed. Just when a
wholly materialistic culture was becoming dominant we were
shaping our lives according to the requirements of the culture it
was displacing.

The object lesson was right under our noses if we had known
what it meant. The lumber boom was over; which was another
way of saying that the bigger part of a state had been treated, not
as a region where people might happily live but as an expendable
resource. The trees were gone and we were left with thousands
of acres of stumps. In the year 1909 old East Hall burned down,
and the academy somehow found the money for a new building.
This was to be a modest affair but slightly more pretentious than
anything the school had owned before, with brick laid on a
wooden frame. As the excavation was being dug the contrac-
tor announced that the needed lumber had arrived—several
boxcar loads of the best-grade Georgia pine, hauled uphill from
the freight station to the building site by wagon. *Georgia* pine—
imported by a builder in the heart of the Michigan white pine
country! The foundations of the society that founded and wanted
to use our town and school had disappeared. We were preparing
ourselves, and the young men and women who came to study
with us, for a world that was no longer there.

If we were in a cultural lag we were nevertheless wholly representative of the nation as a whole; a nation which lived in the
shadow of Thomas Jefferson and Abraham Lincoln but which
was painfully trying to adjust itself to the new era of applied
technology, which creates its own demands as it goes along. Our
Michigan forests vanished in little more than half a century,
partly because the country needed lumber but even more because it had developed new ways to fell trees, move them to the
mills, transform them into boards and get the boards to market.
Because it could do these things faster it had to do them faster.
To repeat: the maddening thing about a technological improve-

ment is that it must be used to the limit. Natural resources have to be treated as expendable. New devices have to be used at full capacity; new processes have to be tuned up, perfected, developed until they can be replaced by something better. Our founding fathers had seen constant improvement as the basic law of life, and the blind force that dominated the new society agreed with them. The difference was that the fathers thought the improvement must take place in people while the new power believed that it should take place in machines. Where the machines would take the people who worked so untiringly to improve them is still an open question.

The thin edge of the wedge can be hard to recognize. I remember one summer day, early in the century, when a ball game was in progress, and an automobile came chug-chugging along and drew up on the grass back of the right field foul line. An automobile was a rare sight in our county; hardly anybody had enough money to buy and support one, and the sandy roads provided almost impossible driving conditions. Anyway, wherever it came from, this automobile drove up and parked, and at once the game broke up while players and spectators gathered around to have a look. The village wit remarked: "The automobile stopped to see the game, and the game stopped to see the automobile," and he said it precisely. In the end curiosity on both sides was satisfied, the automobile went away and the game was resumed. I do not remember who won.

So we had seen the automobile; and there was no way for the most imaginative man to see that here was the perfect symbol of the new era that was going to be so perplexing. It would transform our state with a speed and completeness no one could possibly have foreseen, and it would do the same thing to the country, and nobody could comprehend that; nobody would have been able to believe it if some prophet had explained it. All we knew was that the automobile had broken up a ball game.

CHAPTER THREE

In the Morning at the Junction

Early youth is a baffling time. The present moment is nice but it does not last. Living in it is like waiting in a junction town for the morning limited; the junction may be interesting but some day you will have to leave it and you do not know where the limited will take you. Sooner or later you must move down an unknown road that leads beyond the range of the imagination, and the only certainty is that the trip has to be made. In this respect early youth is exactly like old age; it is a time of waiting before a big trip to an unknown destination. The chief difference is that youth waits for the morning limited and age waits for the night train.

Benzonia was a good place to wait for the morning train. Life was unhurried and unworried. The daily routine was wholly uneventful, and yet there was always a lot to do. We probably had all of the ordinary problems of childhood but we were never bored. There was a boy of my own age who lived in Chicago, and his parents brought him to our town every summer, and he used to protest bitterly when it was time for him to go back home. In Benzonia, he said, there was always something going on, but "in Chicago nothing ever *happens*." His parents chuckled at this, but we children knew exactly how he felt.

So the slow years passed, and we had nothing to do but taste the special flavor of each day. In the spring the south wind carried the scent of apple blossoms and lilacs, and the summer was warm, timeless and peaceful, with clear water for swimming, and fish to be caught. Autumn was somewhat sad, because it was a reminder that even a friendly changeless world had to show a different face now and then; yet the flaming maple leaves glowed through the October haze with an implicit promise that in the end everything would be all right, and even though the winter was long and cold it offered coasting and skiing and skating, and its white fields glittered under the sunlight and caught the glint of the big stars at night. There was nothing to do but grow up, and we could take our time about it. Let that morning train come whenever it chose. We could board it at the proper time with confidence.

Part of this attitude came no doubt because we lived in a hopeful middle-class society that was adrift in a quiet backwater, seemingly removed from the current of change that swept down the mainstream. Knowing very little about the outside world, we accepted it without questioning it; we understood that much was wrong with it, but it was easy to suppose that the wrong was being worked out. I used to hear grown-ups repeat that time-worn, stupendously false sentence of reassurance: Whatever is, is right. I have not heard anyone say that for more than half a century, and it is certain that no one will ever say it again, so that it is hard now to believe that any sensible adult ever felt that way; yet it passed for distilled wisdom at that time. When I was about twelve years old I had a private suspicion that the world might actually come to an end in my lifetime. Why not? The big wrongs were all being righted, the world was steadily getting better, and it probably would not be long before all of the necessary reforms had been made; then the universe, the fullness of God's time having arrived, would be rolled up like a scroll, and as the revival hymn said time would be no more. It figured.

It may of course be true that only a backward child would have had such a daydream. Yet it was characteristic of my time and place. Our town was a tiny fragment of the American whole, sliced off for the microscope, showing in an enlarged form the inner characteristics of the larger society, and my boyhood in turn was a slice of the town, with its quaint fundamentals greatly magnified. On the eve of the terrible century of mass slaughter and wholesale collapse, of concentration camps and bombing raids, of cities gone to ruin and race relations grown desperate and poisonous, of the general collapse of all accepted values and the unendurable tension of the age of nuclear fission—on the very eve of all of this, it was possible, even inevitable, for many people to be optimistic. The world was about to take off its mask, and our worst nightmares did not warn us what we were going to see.

So childhood then mirrored a peace of mind that is not to be found today. But it also mirrored something else—the simple fact that in our town there was always plenty of room for children to play. We had all outdoors at our disposal. All we needed was a trace of imagination, and every child has that. The place to exercise the imagination lay all about us.

In 1909 our family moved into Mills Cottage, which the academy had built after East Hall burned down; it was the girls' dormitory and the central dining hall, and it provided living quarters for the principal of the academy, who was my father. When I went out of the back door of this building I was less than one hundred yards away from what I could easily imagine to be the deep woods—second-growth timber, half a century old or more, its beeches and maples tall and robust enough to give any small boy the feeling that he had gone far into the untracked wilderness. The equipment needed for a venture of this kind was of the simplest. Take an old broomstick, and to one end nail a slim triangle of wood, suitably whittled; you then have a Kentucky rifle, as good as anything Daniel Boone had, and if you can get a fragment of an abandoned cigar box and cut out something vaguely resembling a trigger and hammer, and fasten it loosely to the breech of this weapon with a brad, so much the better. All you have to do is crook your finger and say, "Bang!" loudly, and you have killed a moose, or a grizzly bear, or a redskin.

If you preferred to be an Indian the same shooting iron would serve. There were enough dead sticks lying around in the woodlot to build a wigwam, and if the wigwam was not weatherproof, and was so small that you had to huddle in a cramping squat when you got inside of it, that did not matter; when it rained you went back in the house anyway, and besides the wigwam was just part of the stage setting. As an Indian, of course, you were never shot by Daniel Boone; instead, you shot him, and with a wooden knife whittled out of any stray piece of a packing box you could dash in and lift his scalp. You could not have a real campfire. The woods floor was carpeted with dead leaves, dry and ready to burn, and nobody who grew up in the lumber country needed to be warned about the danger of starting a forest fire. But a campfire was not really necessary.

An Indian sometimes carried a bow and some arrows rather than a gun, but that did not work very well. I had a bow, of sorts—I got it from a friend, to whom I gave one of the Horatio Alger books in fair exchange—but it was deplorably weak, and the arrows were no better. We made them out of dry cattail stalks, gathered in a swamp half a mile east of town, we put wooden heads on them, and we never bothered with feathers. Shot from a bow that was far too limber, these arrows could not be relied on to come within thirty feet of the target, and besides, going around and collecting them afterward was a nuisance. Just as the real Indians had learned several generations before us, we found that the white man's firearm was much better. We never ran out of ammunition, and we never once failed to hit what we were shooting at.

A pal sometimes joined me in this game, and we found that it was best if we were both on the same side—that is, each of us was an Indian, or each was a frontiersman, and our foes were wholly imaginary. Splitting up, and hunting each other, usually led to arguments about who had really shot whom, and the game was likely to break up in a row. Also, it was easier to scalp a victim who did not really exist than it was to scalp a living, active small boy. He was apt to complain that you pulled his hair too hard, and there was always the danger of sticking a wooden scalping knife in his eye. On the whole, it was better to be Indians than to be frontiersmen; we had an excuse to yell, giving the blood-curdling war whoop, and off in the woods there were no adults to lean out of windows and tell us we were making too much noise. We had the world to ourselves.

Now and then we fought the Civil War. The woods were not so good for this, unless we elected to do the battle of the Wilderness, but in the center of town there was a twelve-acre park, officially the academy's West Campus, and it was open enough for any battle. It was not possible to do the Civil War properly with just two actors; at least half a dozen were needed, and it was not always possible to find half a dozen boys who all felt like playing the Civil War game at the same time. We got along without officers, because nobody was willing to take orders, and the enemy of course was always imaginary. We were invariably the Union army, and we never lost. Johnny Reb died by the platoon and the battalion before our unerring musketry. One of the town's authentic Civil War veterans told us that our village cemetery, off on rising ground to the southeast, was a bit like the famous cemetery at Gettysburg; it looked out over the rolling countryside just as the Gettysburg cemetery does, and the main road that came up from the south went past the base of the hill much like the Emmitsburg road that Pickett's men had to cross. But we never went to the cemetery to fight our battles. Our parents would not have approved of boyish fun and games around the burying ground, and we probably would not have tried it in any case. It was a pleasant, friendly sort of cemetery—if you have to be buried I can't think of a better place for it—but it was not a site any of us wanted to use as a playground.

Somewhere along the line my older brother, Robert, acquired an air rifle. It was not exactly a rifle, really—it fired BB shot, one at a time, it was grossly inaccurate at any distance greater than about twenty feet, and at that distance it did not hit hard enough to be dangerous to anything much bigger than a butterfly—but it was a real gun firing real pellets, and one day Robert and I went hunting. (I was equipped with my bow and those unreliable arrows.) We were not playing Daniel Boone now; we were actually hunting, questing for game, and we crept through the woods looking for a victim. At last we saw one; a perky little chipmunk, capering about on an old stump, sitting up now and then to pose, chipmunk-fashion, with his tail flicking.

We approached with proper stealth, and at a distance of perhaps eight feet my brother steadied his gun against the side of a sapling, took careful aim, and pulled the trigger. Somewhat to our surprise the chipmunk fell over, lifeless, drilled through the head. We went up to the stump and examined our prey.

At that moment the fun went out of it all. The chipmunk had been so lively and engaging, and now he was dead, looking pathetic, and we did not know what to do with him. It was unthinkable to take him home, haggle the skin off, clean the carcass and ask our mother to cook it for us; her sympathies, we knew, would be all with the chipmunk, and anyway who wanted to *eat* him? We wound up at last by burying him in the earth at the base of the stump, and we went off home soberly. We had had our big moment as hunters only to learn that success was worse than failure. As an adult I once slew a rabbit with a shotgun, and I have hunted, steadfast but unsuccessful, for pheasant, but from that day to this chipmunks have been safe in my presence.

The game that got most of our attention was baseball, which we played with high enthusiasm and a considerable lack of skill. We were under a special handicap here. For the most part our fathers had never played the game, or if they had they had played some primitive version of it in which you could retire a base runner by hitting him with a thrown ball, and in which nobody wore fielders' gloves; and in their day there was a rule by which the batter was out if someone caught whatever he hit on the first bounce. We used to feel embarrassed when they

talked about that outlandish game; more to the point, we had no one to teach us how to play. (The older boys, of high school age or over, might have done so, but they could not be bothered.) We had to pick it up as we went along, and we did not learn much; watching our elders play, the chief thing we took to heart was that all fielders must keep up a steady flow of chatter, to encourage the pitcher and dishearten the batter. None of our pitchers could throw a curve. Mostly they just lobbed the ball in and trusted to luck. We had no umpire, so there were no bases on balls. If a pitcher could not get the ball over the plate he was denounced by friend and foe alike for delaying the game, but the batter did not get to first because of it.

Another handicap came because our town was so small that it was never possible to create two full teams of small boys. When we "chose up sides" we did well to get half a dozen players on each team, and to play with three infielders and one outfielder was not uncommon. Only the fact that none of us could hit the ball very hard kept us from rolling up tremendous scores. For the most part we did not try to field two teams. We just played scrub.

Scrub was played by one team, and if there were as many as six or seven boys present you could have a game, in which it was each player against the universe. We started out by shouting numbers, which brought on a row if two or more boys called out the same number at the same moment, and the rule was that number one and number two were batters, number three was the catcher, number four the pitcher, number five the first baseman, and so on up the line. Once in a great while there were enough boys on hand to provide three batters and a full complement afield, but that rarely happened. In any case, number one went to bat, and when he got on base number two came up, and at this point the restrictive rule of the game of scrub came into operation. If there are only two batters, and both of them are on base, there is no one to come up to bat and the game is hopelessly stalled, so the rule was that the first base runner had to score whenever number two hit the ball; if he failed to score he was out. Thus it was necessary for the second batsman to stall for a couple of pitches so that the base runner could move on to second or third, proper scoring position. Need I add that it was fairly easy to steal a base in this game? The catcher's peg down to second was not likely to be quick or accurate.

Anyway, when a batter or a base runner was put out he moved into the outfield, the catcher moved up to take his turn as batter, the pitcher became the catcher, the first baseman moved over and was the pitcher, and so on all the way up the line. This worked better than might be supposed. There was no point in keeping score, because there was only one team, but the constant rotation of positions meant that every boy got a chance to play every position and to have his turn at bat, and things moved fast. The chief source of ill-feeling was the rule that the base runner was out if he failed to score when the man at the plate hit the ball; through no fault of his own, the runner was likely to be retired if the man at bat was overeager and swung at the first pitch. The batter who did this was said to sour on the runner, and to sour on the runner was considered more or less a breach of ethics. However, nobody minded much because the rotation of positions was steady and before long the man who had been retired would come to bat again, and the arguments were not really heated.

Now and then some really small boy, age of six or such a matter, would come up and ask to be allowed to play. This was unthinkable, because we scorned the very young the way our seniors scorned us, but we had invented a way around it: junior would be allowed to play pigtail, which meant that he stood somewhere behind the catcher and retrieved all balls which got away from that functionary. This happened about every other pitch, so the pigtail was kept busy. Sooner or later he would realize that this was not much fun—he was not allowed to come to bat—and he would go away and things would go on as before.

Technically there was no end to the game of scrub; it could

go on and on, world without end. In practice it usually stopped after an hour or so, when everybody got tired or the sun became too hot or it was time for dinner. (Dinner, of course, was the midday meal; what you ate in the evening was supper.) If play was resumed after dinner it was a new ball game.

Playing scrub was fun, but it was even more fun to watch our elders in a real game. If the high school team, or the academy team, or best of all the town team, played some team from out of town, it was most exciting. There were no bleachers, and the spectators stood along the foul lines, and we small boys roamed up and down in front of them, shrilling out our comments on the opposing players. It was considered highly effective to scream, when one of the opposition took a cut at a pitch and missed, "Swings like a rusty gate on a stormy night!" and we had other catch phrases; if the rival pitcher seemed to be faltering we would start chanting, "Take me out! Take me out! Take me out!" We must have made unholy nuisances out of ourselves. Looking back I wonder that the grown-ups did not drive us away.

There was one time when we were shut up. Our town team was playing a team from Frankfort, which was the metropolis of our county, a busy little seaport and sawmill city eight or nine miles to the west of Benzonia; because it was three times the size of our town it had three times as many young men able to play baseball, and its team was usually stronger than ours. So one day the Frankfort team was beating our team, and we realized that the Frankfort catcher was a Negro. Black people were scarce. There were none in Benzonia, and not many anywhere in the county, but here was one and we got on him at once. "Chocolate Drop! Chocolate Drop!" we yelled. "You can't play ball, Chocolate Drop!" A small boy who stumbles on what he considers a good phrase can go on shouting it all day, and so it would have been with us, except that after an inning or so the captain of the Frankfort team, a white man, came over and asked us if we would please stop yelling Chocolate Drop: it hurt the black boy's feelings, he was a good boy and everybody liked him, the color of his skin was not his fault, and wouldn't we please be quiet about it? We were as disturbed as my brother and I had been when he killed the chipmunk; trying to rattle an opposing player was all right, but making personal remarks that actually hurt his feelings was not decent or fair. We immediately shut up and stayed shut up, because we were ashamed of ourselves.

Watching our team lose so many games I came to feel that Providence really ought to take a hand. Our boys *deserved* to win more often. They were good young men, even though their skills at bat and afield were limited; they did not chew tobacco or use triple-jointed swear words the way their opponents did, and if there was any justice they would not get licked so regularly. Apparently there was no justice, because their fortunes did not improve. Many years later I realized that watching them lose, and feeling that way about it, had perfectly conditioned me to be a fan of the New York Mets.

Absorbing though it was, baseball more or less lapsed in midsummer. The academy boys had all gone home, the high school boys mostly had summer jobs, and anyway the unshaded diamond got uncomfortably warm under the sun of July and August. Besides, the juvenile element had another interest then—Crystal Lake, which lay just half a mile north of our town and some two hundred feet below it. Then as now, this lake offered as fine a hot-weather playground as anyone could ask.

Crystal Lake is a noble body of water, eight miles long by two or three miles wide, its axis running from southeast to northwest. It was properly named, because it is so crystal-clear that you can count pebbles on the bottom where it is twenty feet deep. It is surrounded by low green hills, and when the sun is out its color is a breath-taking, incredible, picture-postcard blue; spring-fed, it is deep and cold, and only the hardiest would care to swim in it at any time except midsummer, but when the weather is warm to go into this water is like dipping into the fountain of youth. A nice beach runs all the way around it, stony here and there but mostly white sand, and that beach exists because the good people of Benzonia made a profound miscalculation back in 1873.

The lake drains into the Betsie River through a sparkling outlet whose stream is about six feet wide and eight inches deep. This outlet—that is the only name it ever had—wanders aimlessly through the flatlands for a mile or so and then goes into the Betsie, which is more of a river but still an unhurried, modest affair full of sandbars, with occasional islets covered with alders. It occurred to someone in Benzonia, in 1873, that if the outlet were just straightened a bit and relieved of some of its underbrush, and if the ground where the stream left the lake were cut away, the rush of water from the lake would scour out a deep channel in the outlet and the river all the way to Frankfort harbor. Then steamboats could come up into Crystal Lake and the lumber in the surrounding territory could be moved to market. (Saw logs could be moved economically only by water or by rail; there was no railroad anywhere around, and a good deal of usable timber north and east of Benzonia was too far from the Betsie River to use that waterway, and the trees simply stood there, a dead weight on the land.)

So a man who said he was a surveyor went to work. He reported that the plan was perfectly sound. The level of Crystal Lake was only a few feet above the level of Lake Michigan, and once the temporary cascade had done its work a few touches here and there would perfect the waterway. A corporation was formed, money was raised, men with shovels and horse-drawn scrapers were put to work, and one fine day the barrier was cut through and the waters of Crystal Lake were turned loose.

The result was spectacular. The water went out like the Yukon breaking through an ice jam in the spring, the roar of it heard in Benzonia three miles away. The surveyor had miscalculated; instead of being just a few feet above the level of Lake Michigan, Crystal Lake was a good thirty feet above it, and the flood went out in a destroying torrent. It did not scour out any channel; it simply flooded the whole river valley, killing livestock, destroying roads and bringing farmers to the point of revolt. One man was drowned; another, a Baptist minister making his rounds by horse and buggy, lost his horse and barely saved his own life. (People remarked afterward that he was a spirited advocate of total immersion and so probably did not mind what happened to him.)

So it was obvious that this plan was no good. The corporation collapsed in a cloud of debts. A small stern-wheel steamboat that had been built to use the new waterway went ingloriously to work towing schooners and lumber rafts about Frankfort harbor. The level of Crystal Lake was eight or ten feet lower than it had been before, the outlet channel was no deeper than it had always been, a dam was hastily built at the outlet to keep the lake level from going any lower, and there was a general agreement to forget the whole business.

There was one unexpected gain; Crystal Lake now had a beach.

Until then it had not had one. The hills came down steeply banked, with trees growing right to the water's edge, and anyone who tried to go along the shore on foot had to scramble from tree trunk to tree trunk. Now there was a good beach all the way around. At the southeastern end of the lake, near the foot of Benzonia hill, there were acres of dry land where there had been a swamp; a town was built there, given the name of Beulah, and it prospered and eventually became the county seat. When the railroad was built southeast from Frankfort in the 1880s it reached the lake by way of the outlet valley and ran for several miles along land that had been under five feet of water a few years earlier.

All of this, to be sure, had happened long before any of us small boys had been born. We knew nothing about it, or if we heard our elders talk about it we paid no attention; we simply accepted the lake and its unending beach as something put there for our benefit, and all summer long we devoted our afternoons to swimming. There were a good many boathouses along the shore, where people who owned boats stored them in the winter, and we could usually persuade someone to let us use his boathouse for undressing and dressing, but mostly that was too much trouble; we simply went into the woods overlooking the lake, hung our clothing on the branches of saplings, put on our bathing suits, and ran downhill to go into the water. There were two schools of thought about the way to go in. The water was cold, and the first plunge was agonizing. The hardiest ran straight ahead, splashing vigorously and yelling like men under torture, and when it was thigh-deep they threw themselves in, facedown, and took the worst shock all at once. Most of us preferred to wade out slowly, adjusting ourselves by degrees, and the only trouble with this was that anyone who had got in ahead of you was certain to splash you. Whatever we did, we knew that once we were wet all over the water ceased to feel cold. It became just exactly right.

There was much energetic floundering and thrashing about, and all of us learned to swim after a fashion—nothing stylish, but enough to get by. If a gasoline launch was moored somewhere off shore we would scramble aboard and use it for a diving platform; the owners must have been tolerant, because I do not remember that we were ever told not to do this. It seemed to me that the best thing of all was to float on one's back, wriggling the hands just enough to keep from going under. The water was an invisible support, lying there was like floating through the air, and you could look far up into the sky and wonder what it would be like to be up on one of those fluffy white clouds. We stayed in the water until its friendly warmth began to seem chilly again; when our lips turned blue we figured it was time to come out. Then we would scramble up into the woods, get dressed, and go off in search of further adventures.

This usually led us into the town of Beulah, where there was much to be seen. The railroad went through here, and a freight train might be switching cars on the siding behind the station; or the afternoon southbound passenger train might come in, three open-platform cars behind a modest locomotive which panted in a slow, highly realistic fashion during the stop as if the trip down from Frankfort had been exhausting. Here was the point of departure. When you left Benzonia for the outer world you came to this depot and got on a train like this one, and sooner or later all of us would do it, leaving town and lake and woods behind us forever; but that was a long time ahead and we did not give it a thought because the present moment was next thing to eternal. Still, there was a vague premonitory thrill in watching those cars swing off around the curve beyond the station, heading for the unknown.

Whatever else we did in Beulah, we always went to Terp's place. This was a waterfront pavilion operated by a man named Terpining—I don't believe I ever did know his first name: first and last, he was just Terp, a lean, friendly businessman who did not seem to mind having small boys under foot. His pavilion included dressing room cubicles for bathers, a dance hall, two bowling alleys, a T-shaped dock with a long rank of rowboats for rent, and an ice cream bar. Anyone who wanted to go fishing could get a boat from Terp, and if he needed bait Terp would sell him a bucket full of minnows. In a shed somewhere Terp had a gasoline tank, to service the summer people who came in by launch. He also sold cigars and cigarets, and against the wall by the soda fountain there were two slot machines. They seemed singularly innocent, and it never occurred to the authorities to proceed against them as gambling devices. In later years, when I read that Chicago gangsters had taken control of the slot machine trade, I found it hard to believe; surely there could not be important money in this business of getting people to risk a few pennies now and then? I understood at last that the ways of Chicago speakeasies were not at all the ways of Terp's pavilion.

If we were in funds, which was not often the case, we bought ice cream sodas, or pop; if we were not, there was always something to see. There was a steady coming and going out on the dock. The summer people who had cottages at various places around the lake relied on the launch rather than the automobile to come to town and do their marketing. The automobile age had not yet reached northern Michigan, and the road that went around the lake was nothing but a track through the sand and an automobile that tried to follow it was almost certain to get stuck; so the cottager who wanted to go to the grocery or the drug store came down the lake by boat and tied up at Terp's dock. Terp himself owned two launches, open boats with canopies overhead, and side curtains that could be let down if it rained. Anybody who wanted to give a picnic party somewhere on the beach could hire one of these, and Terp had a regular twice-a-day schedule to the far end of the lake. There were more or less regular stops at different cottage colonies along the way, the round trip took about two hours, and as regular commercial carriers operating on fixed schedules these boats were periodically examined by the Federal steamboat inspectors; each vessel had a formal certificate tacked up near the steering wheel, and these were good to look at. They made the whole business seem important.

For all that there was so much coming and going by water, the lake was quiet. The day of the outboard motor had not yet arrived, and all of the power boats on this lake were displacement hulls, not planing craft; there was no loud whining of high-speed engines, and the painful processes of evolution had not yet brought forth the water skier. People went from cottage to town and back by boat because that was the only way to do it, and it was pleasant to go loafing along on that clear lake with the peaceful hills all around it. Nobody was in any hurry, and nobody could have gone fast if he had been in a hurry. Instead of detracting from the general peace the powerboats somehow emphasized it.

Now and then there were boat races. The moving spirit here was Charlie Case, who had a general store in Benzonia, played the tuba in the village orchestra, and devoted most of his spare time in the summer to his two powerboats. (He used to fascinate me, because he looked like the picture of the French revolutionist Danton in Ridpath's *History of the World;* I could see him on the scaffold, waiting to be trussed and guillotined, defiant and undaunted, and I have admired Danton ever since then.) We hardly ever went swimming without seeing Mr. Case, usually with a helper, working on those boats at his dock, tearing the engines apart, putting them together again, tuning them up and then dissecting them once more to file down distributor points, change spark plugs or do whatever else one does to engines at such times. When he was thus engaged I am sure he was one of the happiest men alive.

He was proud of his boats, especially of the larger one, a sleek white vessel some twenty-five feet in length, which I suppose could move through the water at more than fifteen miles an hour, and he vigorously supported an informal yacht club that held regattas from time to time. As spectator sports these were not wholly satisfying, because after all nothing moved very rapidly, but there was a general air of purposeful busy-ness alongshore and Terp's dock was full of official types whose cigars lent an elegant fragrance to the clear air. One of the disappointments of my life has been the fact that no cigar has ever tasted as good as that cigar smoke used to smell there by Crystal Lake.

Out of neighborly loyalty we boys always supported Mr. Case's boat—which in fact usually won—but we had our favorites among the competitors, too; there was one called *Pipedream,* and there was *Undine,* and *Maria Theresa,* and one year a cottager brought in a hydroplane named *Ripper.* Something was wrong with *Ripper's* engine, and she accomplished none of the prodigies of speed she was supposed to be capable of; the motor always seemed to conk out, half a mile from the finish line, so that she would lie dead in the water, exuding thin blue smoke, while Mr. Case's boat swept past to win. A few years later Mr. Case bought a hydroplane and it cleaned up everything on the lake. Then Mr. Case started out for Traverse City to enter a race against real competition. He undertook to get there by way of Lake Michigan, and the big lake was too rough; the hydroplane foundered and sank somewhere in the Manitou Channel, fortunately without loss of life, and that was the end of that. I am sure the man was utterly heartbroken. He loved a fast motorboat the way a Kentucky planter loves a fast horse.

The fishing on Crystal Lake was good if you liked perch, as everybody did. We never bought minnows; it was much simpler to dig in the back yard and get enough angle worms to fill a tin can. With these, with ten-cent hand lines, and with one of Terp's rowboats, we were all set, and an hour's fishing usually brought in a dozen or more fair-sized perch. These fish were docile; they hooked themselves readily and came to the boat without much fuss, and later when they were fried in corn meal they were as good to eat as any fish that ever swam. We had a theory, and for all I know it may have been correct, that the clear cold water of this lake gave the perch's flesh an extra firmness and flavor. We scorned all fish that came from muddy waters, although that did not keep us from going to the Betsie River in March to catch suckers; the Betsie was muddy then with the spring runoff water, and the sucker is barely edible under any circumstances, but it was the first fish in action in early spring and we used to go out and catch suckers just as if they were worth getting.

There had been some notable trout streams in our county, although by the time I came along they were pretty well fished out. The old-timers used to say that in the 1890s it was easy enough to get twenty or thirty brook trout out of the Platte River, half a dozen miles away, in two hours' time; in my day you did well to get three or four in an entire morning. I discovered that there were trout in Cold Creek, a brook that ran through boggy land east of Benzonia hill, and a small boy with a cane rod and some angle worms could usually get two or three small ones if he worked at it—but it was more trouble than it was worth. I was a confirmed rowboat fisherman by disposition, and it was easier and more rewarding to go out on Crystal Lake and catch perch. They never seemed to fail, and there was something extremely pleasant about lounging in the boat, saying nothing, hardly even thinking, waiting lazily for the first faint tug on the hand line to show that some fish, far down below, was doing his duty.

Autumn provided a breathing spell. People did not play baseball in the fall, football had not yet been introduced, it was too chilly to go swimming, and things were more or less disorganized. For the first few weeks getting adjusted to school kept our minds occupied; after school, and on Saturdays, it was fun to wander off to somebody's orchard and eat apples. The unwritten rule was that it was all right to pick up windfalls, because they were usually too bruised to stand shipment, but it was wrong to pick apples from the trees and since there always were plenty of windfalls we observed the rule faithfully.

The older boys were less law-abiding. After dark they liked to go out and steal watermelons. This did not seem like stealing —not to the town's young bloods, who spoke of it as "cooning," although the farmers were bitter about it, and Mr. Mills now and then denounced the evil from the pulpit. Most of the farmers met this threat by putting croton oil in a few melons—nice big melons, usually, conveniently close to the fence, just the ones prowling boys would be most likely to take. The process was simple; cut out a small plug, put in the croton oil, replace the plug, and no one could tell the difference until shortly after he had eaten the melon. It was of course important for the farmer to keep the doped fruit off the market. Croton oil is a powerful cathartic, with explosive, hair-trigger qualities, and it struck without warning; the boy who had eaten a doped melon was apt to lose both his dignity and the contents of his colon, willy-nilly, while he was walking home. No one to whom this happened ever did any more cooning, and in the long run the stealing of melons was kept within bounds.

In some ways winter was the most exciting season of all, especially during the first few weeks. After that it began to seem endless, and by the middle of February we began to feel as if we had been frozen in forever, but at first it was fun. We did not do as much skating as might be supposed, because the unbroken ice on Crystal Lake usually was covered with a foot or two of snow, but we could sometimes clear the surface of a convenient millpond, and a January thaw followed by a hard freeze might make the lake serviceable. A couple of miles to the east of us an electric light company had dammed the Betsie River to provide current for the surrounding villages, and the flooded valley above the dam often provided good skating. That was an eerie place to go. Trees killed by the rising waters stuck their dead tips through the ice, and to skate there just at dusk was like skating through a haunted forest. Once we got around the bend from the dam we might have been a thousand miles from anywhere, with nothing in sight but the ghostly gray dead trees, and no sound except for the ring of skates on ice. It was a little frightening, especially so because there were air holes around some of the trees, although I do not remember that anybody ever came to grief there; anyway, it was good to be on the way back to town again, with skates slung over the shoulder and the mind full of the warmth and the good supper that would be waiting when we got home.

We did a good deal of skiing, in a makeshift sort of way. All of the skis were home-made—a local carpenter would produce a pair for a modest sum—and they lacked modern refinements; there was simply a leather strap on each ski to put your toe through, with nothing to go around your heel and bind you firmly to the skis. Maneuvers that are taken for granted by present-day skiers were utterly beyond our reach, but we could go swinging down the open slopes at a great rate, and glide across country in fine style, and since we did not know that we lacked anything we were completely satisfied. It did not enter our heads that we ought to wear special costumes, or that to go skiing was

to indulge in a sophisticated, socially rewarding activity. We did it because it was fun.

The best sport of all in the winter was coasting downhill. Go where you chose, from the center of the village, and you soon came to a road that went down a long hill. The one to the west went down such an easy slope that it did not offer much; and the one to the north was too dangerous, because it was steep and it led straight into the main street of Beulah, where some farmer was apt to be pulling away from the curb to make a U-turn with a two-horse team and a heavy wagon-box on runners just as a bobsled full of youngsters, moving at better than thirty miles an hour and all but out of control, came barreling along for a disastrous collision. (There was also the chance that a speeding sled might find a freight train crossing the road just at the foot of the hill. If that happened the man who was steering the sled had to take it into the ditch without stopping to think, because otherwise everybody would get killed.) In the end the village council made coasting on the Beulah hill illegal, and the rule was pretty generally observed.

The east hill road was equally steep but less dangerous because there was no town at the foot of it. There was a railroad crossing there, to be sure, but the Ann Arbor railroad did not run many trains and we had a fair idea of the schedules, and there were massive drifts along both sides of the highway in case one had to bail out in a hurry. When a bobsled ran into one of these drifts at high speed there was always a hilarious mix-up; the sled would come to a most abrupt stop and the five or six occupants would be catapulted off into the snow, landing head downward as likely as not. One time Robert and I took our mother down this hill, because she had never gone coasting and wanted to see what it was like. Just as we went down the steepest part, whirling along at a prodigious clip, she concluded that it was like nothing she wanted any more of and she firmly ordered: "Robert! Robert, *stop* it!" We were dutiful sons and always did what our parents told us to do, so Robert obediently guided the sled into a deep drift. As anyone but Mother would have known, the sled stopped but its passengers did not. Mother, who was no lightweight, shot through the air like a rocketing partridge, going completely over Robert's head and coming down wrong-end up in five feet of powdery snow. It took us several minutes to get her out, because she was laughing so hard that she was unable to act in her own behalf. I do not recall that she ever went coasting again.

The best coasting was down the long road that went to the south. Here the slope was more gentle, but when the snow was packed right you could move fairly fast, and you could go on almost forever; with luck, a bobsled could reach the Betsie River bridge, a full mile from the starting point. That meant a long walk back, but nobody seemed to mind. Going down the long slope was effortless and silent, and since we were not more than eight inches off the ground the speed seemed much faster than it really was. A ride like that was worth a long walk.

I remember once some of us went down that hill after dark. We went all the way to the bridge, and as the sled slowed down to a halt we sat motionless as long as there was the least chance of gliding forward another foot. We gave up, finally, turned the sled around, and started pulling it back up hill. It was cold, and a north wind was whipping dry snow off of the surrounding fields with a soft, rustling noise. The wind seemed to come straight down from the north pole—really, there was nothing between us and the pole to stop it—and it came out of the emptiness of the everlasting ice, as if the old darkness once again was sliding down from the top of the world to swallow everything; perhaps that was what made the ghostly creeping little sound out across the snowdrifts. I shivered, not because I wanted a warmer coat but because I wanted some sort of reassurance, which did not seem to be forthcoming. Yet overhead all the stars were out, and on the frozen road I could hear the sound of laughter.

CHAPTER FOUR

Whatever Is, Is Temporary

This is how it was in the old days. A family that wanted to go from here to there went by railroad train because there was no other way to do it. If the distance was short, ten or a dozen miles only, you might hire a rig at the livery stable and let the horses do the work, and if you lived on deep water you might go all or part of the way by steamboat, but as a general thing to make a trip meant to take a ride on the cars. The process was slow by later standards, the journey was apt to be bumpy and dusty, and there were inflexible schedules to keep, but it was exciting, especially for children past the time of actual babyhood. It differed from modern travel in that the mere act of departure was a great event. Nowadays leaving for a distant city is about like leaving to drive across town to have dinner with Aunt Millie, except that you pile suitcases into the car and make sure that the postman and the milkman know you are going to be away, but the old days were different.

We always began by going to the railroad station at Beulah. Mr. Benner had a wagon that left the Benzonia post office in time to meet all the trains, under contract to receive and deliver the mail; he carried our baggage, and his wagon had crosswise seats for passengers, who could ride for a modest fee, so he usually carried us as well. The trip to Beulah was unexciting— no driver in his senses drove down that hill at anything but a plodding walk—but once we reached the depot the atmosphere changed and we began to understand that we were really going somewhere. Actually, we already understood it. Mother felt that her children ought to be presentable if they were going on the cars, so the night before we all had to take baths, even though it was not Saturday night—a gross violation of custom that led us to make vain protests—and when we got dressed on the morning of departure we had to put on our Sunday suits, so that the special quality of the event had already been impressed on us. But when we reached the station platform the reality of the whole business came home to us.

For all that Beulah and Benzonia together made no more than a decidedly small town, this seemed like a busy place at train time. Somebody would be wheeling a platform truck down to the spot where the head-end cars were to stop: empty ice cream freezers going back to the distributor at Cadillac, ice-packed containers from the Beulah creamery bound for assorted destinations downstate, a traveling salesman's sample cases, somebody's trunk, a few suitcases, a mysterious cardboard-bound parcel or two, and so on. People who were going to get on the train stood about looking expectant, while behind the platform teams waited for passengers or packages coming down from Frankfort. The station agent was out, keeping an eye on the platform truck while he assured some anxious woman that this train would infallibly reach Copemish in time for her to catch the Manistee and Northeastern going southwest. Miss Marshall, who collected personal items for the weekly newspaper, would be moving about with pad and pencil, asking people where they were going and when they would be back, and there was always the usual assortment of men and small boys who had nothing in particular to do and had just sauntered over to watch the train go through.

Then at last, just as the tension was almost more than we could take, we could hear the train as it rounded Outlet Point and came along the lake shore, the clear notes of its whistle sounding across the water, and finally it would drift around the last curve and swing up to the platform, smoking and hissing and clanking, with the locomotive putting on its characteristic act of looking and sounding like something alive. A few passengers would get off, and the conductor would call a long-drawn "All abo-o-o-a-r-d!" and we would scramble up the steps and into one of the cars, racing down the aisle for a pair of facing seats. By the time Mother arrived to settle the inevitable argument as to which of three boys would occupy the two places next to the windows the train would be moving again. Wisps of smoke and steam would whip past the windows as we took the first curve and left Beulah behind; then came the familiar East Hill crossing, and Will Case's sawmill with men putting lumber into a boxcar, and we were really on our way. In some ways the mere act of leaving was the high-water mark of the whole trip.

The next big moment came fourteen miles down the track when we reached Thompsonville, where we changed cars. No matter where we were going, we almost always began by changing cars at Thompsonville, where our Ann Arbor railroad crossed the north-south line of the Pere Marquette. The Ann Arbor went all the way to Toledo, two hundred and eighty miles away, but somehow our affairs never seemed to take us in that direction; we usually were going to visit Grandfather in Petoskey, a hundred miles to the north, although once in a while we went south, around the foot of Lake Michigan to Chicago, and in either case we got off at Thompsonville, lugged our suitcases across the tracks to the Pere Marquette station, and went through the whole platform routine all over again. If there was time we strolled down the main street to see the sights. These were not numerous or startling—after all, Thompsonville was a mere village —but in those days it was a busy place, with two hotels, two railroads, a saloon or two and several sawmills, and it struck me as decidedly metropolitan. Compared with Benzonia, almost every town was metropolitan; and anyway this was the gateway to the outer world, bound to the great cities by steel rails, definitely though remotely in touch with the main currents of life from which our city on the hill was so completely insulated. One thing puzzled me: one of the mills at Thompsonville an-

nounced itself as a clothes pin factory, and that seemed odd; how could there possibly be a demand for the unutterable quantities of clothes pins that could be produced by an entire factory working ten hours a day, six days a week? It just did not seem reasonable.

Sooner or later the northbound train arrived, and again we sat by the windows to enjoy the delights of travel. It must be confessed that after a while these began to wear a bit thin. We had to stay in our seats—Mother refused to let us roam up and down the aisle, annoying our elders—and presently we began to get somewhat bored. We never admitted this, because we knew that traveling by the cars was exciting, but it was there just the same and we resented it. What we could see out of the windows took on a monotonous sameness: acres and acres of stumps, low hills covered with uneven second-growth, usually aspens packed so tightly together that you could not imagine playing Indian among them, and weedy farms with tired-looking houses that had lost all their paint and most of their prospects. It was nice to go through a town, because we could see people hanging about and we could reflect in a superior way that we were traveling while they were mere stay-at-homes, but most of these places were dying lumber towns and they were depressing to look at. It was always a relief when we finally reached Petoskey and took the carriage up the hill to Grandfather's house. The trip was a great experience, but it was nice when it ended.

It was even better when we took the night train, because to ride in a sleeping car was to touch the summit of human experience. This did not happen often, but every other summer or thereabouts Mother took us children to Minneapolis for a visit with her sister and the sister's husband, Aunt Vade and Uncle Ed. Aunt Vade's given names, by the way, were Sierra Nevada; Grandfather had quite a few daughters, and he gave the rest of them workaday names like Emma and Kate and Ida and Belle and Adella, but when this girl came along he spread himself. As an aunt, she was as dignified and in many ways as impressive as the mountain chain she was named for, although she was not at all icy; on the contrary, she was warm and affectionate, and although I was a little bit scared of her I was a little bit scared of all adults, including my own parents—they lived in a different world and seemed to be accountable to strange gods, and it was necessary for a small boy to watch his foot in their presence. I realize now, although I did not know it at the time, that my aunt probably sent Mother the money to pay for these trips to Minneapolis, because the academy paid starvation salaries and Father could not possibly have financed them.

In any case when we went to Minneapolis we usually went by way of Chicago, which meant that we got to Thompsonville late in the afternoon and waited there for the night train, and sometimes we had supper in a Thompsonville hotel, which to my mind was another bonus. Later on I came to see that meals in a village hotel in that era were pretty bad. A typical supper would include stringy pot roast with lumpy gravy on a boiled potato, a bowl of stewed canned tomatoes laced with hunks of soggy bread, and rice pudding under blue milk; but small boys eat to get full and not for pleasure, and this stuff at least was filling. After supper we went over to the Pere Marquette station, to wait in the darkness, looking up a track spangled with green switch lights, watching for the far-off glow of the engine's headlight, listening anxiously for the first haunting note of the whistle, which came in like an echo of all the horns of elfland.

This train arrived, I suppose, somewhere around ten o'clock, mysterious and magnificent, long shaft of light shining down the track ahead, red glow from the cab if the fireman opened the firebox to shovel in coal, baggage man lounging in the open door of a baggage car, smoker and day coaches brightly lit with passengers drowsing in their seats . . . and then the Pullmans, vestibule doors open, thin strips of light coming out from below the green curtains here and there, porters swinging down to the platform when the train stopped, planting footstools in front of the steps and chanting quietly: "Pullman car for Chicago . . .

Pullman car for Detroit . . ." It was almost too much to bear. When we went aboard the berths had already been made up, and it was nice to go down the curtained aisle to our own places.

Getting undressed in the berth of an old-style twelve-section sleeping car meant that you almost had to be a contortionist. Getting your pants off, for instance, required you to lie on your back, arch yourself until you were supported by your heels and your shoulders, and start fumbling. I always shared a berth with one of my brothers, and how the two of us managed it I do not quite know, but we always made it, wadding our discarded clothing in the hammock netting over the car window, getting into our pajamas somehow, and then sliding down beneath the covers and turning off the light. Nothing on earth today is quite as snug and secure as a Pullman berth used to be once you were fairly in it, and it seemed to me at the time that to lie there feeling the swaying and jiggling of the car's motion, listening to the faraway sound of the whistle, getting up on elbow now and then to peer out the window when we reached a station, and at last drifting off to sleep, was to know unadulterated happiness. It was best of all if one happened to wake up when the train reached Grand Rapids, which it did along in the small hours. Here there was a cavernous train shed, with cars on other tracks, a switch engine puttering about, people coming and going—none of your small-town depots, where the station agent doused the lights, locked the door and went home after the last train went through: this place was in action all night long. From the car window you could see the station dining room, with its gleaming silver coffee urns, doughnuts stacked under glass domes on the counter, belated travelers here and there having a final snack before going off about their business, and it looked so inviting I used to want to be there myself—except that it was so cozy in the berth, and it would be even cozier when the train began to move again, and it was sheer heresy to wish to be anywhere else.

If we went to Chicago we finished the journey to Minneapolis on railroads which I considered far superior to our lumber country lines. Our roads were deteriorating as the lumber business declined—the Pere Marquette was often in receivership, and was half-affectionately referred to as the Poor Marquette, while the Ann Arbor, although solvent, never did have any pretensions to style—and with their bumpy roadbeds, cinder ballast and aging passenger cars they offered transportation without frills. But at Chicago we boarded the Northwestern, or the Milwaukee, or the Burlington, and these were famous railroads: double-tracked, with rock ballast, automatic signaling systems and steel cars, according to the blurbs on the timetables, which I read with much interest. To ride on these was to be part of the bustling, well-groomed outside world, and it was noteworthy that instead of stopping at every run-down hamlet these trains would go hammering along for two or three hours at a stretch, halting at only the important places. (There did not seem to be any important places in Michigan.) Furthermore, on these trains we ate in the dining car instead of getting along with the shoe-box lunch mother always prepared for lesser trips, and that was highly glamorous. To this day I do not remember anything I actually ate on one of those diners, but the experience was memorable just the same; the table linen was so white and crisp, the waiters so starchy in their fresh white coats, the silverware so impressive and, I judged, so expensive, that what you finally got to eat was not important. Just being there was enough.

The trip back home always had a moment of anticlimax when we left Chicago. After coming down from Minnesota on one of the big-time railroads, here we were, boarding the old, familiar, slightly seedy Pere Marquette again, descending from the first-class to the jerkwater. For the first half hour after leaving the Chicago station the train ran on somebody else's right of way, with two, three or even four parallel tracks flanked by innumerable sidings, and it was possible to imagine that this railroad had miraculously been upgraded so that it was the equal of the fabulous New York Central or Pennsylvania. All too soon, however, our line would branch off and we would be jolting along in the old accustomed way on an unkempt single-track line, leaving the great world, heading for Thompsonville—which, after Chicago, no longer seemed metropolitan. Oddly enough, this letdown always passed away before we got back to Benzonia. This was the home town, and although we understood that in some ways it was nothing much, we liked it, and it was always good to be back. Maybe the warmest, most uncritical patriotism on earth is the feeling a small-town man develops for what he can see when he looks out of his bedroom window.

Railroads were all very well, and I was always glad to ride on them; but there was excitement of an entirely different order when we traveled by steamboat, as we sometimes did. To do this we took the cars to Frankfort instead of to Thompsonville. There was a tidy little harbor at Frankfort, where the mouth of the Betsie River broadened to make a modest lake, and although the town was not large it was most active and a good many vessels called there. Originally it had been an important port of call for schooners, taking lumber from the Frankfort mills down to Chicago, and although this business was just about gone when I was born plenty of steamboats still came and went because the western shore of Michigan was becoming a substantial summer resort area and people from Chicago liked to come north and escape the Illinois heat. There was a line of passenger steamers that cruised north from Chicago from early summer until well along in autumn, putting in at any number of unimportant towns and going on to the straits, and sometimes we took this way to go to Petoskey; two or three times we went down to Chicago on one of these boats instead of taking the sleeper from Thompsonville, and this twenty-four-hour trip on the lake beat even the Pullmans. Here again the moment of departure was the big thing. To wait on the beach and watch the boat come over the horizon from the southwest, to scamper back to the dock while the vessel came in past the pier heads, to stand there while it came alongside—so silent, so unhurried, so purposeful, coming

so close that you could read the name on the bow and see the words "U. S. Mail" just below—and to watch while the heaving lines came spinning through the air, and the dock hands drew in the hawsers and made them fast: this was even more exciting than watching the night train come in, because it was touched with the invisible perils of the open water.

For there was always something faintly scary (to me, anyway) in going aboard a boat for an overnight passage. We went up the gangplank through an open port in the side, aft, and found ourselves in a lobby on the lower deck, purser's office on one side, stairway to the upper decks on the other, and between the two the slanting column of a mast came up through the deck and disappeared through the overhead. It was usually fluted, painted white, sometimes with gilt trimmings, but it was obviously a mast—if I asked, reliable adults told me so—and that was certain proof that we were leaving the certainty of dry land behind us and entrusting ourselves to a *ship*. In Great Lakes parlance, to be sure, it was a boat, because the word ship was never used, but I had read books about journeys at sea and I knew that masts went with ships. I also knew that ships were subject to unpredictable perils, including one that was incomprehensible and apparently beyond remedy—if nothing else happened, a ship could always "spring a leak" and go to the bottom before anyone realized that anything special was wrong. That might happen to us. I did not really think it would, and once the boat got under way and steamed out into the lake I forgot all about it, but the faint tinge of unease that it created gave a special flavor to the excitement of the occasion.

People who lived near the Great Lakes had plenty of reason to know that these seas were dangerous. In the summer months, to be sure, when all this vacation travel took place, they were usually harmless enough, but at other times they were definitely to be respected. Literally hundreds of commercial craft have been lost in Lake Michigan during the past century, and some of them were passenger liners—like the side-wheeler *Alpena,* which disappeared without a trace in an unexpected storm on the run from Grand Haven to Chicago, and the *Chicora,* lost with all hands somewhere between Milwaukee and Benton Harbor. My own family's history had a case in point; Uncle John went to the bottom of the lake when his boat went down in the 'nineties.

This happened before I was born, and the circumstances were a bit special, not likely to be duplicated on any passenger craft, but it was something to remember. Uncle John was Mother's older brother, and he was sailing on some freighter, and the story in our family went as follows: his boat was in harbor at St. Ignace, up at the straits, taking on a load of pig iron, and a howling autumn gale was coming in from the southwest, but the captain fancied himself as a dauntless sea dog and elected to put out into it, regardless. Furthermore, the captain was drunk, and he cast off his mooring lines and went out to sea without bothering to close the cargo hatches—time enough for that, once they got clear of the land. Unfortunately, there was not time enough. The big waves swept solid water in over the decks, the water poured down the open hatches, and the ship sank like a stone, taking the wooden-headed captain, Uncle John and all but one member of the crew down with her. The man who escaped floated ashore on a wooden hatch cover; according to one version his hair turned white because of this experience, and according to another he became insane, although I could not understand how he could tell his story if he had lost his wits. But whatever the truth about the survivor may have been it was undeniable that the steamer had sunk and that Uncle John had gone down with it, and the story remained at the bottom of my mind, along with all the bookish tales about losses at sea, to stir fitfully whenever we boarded a steamboat. Lake Michigan was beautiful, but like those starry winter nights there was a subtle understood menace somewhere in the offing.

However, none of this made me lose any sleep. Once the steamer got out into the lake my fears vanished; the boat was just too real, too solid, too much a part of the established order of things, and the officers and crew were too matter-of-fact and active, to leave any room for worry. If bad things did happen on the big lake they obviously were not going to happen on this trip. There was nothing to do but relax and enjoy it. I do not remember that these boats gave us the feeling of luxury that seemed to go with Pullman sleepers and railroad dining cars, but they were always comfortable and the staterooms were undeniably snug and inviting. Also there were things to see. If we were coasting along the Michigan shore there was the endless line of sand bluffs, all white and shining when the late afternoon sun touched them, and out to sea one could almost always see a freighter trailing a plume of lazy smoke. These freighters were often spoken of as "lower lakers"; they were long, low in the water, pilothouse and officers' cabin in the bows, smokestack and cabins for lesser folk at the stern, with several hundred feet of open deck in between, and they got their name because they carried bulk freight to and from the lower lake ports like Chicago, Detroit, Cleveland and Buffalo. They were not fast, and seen from a distance they did not seem to be moving at all, and I used to wonder how anyone could stand it to go on boats that moved so slowly. When I grew up I spent a summer as a deck hand on a lower laker and learned that that leisurely progress was one of the best things about them. Besides, they were not quite as leisurely as they looked; they lost precious little time in port.

Some of the things you could see from a Great Lakes steamer were not really there; now and then you skirted the enchanted isles, although as far as I know no one ever actually went ashore on any of them, and nobody talked about it because there was no sense in getting a name as a romantic. But there were moments . . . One time we took a car ferry from Frankfort to go to Manitowoc, Wisconsin, whence by shuttle train we could reach some town where we could board a Soo Line express for Minneapolis, and we sailed at midnight or a little later. We had to get up early, because this crossing of the lake took less than six hours, and I got out on deck just at dawn and looked west at the Wisconsin shore, seven or eight miles away. We were passing the town of Two Rivers, a small manufacturing and shipping center, and the sunlight came up behind us, reached over us, and touched this unremarkable place with a magical light. The factory chimneys became slim golden pillars against the western sky, the buildings were all transfigured, and suddenly this was a seaport in the land of fable, the place everybody sailed for but never reached, unattainable, existing only at the moment of dawn. Roads no doubt led from it to the Land of Oz, or to the Island Vale of Avalon, but you could not actually get there; you could only remember what it looked like. One of the ship's officers came along the deck, saw me staring, and stopped to take a look himself. Then he turned to me, grinned, and said, "Pretty, isn't it?"

In certain lights the lakes could produce mirages. A freighter on the skyline would suddenly break up, midships section vanishing altogether, pilothouse and after cabins becoming extremely tall, reaching up like lighthouses in the deep water; then, after a minute or two, the lighthouses would disappear and there would be a steamboat again, prosaic as any other cargo carrier. On the north shore of Lake Superior the Canadian cities of Fort William and Port Arthur lie at the end of a broad bay, and on the seaward side of this bay there are islands; and if you sail from one of these cities late in the day these islands suddenly multiply so that each one is accompanied by a twin, each rock and tree perfectly duplicated, and no matter how hard you look you cannot tell which island is real and which is not. The navigator, I suppose, has to stick to his chart and his compass even though he has hardly passed the pierhead; the only problem is that the compass on Lake Superior sometimes does tricks because there is so much iron under the bottom of the lake and in the surrounding hills. After a while the imitation islands rise into the air, get all streaky and distorted, and then go away entirely, and the lake is clear once more. I feel sorry for people who have never cruised the Great Lakes by steamboat.

Those car ferries were unusual vessels. They were not in the least like the car floats visible in New York harbor; they were (and still are, for they have survived three quarters of a century of change) seagoing steamers, the car deck all enclosed to make a gloomy cave as long as a football field, with four tracks on it, able to carry two dozen boxcars at once. Above there is a steel deck bearing staterooms for passengers, galley and dining room, officers' quarters, and nowadays accommodations for the "unlicensed personnel," or crew. In the old days the crew was housed below the car deck, down along the waterline, and it was uncomfortable down there, but today they are more pleasantly situated; and this is just as well because these ferries are icebreakers, keeping schedule all winter long, and what with the grinding ice floes and the midwinter gales a sailor's life on Lake Michigan can be rugged in January.

Sailing at midnight on one of these boats was somewhat eerie, because my capacity for scenting danger where it did not exist became enlarged. The loading slips were on the south side of the harbor, and across the water the town of Frankfort was completely silent, nobody astir, houses all dark, only the street lights giving any sign of life. At the loading slip our ferry would heel to port and then to starboard as the switching crew pushed the cars aboard; then the loading was complete, and for five or ten minutes there was a muffled thumping and clanging as the crew fastened rail clamps, fixed jacks at the corners of the cars, attached chains, and arranged things so that the cars would stay where they were supposed to stay if a stormy sea made the boat roll heavily. In summer months there was not much chance that things would go wrong, but in bad weather it was another story. If a car ferry captain found a heavy beam sea running when he came out of the harbor he would cross the lake in a series of tacks, taking the wind on the bow and then on the quarter to avoid wallowing along in the trough. If the cars ever broke loose there would be serious trouble, with outright loss of the steamer and everybody aboard a distinct possibility. Many years have passed since anything of the kind has happened, but it is necessary to be careful.

On the particular night that I remember preparations were at last complete, and after a warning note on the deep, husky whistle the boat departed. We had come aboard an hour or so before departure time, and of course I could have gone to bed at once, but I was not going to miss the moment of sailing so I was out on deck as we steamed past the lighthouse and committed ourselves to the open lake. It was unsettling, for even though it was the calmest of summer nights I had my doubts about what might be lying in wait for us out there in the pathless dark. At last I looked up at the unlighted pilothouse. I could just make out the figures of men standing there; at an open window in front an officer lounged with his elbows on the sill, pipe in his mouth, gazing straight ahead, looking as if he had not a care in the world, and I went off to bed comforted. We were in the care of men who knew what they were doing, and if there was trouble ahead they would see it and do something about it before it got to us. It would be nice to feel that way today.

With the perils that might arise on the seas, or on the steel-bound rights of way through the stumpy plains, the boat and train crews were well qualified to deal. However, they could see no farther into changing times than any of the rest of us could see, and what they and we looked upon as an established order of things was in fact subject to constant alteration. Nothing that we considered fixed was really settled. We lived by the best light the past could give us, but we were going to live in the future and the proper guiding lights were veiled. We might understand it when it came or, for that matter, we might not—but we could neither foresee it nor influence it. We were at the mercy of a series of accidents that had already happened.

We lived where we lived because the wealth of the state's pine woods had been discovered just when the nation needed un-heard-of quantities of pine boards. The exploitation of that resource had gone more rapidly than anyone supposed it would go because as rising demand met unlimited supply the growth of technological knowledge made it possible to turn trees into boards faster than had been done in all the history of mankind. The unlimited supply disappeared altogether, but the technological progress remained and exerted its own pressures. The one certainty was that everything was going to change. We might well have altered that old saying: Whatever is, is temporary. That is a hard truth to live by.

What came next, as the forests died, was the era of the summer hotel.

The transportation network that had been built to get the timber out now served to bring the summer people in. They came to our impoverished land in a healing flood, pouring out on station platforms as the "resort specials" arrived, swarming down the gangplanks as the steamers docked, with horse-drawn carry-alls waiting to take the visitors to the summer hotels, drivers standing by with long whips at order arms, calling out the names of the places they served: "Island House . . . Arlington Hotel . . . The Belvedere," and so on.

Every city on Lake Michigan and many more on the inland lakes had one or several summer hotels; huge, brightly painted, made of wood, with broad verandas all about, commanding a fine view of sunset over the water. The visitor at one of these places usually stayed put, once he checked in, because there was not really much to do; life was comfortable but it must have been a trifle dull. The children could play on the beach, sometimes a family could rent a boat for a cruise along the shore, and in the evening there were usually sedate dances for the college-age crowd, but on the whole nothing much happened. An adult put in most of his time in a rocking chair on the porch, reflecting that he was at least keeping cool and that he was north of the hay fever zone, placidly digesting the huge meals of whitefish and lake trout that were placed before him every day.

Some of these hotels, like the Grand on Mackinac Island, were luxurious and imposing after the manner of Saratoga Springs, although I never heard of any gambling casinos at any of them. Most resort towns had cottage colonies, some of which had a strong evangelical coloration, with improving concerts and lectures and innumerable religious services. I can remember four —Epworth Heights, for the Methodists, at Ludington, the Congregational and Christian Summer Assemblies on Crystal Lake near Frankfort, and the Baptist show place, Bay View, near Petoskey—and I suppose there were a good many more. A few wealthy folk had expensive summer homes at places like Charlevoix and Harbor Point, and quite a few lesser folk had cottages on the inland lakes and rivers where there was good fishing, but there was not much moving around at any of them. There simply was no good way to go flitting about. When you reached journey's end you dug in for the summer.

This was a middle-class vacation country, for the most part. The wage earners in the great factory cities to the south did not take vacations. They were busy making things, among them the automobiles that were about to change the entire pattern, putting the passenger steamers out of business, doing the same to the railroad passenger service, and in the end compelling the state to build a network of hard-surfaced roads that doomed most of the summer hotels. (If they were easier to reach by automobile, they were also easier to leave; why anchor yourself in one spot when it was so simple to drive a few dozen miles up the road and try something else, preferably a furnished cottage that you could rent by the week, spending much less money than you would have to spend at a hotel?) These hotels suffered, in any case, from the fact that they were essentially luxury accommodations serving a clientele that found the price of luxury a bit too high. They were closed for nine months in every year, and unless the summer trade was really lush the hotel owner lost money. More and more of these places went out of business in the years just before the first World War. Many of them burned down, in the winter season, and local people would wag their heads and make remarks about insurance money. The automobile simply added the finishing touch.

So the worn-out lumber country had turned to the summer visitor for its economic salvation, and now the summer visitor adopted new ways; he went to different places and he did different things after he got there, he was likely to move on at a moment's notice, and the land that lived on him had to adjust itself accordingly. Nobody realized it for a while, but the overpowering era of the internal combustion engine imposes a law of its own which grows more rigorous with age. Simply stated, that law is as follows: If it is at all possible, at no matter what inconvenience or expense, to get from this place to that place by automobile, it will eventually become impossible to get there by any other means whatever. (The airplane is not an exception to this rule, because it is nothing but an automobile with wings.) If a society is built around a certain transportation network, and that network is destroyed and replaced by something very different, the society itself has to change from top to bottom.

So the town that used to be important because it was on the railroad or had a good harbor finds its importance gone; it shrinks, and sometimes it dies altogether. The boats and the trains die, and so do the elaborate summer hotels, and all the ways of life that were built on these things disappear. The world we were used to suddenly becomes the world we lost—or the world we escaped from; you can say it either way, depending on how you look at it. The change may indeed be for the better. The point is that the society that is being changed has no control over the process.

The boat clears the harbor and steams out into the windy dark, and all of the charts are unexpectedly found to be worthless; the officers have to guess where the opposite shore is, and they have no idea what sort of landfall they are going to make. All they really know is that it is impossible to turn back. The land they knew has gone below a horizon that can never be regained.

This struck us in Benzonia with especial force. Ours was not a lumber town, but it had been built to meet the needs of the lumber country and as the new century grew older our reason for existence quietly evaporated. It was a long time before we realized this. We could see that changes were taking place, and we understood that we were more closely connected with the outside world than we used to be, but what it all meant was beyond understanding. The little academy went ahead, training young people to make their way through the nineteenth century on the theory that the century that was opening would be essentially like the one that had gone before it, and it took a while to see that what lay ahead was going to be different in every single detail. A backwoods community that has lost its woods can be a confusing place.

CHAPTER FIVE

The Ax, the Log and the River

My sixth birthday was a special occasion. We were staying with grandfather in Petoskey just then, and for a birthday celebration my parents took me to the theater for the first time in my life. There was no theater to go to anywhere near Benzonia, and in any case most people in our town considered the theater more or less sinful, and spoke against it in prayer meeting. My parents were less strait-laced than that, and anyway the show I was taken to was highly moral—*Uncle Tom's Cabin,* no less, complete with tossing ice floes, bloodhounds, and the transfiguration of Little Eva; all very edifying and painfully exciting as well. I enjoyed every minute of it, rising in my seat once to scream, "Give it to him!" when the forces of right closed in on (I think) the villainous lawyer, Marks. I was just a bit disillusioned when I heard my elders say, on the way home, that Little Eva was not really a small child but a grown woman; they had seen her in the lobby, after the performance, selling photographs of herself.

Besides going to see this play, I was given the birthday gift I wanted most of all. I was presented with an ax.

It was a child's-sized ax, of course, bearing about the same relation to my height and strength that a lumberman's ax bore to the height and strength of an adult, but it was no toy. The shape and balance were the same as with the grown-up's model, and the head was made of good steel capable of taking and holding a keen cutting edge. (Let a child learn to use an ax with a dull blade, and the first time he swings a sharp one he is apt to cut his foot off.) The ax was a highly respected implement in Michigan. You had to know how to use one, even if you had no intention of ever working in a lumber camp; at the very least you would have to split stove-wood for the kitchen and living room stoves, and from boyhood to old age you could expect to split many cords of it, a cord being a stack of wood four feet high and eight feet long. Having an ax of my own showed that I was no longer a baby. I have never received a birthday gift that pleased me as much as that one did.

There was another way in which my sixth birthday marked a milestone. We moved away from Benzonia—temporarily, as it turned out, although we did not know that at the time—and settled in Boyne City, which seemed to be the precise opposite of Benzonia in almost every respect. For Boyne City was just about the last lumber boom town in the lower peninsula, and when we got there it was busily engaged in cutting down and sawing up one of the last stands of virgin pine. It contained three or four sawmills, a chemical plant where wood alcohol, or turpentine, or possibly both, was extracted from recently felled trees, a tannery which consumed the bark of thousands of hemlocks, and a blast furnace fueled by charcoal made from the hardwoods that did not seem to be good for anything else. I suppose it had a population of twenty-five hundred, or thereabouts, and it was noisy, odorous—between the tannery, the chemical plant and the mountains of pine-wood sawdust that piled up by the mills its air held a wonderful and inescapable combination of smells—and to a six-year-old, especially one who had been living in one of the quietest villages in North America, it was marvelously vivid and exciting. I heard my elders say that it contained no fewer than thirteen saloons, and although this was a fact that they deplored it seemed to me to be a mark of distinction; it might be a sign of wickedness, of course, but what other place could show such an impressive total?

Boyne City is situated at the eastern end of Lake Charlevoix, some twenty miles south of Petoskey. Eighteen miles to the west, at the resort town of Charlevoix, the lake communicates with Lake Michigan by a deep-water channel, and in the early 1900s steamboats from the big lake came in and docked at Boyne City. There were boats and barges to take lumber to Chicago, bulk carriers bringing iron ore down from Escanaba, and a number of small passenger steamers that cruised up to Petoskey, Harbor Springs and Mackinac Island. This meant that the waterfront was a stimulating place for a small boy. It was not extensive, but something always seemed to be going on there.

In addition, the city was the point of origin and principal terminus of a typical pine country railroad, the Boyne City, Gaylord and Alpena, a standard-gauge line whose name had a fine, triple-jointed lilt to it even though the places it connected were comparatively unknown to fame. In 1906 it was still threading its way across the northern part of the lower peninsula, and I believe it finally made it before the great railroad blight descended, but its chief functions were two: it offered freight and passenger service between Boyne City and Boyne Falls, eight or nine miles to the east, where it crossed the north-south line of the Grand Rapids and Indiana, a subsidiary of the mighty Pennsylvania, and it went zigzagging through vast stands of pine and hardwoods, bringing saw logs to the Boyne City mills. It ran within sight of our house, day after day the trains of flatcars carrying logs went rumbling past, and I could sit on the woodpile by our kitchen door and admire them. I was able to do this because I was deemed just too young to go to school and I had most of the day at my disposal. I have never felt on such intimate terms with any railroad as I did with this one. It was as busy as could be, and yet it had a homemade, improvised character that was immensely appealing.

The Boyne City, Gaylord and Alpena had apparently picked up its motive power where it could find it. It owned ten locomotives, and no two were alike. They did not even sound alike. In no time at all Robert and I got so we could tell which engine was coming just by hearing it whistle. Most of the locomotives were like nothing I had ever seen before. Only two or three seemed to be orthodox in design, and some of them struck me as positively eccentric, as if they had been put together by someone who never made a steam engine before. There were two Shays, for instance, a big one (Number Nine) and a little one (Number Three), and the up-and-down motion of their vertical piston rods was both perplexing and fascinating. One locomotive was fairly normal except that it carried its bell on top of its sand dome, which gave it an oddly humpbacked appearance and seemed to me to be grossly irregular. I do not now remember just how the other engines departed from what my six-year-old mind considered proper standards, but almost all of them did. There were two regular 4-4-0 types, but one of these had lost its cowcatcher in some accident and they had never bothered to replace it. All in all, the steam engines of this little railroad gave my brother and me a great deal to talk about.

If the railroad palled on us, as I do not think it ever did, there was always the Boyne River. Our back yard sloped down to the edge of this river, which was not exactly spectacular but which made a profound impression just the same. It prodded our imaginations, as a flowing stream always does, and it seemed dangerous; a moving flood that could drown a small boy if he took liberties with it. I revisited that back yard a few years ago, looked out on a placid, sparkling, friendly little stream, and wondered how I could ever have found it so menacing. At last I realized that when I originally saw it I was no more than half as tall as I am now— the river, in other words, really was twice as wide and twice as deep, in relation to me, as it is now, so some of the peril doubtless was real enough. I suppose, too, that my parents had issued stern warnings about the bad things that could happen to children who played carelessly on a river bank, and this may have strengthened my native timidity.

However that may have been, the river was impressive. In the spring, just after the ice went out, an old-fashioned log drive came down this river, and men with peaveys and pike poles, wearing ferociously spiked boots, came along the banks or trotted lightly across the shifting carpet of logs that covered the stream's surface from bank to bank, and we had it all where we could see it in a continuous close-up. This was not one of the great log drives of lumber country legend; the Boyne River after all was not big, and by the time they reached us the logs had practically come to the end of the line. The danger of a ruinous log jam was over, and all that remained now was to get the logs a last half mile into the storage ponds from which the endless-chain conveyors would send them up to the whining buzz saws and the voracious, earth-shaking gang saws. The river men on duty here had a fairly easy task.

But the business was worth looking at, especially if you had never seen anything like it before. Day after day the logs went drifting past, and the men who worked to keep them moving went about on them so effortlessly, and apparently so casually, that small boys who had slipped the leash at home were often moved to go out and walk the logs themselves. This actually was a dangerous game. With the runoff of the melted snow back in the hills, the river was deeper and more turbulent than it ordinarily was. Furthermore, that moving carpet was treacherous. In addition to saw logs, the drive contained numbers of slim cedar and jack pine poles hardly bigger than saplings—for fence posts, or for the chemical plant, perhaps even for the pulp mills farther down Lake Michigan—and these were by no means sturdy enough to keep a log-runner afloat. To an experienced river man they were of course no problem, because when he moved out across the logs he knew where he was going and chose his path with automatic expertise, but to a boy who was simply scampering blindly for the opposite shore they were a mortal hazard. They could drop him into the water in the twinkling of an eye, and if that happened the moving logs were all too likely to drift in over him, trapping him under water and drowning him.

For this reason, small boys were ordered to keep off the logs—

by their parents, by the town authorities and by the river men themselves. Small boys being what they are, this prohibition was not always effective. As far as I was concerned it worked pretty well, because I was afraid of the river in any case, but with the older boys better enforcement was needed. Robert nearly lost his life that way; skipping logs one day, he came upon one of these danger spots, went into the water over his head, and was fished out only because some river man happened to see what had happened. Dripping wet, Robert went home. The first thing Mother noticed was that he had got his new shoes wet, and she was upbraiding him for this when it suddenly dawned on her that her cherished first-born had just had a narrow escape from death; this gave Robert a moral advantage that made the scolding completely ineffective. However, he did abandon the practice of going out on the logs.

Somewhere far out of our sight—up the river, up the railroad track, back in the distant rolling hills—was the country where these logs came from; the dim, cathedral-like forest where trees that had been three centuries getting their growth rose from a carpet of brown pine needles, straight trunks going up through a quiet dusk to support a rustling green canopy far overhead. People in Boyne City subscribed to Michigan's most cherished delusion: they thought that the supply of lumber was inexhaustible. That word *inexhaustible* had been on men's lips since before the Civil War, and by 1906 most of the state had stopped using it because most of the virgin timber had in fact been exhausted long since, so that big sawmill towns like Saginaw and Muskegon and Manistee were desperately looking for some other way to stay alive. But in Boyne City, the word was still good.

Or at least it still seemed to be good. The men who owned the mills and the lumber camps and the railroad doubtless had a clear idea of the real situation, and they were prepared to follow the lumberman's oldest rule—*cut and get out.* But to everybody else the setup looked permanent. The mills themselves, noisy, constantly busy, with blue-gray columns of smoke leaning away from their tall stacks, and the endless snake-dance of logs going up the inclines to the machinery that would reduce them to boards, had so obviously been built to last; and in winter the parallel lines of the railway iron, precisely drawn in India ink across the white fields, converging to a vanishing point far off under the frozen sky, looked like part of the natural order of things. This was bound to endure because if it all vanished there would be nothing left that one could count on and helpless folk would confront a world all of whose certainties had collapsed. Michigan had been brought up on the belief that its riches would last forever. The great forests, the copper and iron under the hills, the salt mines far underground, the vast hills of limestone, the wealth of fish in the streams and lakes, the crystal purity of air and water—they were there to be used, it was man's duty to exploit them to the full, and to doubt their permanence was to doubt the solidity of the great globe itself, cloud-capped towers and all.

We had no doubts; or if now and then people did have some they quickly suppressed them. The future that was coming in would (we were confident) be shaped on the present—and so indeed it was, when we finally got it, although the shape of it was not quite what everyone had been looking for because the present contained elements that had not been carefully appraised. The trees were cut down, most of the copper was used up—some mines had mile-deep shafts, with galleries reaching out under the bed of Lake Superior itself, which proves that the acquisitive instinct knows no limits—the fisheries were pretty largely exhausted, the air and the water were getting soiled, and year by year there was need to use larger quantities of the iron and the limestone. Some of these resources were irreplaceable and others could be replaced only by a greater effort than anyone wanted to make, but that made no difference. Our society lived by making war on its environment; it won the war only to find the struggle intensified.

We had moved away from Benzonia because father wanted to try the experiment of making some money.

He had been on the Benzonia College faculty during the last few years of the nineteenth century, conducting courses designed to prepare young men and women for the work of teaching in the public schools. The ordinary college then had what was called a "normal department"—a college that devoted itself entirely to such work was known as a normal school—and Father in his own person was the normal department of Benzonia College. When the college was discontinued and the academy took its place Father's department of course ceased to exist, and for a few years he made a living by selling insurance. The immediate neighborhood offered a mortally poor field for this because the population and its wealth were steadily declining, so Father was on the road a good deal, pursuing prospects up and down the western part of the state; he did not especially like the work but he did it well, and late in 1905 the insurance company he represented established an office in Boyne City and put him in charge of it. This offered a chance to make a decent living, after years of subsisting just above the level of outright poverty, so Father took us all up to this bustling lumber town with high hopes.

Getting the new office in operation, Father needed printed material—brochures, hand books and I do not know what all—and he made a bargain with the publisher of the local newspaper. The publisher agreed to do Father's job printing, and in payment Father wrote weekly articles on Boyne City, its assets, its prospects and its interesting ways of life. Father wrote clearly and easily and the deal turned out to be a good one. The part that affected me personally was that he was taken on conducted tours of the sawmills, the blast furnace, the tannery, the railroad shops and so on, and he usually took Robert and me along to see what was to be seen. The sawmills appalled me: they were noisy, the heavy jolting of the big gang saw which could take two logs at a time and turn them into boards with one prodigious effort seemed likely to shake the whole building apart, and there were altogether too many moving, whirring, deadly looking pieces of metal that could hurt a small boy—or a grown-up man, for that matter—to suit my taste. I was glad to have seen it all, but I was also glad when we came out. The blast furnace was not quite so bad, although it too had a nightmarish quality. We went to the highest level of the silo-shaped furnace and stood there on a gallery of slotted iron, eyes popping out, while a door was opened and a hand cart of ore or limestone or charcoal was dumped into the glowing interior; whereupon a big tongue of flame shot up, and I felt the heat in my face and shrank away, trying not to think about what it would be like to fall through that infernal trap door. It was frightening enough, but somehow it was not quite as bad as the sawmills; it lacked the hint of uncontrollable violence that seemed to go with the whining saws. Of the tannery I remember nothing at all except that it had an odd smell and that somebody gave me a little two-inch square of tanned leather, which I kept for years for no good reason.

The big day was the day Father took us out to a lumber camp.

We rode out in the caboose of a freight train, which by itself was enough to make this a great occasion; past Boyne Falls, and off on some temporary branch line that led to the lumber camp, where our engine was to drop its empty flatcars and collect loaded cars for the return trip. While the train crew did this, Father took us up to the cook shack for a midday meal. Some representative of the lumber company was either waiting for him there, or had accompanied us from the start; I do not remember which way it was, and it does not make much difference. In any case, I got my first look at an old-time Michigan lumber camp.

I did not actually see a great deal, and anyway a scene remembered from early childhood is glimpsed as through a glass darkly, with the real and the unreal looking much alike. Looking back now I can recall little more than a set of log-and-tarpaper buildings in a clearing on rising ground, a wilderness of stumps and unwanted saplings all around, and somewhere in the distance a swampy plain where spiky dark trees without leaves or needles stood bleak and lonely against the snow—tamaracks, undoubtedly, although I could not have identified them at the time. The camp was singularly quiet, and hardly any men were in sight. The men, of course, were off in the woods, hard at work; from first to last, the lumberjack never saw his camp in daylight except on Sundays—he went off into the forest before sunrise and he came back after dusk, and he knew his home place only as a warm spot in the cold darkness, where he ate and slept and on Sunday boiled his socks and long johns and waged ineffective war on the bedbugs that infested the bunkhouse.

What does stand out in my mind is the memory of eating in the cook shack, an oblong building with an enormous wood-burning range at one end and long tables flanked by backless benches running the length of the room. Here the men were fed, morning and night; in the middle of the day the meal was taken to them in the woods, where they sat on logs and stumps and ate big bowls of stew, stacks of fresh bread, and incredible amounts of pie, doughnuts and cookies, with gallons of coffee out of soot-blackened pots. Our little party sat at one end of a table and got the same fare, and it seemed to me that this was the way to live because there was so much of everything. I was especially impressed by the coffee and the cookies. The coffee came in tin pannikins rather than in cups, and the pannikins looked big enough to serve as washbasins. At home I was hardly ever allowed to drink coffee, because Mother felt that it was not good for growing boys, but Father was more easy-going, and besides there was nothing else to drink there, so I lifted the pannikin with both hands and gulped until it was empty. The cookies were even more noteworthy. They were as large as pie plates . . . well, perhaps not quite that large, really, but I saw everything bigger than life-size in those days, and it seemed to me that for the first time I had found cookies that were as big as cookies ought to be.

At the table, and later, I heard all about lumber camp cook shacks. The cook was undisputed boss of the shack. His word was law, and even the camp foreman himself—a slave-driving autocrat who had to be willing and able to enforce his commands by beating up some of the stoutest rough-and-tumble fighters in existence—would not dream of overruling him in the cook's own bailiwick. The cook's first rule invariably was that

there could be no talking at the table. A man might ask another to pass the bread, but beyond that he could say nothing; the meal was eaten in silence, except for the incidental noises made by seventy-five or one hundred ravenous men stuffing themselves, clumsily but with awe-inspiring effectiveness, consuming a prodigious meal in no more than fifteen minutes. As a matter of fact the cook was one of the most important men in the entire crew, and usually he was among the most highly paid. The worst calamity that could befall a lumber camp was for the cook to quit in midseason, because if that happened the men were apt to go away forthwith, leaving the foreman without a work force. Because of this the management generally handled the cook with kid gloves on, and what he wanted he was likely to get.

For a lumber camp would stand or fall on the food it provided. The men who worked there were exploited as ruthlessly as any workers in American history—the work was hard, often it was dangerous, the hours were long, the pay was low and there were no fringe benefits whatever. The one compensation was that there was always plenty to eat. The quality might vary, from camp to camp, although the men knew good cooking from bad and a firm that was known to use inexpert cooks generally had trouble recruiting its working crew. One of the biggest companies logging the Manistee River got a bad name because it served baked beans three times a day, with everything else regarded as trimmings. The men made up an irreverent jingle about it, and to this day there are people around Manistee who can sing it for you, to the tune of "Maryland, My Maryland":

> *Who feeds us beans until we're blue?*
> *Louie Sands and Jim McGee.*
> *Who thinks that nothing else will do?*
> *Louie Sands and Jim McGee.*
> *Who feeds us beans three times a day,*
> *And gives us very little pay?*
> *Who feeds us beans, again I say?*
> *Louie Sands and Jim McGee.*

The lumberman lived mostly on meat, potatoes, bread and pastry. One historian of the logging era estimated that a hundred-man camp would consume six barrels of flour every week, plus two and one-half barrels of beef and an equal amount of pork, eight bushels of potatoes, three bushels of onions, a barrel of sugar and forty pounds of lard, along with incidentals like canned tomatoes, pickles, prunes and sausage. The chief breakfast staple was the pancake, covered with molasses or pork gravy and accompanied by whole pans full of fried potatoes and fried salt pork. A cook who served a sixty-five-man camp in the Grand Traverse Bay area baked thirty-five loaves of bread and three hundred and fifty buns twice a week, got eighteen pies out of the oven every morning before the sun was up and produced two kegs of cookies each day. A cook in an upper peninsula camp complained —or boasted—that he had to make a barrel of doughnuts daily. Besides the salt meat a good deal of fresh beef and pork was eaten. In the early days, when game was plentiful, a camp sometimes hired a hunter to provide a supply of venison. All in all, the woodsman got plenty to eat.

He needed it, because his life was hard. In the early days, conditions were downright rugged. The bunk shanty originally was simply a rectangular building of chinked logs, with no floor but the packed earth. Bunks were ranged along the walls, and the heat came from an open fire in a shallow pit in the middle of the room. There was no chimney; overhead there was a slot in the roof, and most of the smoke went out there. Windows there were none, and the bunk shanty was as smoky, ill-ventilated and generally smelly as any living quarters man has ever used. As a matter of fact, in its essentials a shanty like this was much like the traditional long house of the Iroquois Indians, except that the long house was probably more comfortable. The point to remember is that the Indians were a stone-age people giving themselves the best housing they could devise; the lumbermen were nineteenth-century Americans occupying the worst quarters their society had to offer.

As years passed, of course, conditions improved. The bunk shanty was given proper flooring, and a stove with a regular chimney replaced the open fire pit. The bunks remained about as they had been—oblong wooden boxes, with evergreen branches and a sack of straw for mattress and springs, and woolen blankets for covering, the whole offering a secure refuge for the vermin that were a plague of every camp. Except for the fact that there was no smoke in the air, ventilation remained about as it had been. The shanty was usually crisscrossed with clothes lines, on which wet socks and boots were hung up to dry, and by bedtime the air was thick enough to a float a canoe. There were rarely any windows, and when there were windows they were kept closed; it was cold, outside, and anyway the men spent the entire day out in the open so who wanted fresh air at night?

To the men who occupied it this shanty gave the name to the entire trade. The man who worked in the woods rarely spoke of himself as a lumberjack, because he considered that a city man's expression. Sometimes he called himself a logger, but most of the time he spoke of himself and his fellows as shanty boys. If you lived through a winter in the steamy, malodorous dimness of a lumber camp shanty, you belonged; you were a shanty boy, then and thereafter.

Though the housing improved, the life remained hard. The men were out in the woods as soon as the sun came up—the get-'em-up cry in the bunk shanty was a chanted "Daylight in the swamp!"—and the foreman went about indicating the trees that were to be felled. (Until fairly late in the game the lumbermen wanted nothing but tall, straight white pines; lesser pines, and all of the hardwoods, were left standing. Before the logging era ended, to be sure, they took everything, but as long as there was plenty of pine it was the only tree that really mattered.) When a tree had been chosen, two ax-men came up, standing facing one another, one of them swinging his double-bitted ax from the right shoulder, the other swinging from the left; it was their job to cut an eight-inch or ten-inch notch on one side of the tree to

SHARP.

control the direction in which the tree would fall. Before they began to cut, the axmen took pains to clear away any under-growth that might be standing by the trunk; to strike a limb or a sapling by accident, either on the back-swing or on the cutting stroke, would produce an out-of-control glancing blow that might maim a man for life, and these men took no chances. When everything was ready the men began to swing their axes, striking alternate blows in a remorseless rhythm, cutting a deep triangular notch whose edges were as smooth as if they had been planed; an ax was a precision instrument in the pineries.

Once the notch was deep enough to determine the direction in which the tree would fall the axmen laid aside their axes and took another weapon, with which they actually brought the tree down. The new weapon was a cross-cut saw seven feet long—limber, with sharp jagged teeth, bowed out along the cutting edge, thicker at the back than it was where the teeth were, with a handle at each end. The sawyers attacked the tree on the side opposite to the notch; they drew the blade back and forth lightly a few times, to provide a guiding groove, then settled down to work in a steady rhythm like the one made by the axes, and the blade made a musical zing-zing as it cut deeper and deeper into the wood, spurting a handful of sawdust with each stroke. This part of the work went fairly fast. If pitch from the raw pine clogged the teeth of the saw the men used a rag and a bottle of kerosene to clean the blade, and if the weight of the tree pressed down on the blade as the back edge went in out of sight, a hard-wood wedge would be driven into the cut to relieve the pressure. And at last the top of the pine, far above, would quiver and give a sudden movement, and there would be a sharp cracking sound from the trunk, at which moment the sawyers would remove the blade, step backward, and raise the warning cry of the pinewoods —"Tim-m-ber-r-r!"

When this cry was raised everybody within range took cover, because a tall pine came down with a mighty crash and nobody was quite certain what might happen. Sometimes the heavy trunk rebounded when it hit the ground, sometimes it struck another tree on the way down and fell off, unpredictably, sideways, and now and then it bore an unexpectedly long branch, sticking out at right angles to the trunk, to strike a man who had thought himself out of danger. (A long branch of that kind was known, significantly, as a widow-maker.) Usually, of course, the tree came down the way it was supposed to come, and as soon as it had come to rest, work on the other trees went on as before.

Once the tree was on the ground, men with axes attacked it, cutting off the branches and the too-slender tip; then the trunk was marked off into sixteen-foot lengths and the sawyers returned to cut the trunk into logs. The sawyers were veterans, owning that finely wrought skill that makes a hard job look easy. The rule was that a sawyer simply pulled the saw toward himself; he did not press down on it, because the weight of the saw itself was enough to keep the teeth biting into the wood, and he did not push it away from him at the end of the stroke because that made his partner's job harder. (To push on the return stroke was known as riding the saw, and it was enough to get a man demoted.) A pine tree two feet thick could be reduced to logs in short order.

Now the first step in the destruction of the forest and the creation of useful building material was over. From this point to the moment the logs entered the sawmill the lumber business was a matter of transportation. That does not mean that it was simple. Logs are hard to move, moving them is subject to all manner of evil strokes of chance, an aspiring lumber baron could go broke if his luck was bad, and year in and year out the business killed a few of the baron's hired hands no matter how the boss's luck was running.

The initial move in this business of transportation was to get the logs out of the trackless timber and over to the roadway the lumbermen had created. Teamsters came in, a device much like an oversized pair of ice tongs was attached to one end of a log, and a pair of stout horses—oxen, in the early days, but usually horses toward the end—dragged it off through the trees to the skidway, a pile of logs by the roadway. This roadway was an affair of packed snow, turned to ice by water that was sprayed on it at night from a tank cart in zero weather, and it was built for just one purpose: to make it possible to move the ponderous logs over to the river that would carry them off to market once spring came and the ice was out. The roadway snaked its way through and around the stand of timber that was under attack, it avoided up-hill drags as much as possible, and it could be used only in the wintertime. No wagon ever built could carry the incredible loads that could be moved by sleigh on an icy road; a mild winter without enough snow or freezing weather to keep the roads well iced offered the boss lumberman a sure route to bankruptcy.

Naturally the lumber camp sleigh was a heavy-duty affair. It consisted chiefly of two pairs of steel-faced runners, in tandem, bound together by ponderous beams, the forward pair of runners of course working on a pivot. Each runner was set some eight feet away from its partner, and the pair carried a heavy transverse beam, known as a bunk, twelve or fourteen feet in length, and the two bunks, one on each pair of runners, were what the sixteen-foot logs rested on. The sleigh was loaded at the skidway, and the record of the weight a sleigh could carry would be un-believable if there were not plenty of photographs of loaded sleighs to prove it. A load of logs piled three times the height of a man's head and weighing thirty tons was not especially unusual.

The first logs were rolled onto the sleigh's bunks from the skidway; the rest were hoisted up by horse power, while men with cant hooks guided them into place. The cant hook was the indis-pensable tool here. It had a handle of tapered ash or rock maple, from four to six feet long, iron-shod at the base, with a sharp steel hook a foot long swinging from a hinge ten inches above the base. It gave a man a grip on a log so that he could turn it over, hold it in place, inch it over into the spot where he wanted it to go, and in general keep it under control. He could do these things, that is, if he knew precisely what he was doing and had the strength, skill and nerve to do it properly; inert logs tended to be cranky, and a cant hook man could get mashed if a log got away from him. (Given a sharp spike at the business end, a cant hook became a peavey; the cant hook was the favored instrument in the woods and the peavey was used after the logs had been put into the river.) When the sleigh was fully loaded the logs were bound in place with chains, and the teamster took over.

It was up to the teamster to drive the sleigh along the glare ice of the roadway two or three miles to the banking grounds, an open place on the bank of the nearest river where the logs were stacked in enormous piles that would be tumbled into the water when spring came. The teamster was another man who had to know what he was doing. His horses were shod with calked shoes so that they could work on the ice, but the sleigh had no brakes whatever and on a downhill drag the load could take charge if the teamster was the least bit careless. As a safety measure, one or two men went out at night and spread horse manure on the icy ruts on all descending grades; a man who held this job was known, for some reason, as a chickadee. If a thirty-ton load once picked up speed on a downgrade the horses could not hold it back, and the result was a wild smashup, sleigh running over the team, heavy chains snapping like thread, logs scattered all about, teamster and horses buried under everything as likely as not. If the teamster survived he was in danger of being either fired outright or turned into a chickadee, but his chance of survival in a downhill wreck was not good. It was bad enough to lose a teamster, but the loss of the horses was what really hurt. A good team of Percherons represented a cash investment of six hundred dollars or more.

In one way or another the winter's cut of logs was finally stacked up along a river, and when spring came the camp's work was over. Until near the end of the lumber era in Michigan, the work was strictly seasonal. The men were hired late in the fall, when a new camp was built, and they were paid off in the spring, and what they did in the warm-weather months was entirely up to them. Many were farmers, raising potatoes and beans and anything else the thin soil of the lumber country would produce from spring to mid-autumn, and then going back into the woods for another winter of it. Most of them were subsistence farmers, although they would not have recognized the expression if they had heard it. When the lumbering era was over, a great many discovered that their hardscrabble farms would not support a family unless the farmer could earn money on the side, and in the first quarter of this century they abandoned their farms by the dozen and by the score, letting unpainted houses and barns fall in, letting the fields grow up to weeds and sumac, letting the state take over for unpaid taxes. Many a county in the lumber country has a smaller population today than it had fifty years ago.

The man who worked in the woods was caught in a bind. The lumber camp did not offer a decent annual income. Wage rates varied, of course, from year to year and from place to place, but the logger generally got twenty-five or thirty dollars a month and his work year was only six months long. Even if he did not give way to the impulse to spend his pay in a grand blowout in the saloons and dives of the nearest lumber town when he got paid off, he obviously did not have enough of a stake to carry him through six months of idleness. He needed a job. Sometimes he worked in a sawmill during the off season, but it was precisely the man who was most anxious to protect his future and take care of his family who was most likely to turn to farming. This made him more vulnerable rather than less. He had two jobs, and each one was propped up by the other. Take one away and he was lost. A few men, of course—prodigiously hard workers, and luckier than most in their choice of farm land—managed to make a go of it as farmers, but most of them simply got out when all of the trees were gone.

Meanwhile, as the lumber camps paid off their men and closed, the business of transporting the logs to the mills got under way. Originally everything went by water, and right down to the end a lot of it did, and now it was the riverman who was all important.

A crew of rivermen was usually composed of the coolest and handiest veterans of the lumber camp. They carried peaveys and pike poles—long poles with a metal spike and crosspiece at the end, like oversized boat hooks with sharpened points—and they wore spiked boots so that they could keep their footing on the floating logs; and it was their job to bring the logs downstream from the banking grounds to the log booms at the river's mouth, where the logs were sorted out and sent on to the different mills that were waiting for them.

This called for hard work, on a dawn-to-dusk basis, and at times it was extremely dangerous. When logs grounded on a sand bar or some other obstruction, or got into some other sort of tangle through the natural cussedness of logs adrift in moving water, a log jam developed, with logs at the rear of the drive piling upon the logs in front, the force of the current packing them together, the whole thing acting like a dam, with the river's flow downstream reduced to a trickle while the water level upstream rose higher and higher so that many logs floated off and became stranded in the swamps or undergrowth some distance away from the ordinary banks. The sheer weight of the logs impounded in a big jam could be prodigious. A log drive that contained one and one-half million board feet of lumber, a winter's cut for an average camp, would fill a major river, bank to bank, for two miles.

Naturally, a log jam had to be broken as quickly as possible, and it was the riverman who had to break it. He did it usually by going out along the downstream face of the jam with his peavey, prying and poking and tugging to get the logs loose. He started at the riverbank, and often enough careful work there would do the trick; the pent-up water would come surging through, loosened logs would go floating downstream, and the jam would fall apart. (Afterward, some of the men would have to go back upriver and get the stranded logs back into the water, but this was not dangerous; it was just drudgery.) Sometimes work along the bank was not enough, and it was necessary to attack the jam in midchannel. Here the logs might be piled up in a jack-straw heap twelve feet high, and the riverman had to keep his wits about him. There was always the chance that when a key log was moved the whole jam would start tumbling down with explosive force, like a water-borne avalanche, and a man who could not see this coming and get ashore with all speed did not have long to live.

Behind the logs came the wanigans—rafts or scows, one carrying the cook shanty and another bearing sleeping quarters: tents, sometimes, to be put up on the bank. The rivermen came to the wanigans when the sun went down, ate the traditional outsized meal, smoked their pipes and yarned briefly, and then tumbled into bed. Men frequently finished the day in wet clothing—it was common to have to stand waist-deep in icy water, dislodging logs that had piled up on some submerged obstacle and seemed likely to cause a jam if not removed—and these men rarely changed to dry clothing when they reached camp. It was the riverman's belief that if he did this he would catch cold, so he simply went to bed soaking wet and let his clothing dry on him.

Sending logs downstream called for careful organization. No single drive had the river to itself, especially on a large stream like the Muskegon or the Manistee. A dozen separate drives might be afloat at the same time, and the lumber companies usually arranged things so that each river crew was responsible for a certain part of the river, receiving everything that floated down to its beat and sending the logs on to the next crew downstream. Since one pine log looks much like another, this was an invitation to chaos when all the logs reached the sorting grounds at the river's mouth and each company had to collect its own logs. The companies met this problem just as the western cattlemen met a similar problem arising from common use of an open range: each one put its brand on its own stock.

At the banking ground there was always a man with a marking hammer—a heavy sledge whose metal striking-face bore, in sharply defined raised characters, the distinctive mark of the company that owned the logs. One hard blow on each end of the log left that mark stamped on the wood, and when the logs got to the end of the trip it was comparatively simple to determine who owned what. There were certain problems, of course; just as rustlers afflicted the western cattle ranges, river pirates infested some of the logging rivers, slipping floating logs up creeks or into backwaters, sawing two inches off of each end, applying a new mark, and sending the pirated log back into the current again. A logging outfit generally made a certain allowance for shrinkage when it sent a drive down the river.

It was important, of course, for a company to know just how much lumber it actually had afloat, and at the banking ground an official known as a scaler kept track. He carried a special metal-capped yardstick (irreverently known to the rivermen as a cheat stick) and with this he measured the diameter of a log; then he used an intricate formula to estimate the number of board feet of lumber each log contained. The estimate was based on the assumption that the log would be cut into planks twelve inches wide and one inch thick; a board foot of lumber, accordingly, was one foot of a plank cut to those dimensions. An average log, sixteen feet long and sixteen inches in diameter, was expected to scale 144 board feet; a bigger log, twenty-eight inches thick, was supposed to scale 576 board feet. At the mill, to be sure, a log might be cut into four-by-fours, or two-by-fours, and it was bound to yield some planks less than a foot wide, but the board foot concept offered a reasonably accurate way to figure its worth.

Duly measured and stamped, then, the logs went down the river in care of the rivermen, and they were workers who took immense pride in their calling. They had to be daring and skillful, with stamina enough to bear up under exposure that would have sent the ordinary mortal to a hospital with pneumonia in short order, and they gloried in their own toughness. When the drive ended, and the rivermen collected their pay and descended on the barrooms and other places of amusement at the end of the line, many fights resulted. Put a few slugs of whisky under

the belt of one of these men and he was likely to find himself in a state of grace; in which condition, as he lounged with his elbows on the bar and a shot glass of this or that in his fingers, he was apt to reflect that he could lick any man in the house, perhaps any man in the state, and sooner or later he would mention it, not to brag but just as an interesting item for conversation. Put a dozen such men in one saloon, with whisky giving everybody the gift of tongues, and interesting things were bound to happen. In the encounters that resulted, no holds were barred. When one man got another down he would choke him, gouge him, or (by preference) stamp on him with his spiked boots. Veterans of such brawls usually had sinister pockmarks on their faces. They had suffered, it was said, from logger's smallpox.

But hard living and hard fighting were not the whole story. There were easy stretches on every drive—times when the logs floated smoothly down a steady current, with no tangles, no jams and nothing to worry about. At such moments a riverman would jab the spike of his peavey into one end of the log he was riding, stretch out on his back along the length of the log, light his pipe, look up at the clouds, and let all of tomorrow's problems take care of themselves. This was the time when he saw the glamor of his own existence, and reveled in it.

CHAPTER SIX

Death of a Wilderness

When my brother and I watched the rivermen take the logs past our yard in Boyne City we were looking at the closing scene in a pageant that would not be performed again. The lumber era itself was coming to an end because the last of the trees were being cut down, but the romantic, perilous, highly specialized craft of the men who took the logs downstream had become obsolete even before the forests disappeared. The business of turning living trees into logs, getting the logs to market and then reducing them to the lumber the builders could use—dating back, in its essentials, no doubt, to the distant past when Hiram of Tyre sold the cedar timbers that helped Solomon build his temple—had been modified, quickened and at last completely transformed by technological progress. The remote backwoods of Michigan felt the effects of this progress as directly as the most up-to-date factory in the industrial belt. All of the customs and techniques of a sprawling, primitive industrial process were profoundly changed, in one explosive generation, as men began to see what could be done with machinery. The work went faster and reached farther, the wasteland that finally covered thousands upon thousands of acres was created more quickly, and the human adjustments that had to be made after the pageant ended were made immeasurably more challenging.

For the fact is that in the final third of the nineteenth century the lumber industry ceased to be limited by the strength of men's biceps and the power of running water. It had broken the bonds that restrain physical achievement. In an unplanned, clumsy, unrecognized way it had led the lumberman up to the edge of the headiest, most dangerous knowledge man has ever had—the knowledge that all of the old limitations are gone and that quite literally he can do whatever he wants to do. Anything he can imagine he can accomplish; king of infinite space, except that he has bad dreams. Living in a wholly material world he suddenly finds that his powers are infinite, and he neglects to note that what he does will have abiding consequences in the world of the spirit. These powers can take him to everlasting heights—or, if his luck is out and his wisdom fails him, down into the bottom-less pit. This is the fearful heritage of the twentieth century. We have it, and like the Indians we are trying to adjust ourselves to a horizon that is too broad for us. You can see a small bit of it approaching in the matter-of-fact story of the lumber industry.

By the early 1880s, or perhaps a bit earlier, this industry found itself limited by nothing whatever except two things that were utterly beyond its control—the appetite of the market, and the supply of its raw material. The appetite of the market, taking the good years with the bad, seemed to be unlimited; the source of supply, unfortunately, was not. The Michigan lumber industry ran full tilt, faster and faster year by year, until at last it struck this irremovable obstacle. Then, just as it was reaching top speed, it collapsed.

The figures are impressive. By the 1870s more than a hundred sawmills were operating in the Saginaw-Bay City area alone. They worked a twelve-hour day, six days a week, and some of them had night shifts. In 1882, their peak year, they turned out more than one billion board feet of lumber; between 1851 and 1897, when the final tapering-off period was at hand, they cut just under twenty-three billion board feet. They were not work-ing alone. There were other busy sawmill towns—Muskegon, Manistee, and a score of smaller places up and down the shores of Lake Huron and Lake Michigan, and in the interior as well. By 1897, in less than half a century, Michigan as a whole had turned out more than a hundred and sixty billion feet of pine boards. Only six billion feet remained to be cut, most of it in the upper peninsula. The end was in sight.

Obviously, one hundred and sixty billion board feet is an enormous amount of lumber, but the figure is as hard to grasp as the estimate of the age of the pre-Cambrian reefs up in the copper country. It becomes clearer when you realize that that is enough lumber to build ten million six-room houses. One fanciful statistician once estimated that it was enough to build a solid pine floor over the entire state of Michigan, with enough left over to floor all of Rhode Island as well; or, such ventures being ruled out, to build fifty plank roads, each fifty feet wide, from New York to San Francisco. Actually, most of it went to build houses and barns all over the United States east of the Rockies, meeting the needs of a time when the nation's population was expanding beyond anybody's expectation.

Much has been written about the pitiless greed of the lumber barons, and most of it is quite true. Certainly their ranks included some of the least inhibited money-seekers in America, and the record of the way in which the industry consumed a priceless resource and then left the debris for other people to pick up is instructive but not edifying. At the same time it ought to be clear that these men were impelled by irresistible forces. The country had to have housing and it had to destroy forests to get it, and the lumberman was obliged to act accordingly. Even stronger than this was the force exerted by the machinery the lumber industry had created. This machinery could move faster than ever before, and it would not operate properly at half throttle. What the lumberman could do he had to do. In the end he killed himself by his own efficiency.

It began in the forests. Up to about the time of the Civil War, trees were cut down by axes, which was slow, laborious work. The arrival of the crosscut saw speeded this process immeasurably, and the cant hook and peavey, perfected in the pineries of Maine at about the same time, made it much easier to handle the logs. A given work force could fell, cut and stack more timber now than ever before; though these tools were elementary they were highly effective. In the same way the equipment at the sawmills was vastly improved. A high-speed circular saw with replaceable teeth could rip logs apart faster than before, and the engineers devised conveyor systems to move logs to the saw, carry away scrap lumber and get the finished boards out to the yards and loading docks with a minimum of human effort. The gang saw came before long, and the mill's capacity for processing logs was almost unimaginably increased. At both ends of the line, in other words, the industry was able to turn more trees into lumber, and do it faster, than had ever been possible before.

The real stumbling block was the need to rely on the rivers to bring the logs to the mills.

This furnished the riverman with an interesting way of life, to be sure, and in a sense it was the cheapest way imaginable to move logs, but it imposed severe restrictions. It cut the work year in the timber country to six months, for the haul to a river-bank could take place only on icy roads. Worse yet, only those trees that grew near an adequate stream could be cut down. The haul on icy roads had to be a short one, or the lumberman would go bankrupt; to build a good ice road cost upward of a thousand dollars a mile. Finally, it meant that over most of the forest country nothing but pine trees could be used. Pine boards, of course, were what the building industry wanted, but there was a market for hardwood timber and eventually it was ex-ploited to the full; the trouble was that green hardwood logs either would not float at all, or floated so sluggishly and so nearly submerged that they constantly ran aground where pine logs would go clear, and hence created dangerous and expensive log jams. As a result of all of this, in a state where trees grew like weeds, the lumberman for a long time could use only the pines that grew near running water. Everything else was out of his reach.

Now the railroads began to come to the rescue.

Michigan's first railroads ran across the extreme southern part of the state, far below the lumber belt, tying the prairie towns together, opening the way for traffic between Detroit and Chicago, and binding the whole area firmly to the rest of the middle west. Roads into the lumber country came later, and it was not until after the Civil War that they began to penetrate the region where there were pine logs to be hauled. They were built partly because of a generous system of land grants (since most of the acreage in these grants was heavily timbered, this put the railroads into the lumber business right up to their eyebrows) and partly because the pine lands offered plenty of freight; and it was fondly believed that once the trees were gone the cutover region would blossom out with farms whose people and produce would keep the roads profitably busy for all time to come. By 1874 a railroad from Saginaw to the new Lake Michigan town of Ludington cut straight across the timberlands; less than ten years later two lines reached all the way to Mackinac City; another line from Chicago came up through Grand Rapids and went on to Traverse City, continuing north to Petoskey by 1894. The familiar road of my childhood, the Ann Arbor, came up on a long diagonal from Toledo to Frankfort in 1889.

These roads made it possible for the lumbermen to exploit thousands of acres of pine lands that had been inaccessible. In many cases they literally brought the sawmills to the forest. Little towns came into being along the rights of way, each with one or more mills, and although some of them vanished quickly once the nearby pine trees were cut down a few got enough vitality to live on after the lumber era ended. The railroads sent out tentacles in the form of branch lines, and places that never saw a riverman or a log drive lived by the clanking of endless lines of flatcars coming in loaded direct from the pineries.

A second development, going hand in hand with all of this, had even more far-reaching effects. This was the construction of dozens of narrow-gauge lines—stubby little railroads, short and narrow, cheaply built and cheaply operated, some of them touch-

ing no city or town anywhere, running from nowhere to nowhere, crossing no highways and passing no farmhouses but
carrying during their short lives immense quantities of logs. The
first of them, setting the pattern for all, was built in 1876 by an
energetic young lumber operator named Winfield Scott Gerish,
who owned thousands of acres of good pine forest near Lake
George, in the central part of the state, and unhappily realized
that the Muskegon River, the only practical waterway in that
area, lay six miles away. This meant a ruinously expensive long
haul even in wintertime, and put the timber hopelessly out of
reach in summer.

Gerish turned his mind to the narrow-gauge railroad. It is said
that he first saw a narrow-gauge locomotive at the Philadelphia
Centennial Exposition that summer and was impressed by the
fact one of these undersized railroads could be built and operated
for far less money than would be needed for a standard-gauge
line. He raised a little capital and went to work, and before long
—at a cost below forty thousand dollars—he had a three-foot-
gauge railroad reaching back from his banking ground on the
Muskegon River to the heart of the pine forest. He got the line
into operation during what other lumbermen found a disastrously
mild winter, when there was hardly enough snow and ice to
move loaded sleighs at all, but with his two locomotives and fifty
flatcars Gerish was able to move logs without difficulty. Nearly
all of the logs carried downstream by the Muskegon that year,
it was said, had been brought to the bank by this narrow-gauge
railroad. In its first full year the line carried twenty million board
feet of timber; a year later it carried one hundred and fourteen
million.

Nobody could ignore a demonstration like that, and the industry got the idea at once. In 1882 thirty-two logging railroads
were built and by 1889 there were forty-nine of them, able to
move more than a billion board feet of timber annually. Eventually there were more than eighty lines in operation in Michigan, and the lumber business had been revolutionized. Some of

these roads, like the one Gerish built, existed solely to get logs from the forest to running water. Others served as feeders for the standard-gauge railroads; there was one that came into Beulah just before the turn of the century, bringing logs down its four miles of track for transshipment by the Ann Arbor to Frankfort. It had a short life—it was gone and all but forgotten by the time of my boyhood, and I never even heard of it until I was a grown man—but while it lasted it brought a good deal of timber down to the mills. A few narrow-gauge roads were more pretentious and served as common carriers, even providing passenger service on fixed schedules. Such a one, for instance, was the Mason & Oceana, which served mills and docks at Ludington, with upwards of thirty miles of line and—for a time—had visions of extending itself all the way to Grand Rapids and becoming permanent.

Still others went from the forests direct to the mills. Portable sawmills appeared, planting themselves on some tiny logging railroad, cutting logs until the supply was exhausted, and then moving on. The narrow-gauge roads also moved from place to place, taking up their rails as soon as one field was played out and moving off to find some new area that needed them. Compared with standard-gauge lines, these undersized roads were inexpensive. A locomotive could be bought for four thousand dollars, flatcars cost no more than a hundred and sixty-nine dollars apiece, and to prepare and metal the right of way averaged no more than four thousand dollars a mile. Few of these lines were more than six or eight miles in length.

As an immediate result, the industry was no longer confined to the pineries that lay close to the rivers. Now the lumbermen could reach back into forests that could not be touched before, so the source of supply was prodigiously increased. Furthermore, logging became much more of a year-around operation, because a railroad could move logs in summer as well as in winter without relying on snow, ice and cold weather. (Most railroads could; where a line ran through swampy ground, as many of them did, the roadbed was apt to sag badly when the winter ended and the soil became spongy. A rock-ballasted right of way was unheard-of in this business.) The old problem of getting logs from the place where a tree was felled to the skidways where they could be put on carriers still remained. To an extent this was solved by the use of "big wheels"—a pair of wagon wheels ten or twelve feet in diameter, which could straddle a felled tree or several logs, lift one end of the load off the ground, and so make it possible for a team of horses to drag the timber to the place where it could be loaded. A factory in Manistee made thousands of sets of these big wheels during the last quarter of the nineteenth century. Toward the end of the lumber era some ingenious operator thought of an overhead conveyor system—cables strung from one tall tree to another several hundred feet away, with a device suspended from grooved wheels that rode on the cables. With this a fallen tree could be hoisted clear of the ground and the underbrush and whisked through the air to the skidway. This was devised too late to do the Michigan industry much good, and it came to full development several years later in the forests of the far northwest.

The first consequence of all of this was a mighty broadening of the territory where the lumber industry operated; thousands of square miles of timberland previously out of reach were now available. In effect, the supply of the basic natural resource became greater than it had ever been before. But a second consequence swiftly canceled out this advantage, because the industry's ability to destroy the forest grew much faster than the increase in the source of supply.

On top of this, one of the baffling factors of the age of improved technology now made its appearance. The cost of production became lower but only on condition that the producer was able to put more and more money into it. (In other words, it was cheaper, but it cost more to do it.) The day of the small jobber, who contracted to cut a man's pine and get it to the riverbank, began to end. He and his employer could not compete with the big operators, or combinations of big operators, who could lay their own railroads, move them from this place to that place as need arose, hire big crews and get logs to the mills at a lower cost per log than the jobber could manage. These big operators in turn had to invest a lot of money, and they could not get it back unless they operated at capacity. A narrow-gauge railroad may be comparatively inexpensive, but it loses money when it is not used and so it was used all the way to the hilt, and a firm that had been cutting five million board feet in a season found that it could cut as much as twenty-five million. What could be done had to be done, and so the "inexhaustible" supply of timber began to look like what was left at the bottom of the barrel. To paraphrase the law of Malthus: production tends to increase faster than its means of subsistence.

This was the crack of doom for the great Michigan forest, no matter what sorts of trees it contained.

The state was never covered—not within living memory, at any rate—with one unbroken stretch of pine trees. The growth was mixed. A big hardwood forest would contain isolated ridges, low hills or swampy areas where nothing but pines grew—a few dozen acres here, a hundred acres there, sometimes a whole square mile, six hundred and forty acres—but for the most part the pines grew up along with the other trees, maple and beech, elm and oak and ash, hemlock and birch and black cherry and walnut, and originally the lumberman was highly selective. He wanted nothing but pines, and they had to be fully grown; he took only the larger ones, and only those that grew near running water. Now he realized that he wanted everything, and so he took everything. He could use small pines as well as big ones; more important, he could use hardwoods as well, because the railroad could move hardwood logs as readily as logs of pine.

All of the old limitations were gone. The lumberman could go into every corner of the forest and cut down all of the trees, and that is exactly what he did. He still preferred pine, but by the 1890s the end of the pine supply was in sight, and so while a number of operators dismantled their mills and tracks and moved out of the state in search of virgin timber farther west, a good many remained and went after the hardwoods. Grand Rapids took walnut, oak, maple and black cherry and before long was boasting that it was the furniture capital of the United States, or possibly of the entire world. Cadillac found an extra twenty or thirty years of life for its mills by specializing in maple flooring. Traverse City suddenly discovered that it largest single employer of labor was a mill that made hardwood chopping bowls, salad bowls, butter bowls and so on. Out of the dwindling forest came railroad ties, telephone poles, fence posts, shipyard timber, and blocks cut from pine stumps to be used for match-sticks. Even the supposedly worthless aspen, that came up in matted profusion when a stand of pine was removed, became an article of commerce; men could use it to make boxwood, or feed it into the pulp mills to make paper, and boats and trains that once carried saw logs went off to market loaded down with the slim logs of aspen.

So over most of the state of Michigan the forest was de-stroyed, with single-minded dedication and efficiency. Sometimes it seemed as if men of that time actually hated trees, although it was noted that once a lumber town was built its people hastened to set out saplings in the yards and along the streets to soften the harsh outlines—which could be extremely harsh, in a jerry-built backwoods village—and to provide shade. But the original growth was made up of enemies, and no quarter was given. I remember a characteristic incident from my innocent home town of Benzonia.

On a hillock back of the girls' dormitory there was a nice stand of second-growth hardwoods, mostly maples and beeches—the same in which I played the part of Daniel Boone with my trusty broomstick rifle. In the middle of this little woodlot there was one towering tree that had somehow escaped the ax and saw when the village was built. I do not recall what sort of tree it was except that it was a hardwood, and it was a noble tree,

rising far above all the other trees, a landmark visible from anywhere in town. Now there lived in Benzonia a man who served
in some official capacity; member of the county road commission
or the county surveyor's crew, or something similar. This man
looked upon this tree every day, and apparently it offended him.
It had survived, the only tree in the whole township that dated
back to the original forest, and he seems to have felt that he
ought to do something about it. He consulted the blueprints
on which the village had been platted and discovered that this
tree grew right in the center of what had been marked out as a
highway. The highway had never been built, and never would
be built, because it would be a dead-end street at each end, it
led neither to nor past anything of consequence, and to build it
would have required the builders to cross two deep ravines. It
was wholly impractical, and everybody knew it, and to this day
it remains unconstructed. But the plat said there was a roadway
there, and the big tree was a trespasser. So this petty official
got a few men with saws and axes, went up to the hillock, and
cut the tree down.

It came down with a soul-satisfying crash and it lay, butt-end
upward, on a steep hillside, leaving a flat stump as broad as a
dining room table. It stayed where it fell, slowly rotting. Nobody cut it into logs or did anything else with it; nobody had
ever intended to do anything with it, it was just a big tree that
deserved to be laid low. A number of people shook their heads
and made noises of disapproval, and my father, thinking that the
tree was on ground owned by the academy, lodged a protest. But
there was the plat, the tree grew in the middle of what had been
laid out as a public highway, and nothing could be done. Presumably its destruction satisfied something in the soul (if that is
the word for it) of the man who felled it. Anyway, what was
one tree more or less in Michigan? It was gone, and my small
sister found that the big flat stump made a fine place for her to
play house with her dolls.

It was not often necessary to hunt down survivors in that way because as a general thing survivors were most uncommon. Land that had been combed over for its pines got another combing, and if necessary it got a third, and in the end the lumber crews missed nothing. (If it has roots, cut it down.) The narrow-gauge network that had expanded so mightily contracted with equal speed, rails and rolling stock carried away, ties left to crumble where they lay. Open places surrounded by second-growth saplings, unspeakably desolate yet at the same time throbbing with life, terminal points once for busy little carriers, complete with sidetracks, water tank, an uneven wye to turn locomotives around, and donkey engines to pile logs on flatcars—these disappeared altogether, everything removable gone, tangled underbrush covering the barren ground, roadbeds turning into low grassy ridges and at last losing their identity entirely, so that now only a local antiquarian or two can come within a mile of saying where they were.

The lumber towns often went the same way. Some of them simply evaporated, leaving hardly trace enough to make a traveler say: Ghost town. Others went into a long decline, surviving today as a couple of houses, a filling station and a barbecue stand. Along the shore of Lake Michigan you can find stretches of sandy beach with a few half-submerged pilings out in the water to mark the place where schooners once loaded lumber for Chicago. It was not always necessary to have a harbor to make a seaport in the old days. There would be a sawmill on the beach, and in front of it a wooden pier running out into the lake; a schooner coming in for a load would anchor five hundred feet offshore, drift in to the pier, make fast there, and take on as many planks as it could carry. If an onshore wind came up the schooner would cast off its moorings, kedge out to deeper water, get its anchor aboard, and tack off and on until the wind subsided, when it would return to finish the job. This could be done only in the mild warm-weather months, of course, but a lot of lumber got shipped that way.

In one way or another, however, most of the lumber towns

survived, even though they had hard sledding. As the industry that once supported so many people ceased to exist, men lived by such expedients as they could arrange. In parts of the cutover country, where men went out to make farms amid the rows of stumps and found that it was mortally hard to get enough to eat, let alone make a little money, some of these expedients were unusual. Along the northwest coast of the lower peninsula, for instance, many people were saved from outright starvation by the passenger pigeon.

This fabulous bird used to come up to that part of the state in the summer, flying from its haunts in Indiana, Kentucky or wherever, and it came in numbers whose totals would be beyond belief if they were not so abundantly confirmed by contemporary accounts—by the million, by the hundred million, by the billion, by practically any number you care to name. They flew slowly, clumsily, close to the ground, in flocks so dense that a man could kill enough to make supper for his family just by throwing sticks and stones at them. Men with shotguns could bring down half a dozen or more with one shell, and when men were firing in company nobody bothered to try to identify the birds he himself has shot; so many were falling that every hunter could pick up all he could carry. In the late 1870s farmers near Petoskey —so hard pressed by a bad crop year that a relief train from Grand Rapids came up with gifts of food—got a new lease on life from one of these flocks. They ate the pigeons, and they made a cash crop out of them by packing hundreds of thousands for the city markets downstate. A newspaper reported in 1878 that from three to six tons of birds, plucked and packed in barrels of ice, were shipped south every day. Men caught birds alive by fastening big nets to the tops of springy saplings, fastening the nets close to the ground, baiting the area and then springing the trap when the birds came in to eat; it was said that when the nets were sprung a single trap would catch from three hundred to five hundred pigeons. At Traverse City live birds were shipped away in wicker cages to sportsmen's clubs all over the middle west; at the clubs they were released one at a time and shot down—or at least shot at—just as clay pigeons are used today.

It was a good business while it lasted, which was not long. Live birds were worth a dollar apiece, and dead birds packed in ice brought from twenty-five to thirty-five cents a dozen. There were times when the platform of the Grand Rapids and Indiana railroad station at Traverse City was piled so high with crated birds that there was hardly room for human passengers.

The inevitable result was the extinction of the passenger pigeon, which was doomed by the same thing that killed the wilderness. The flights stopped coming. By the end of the nineteenth century they were no more than a memory, and a few years later the last passenger pigeon in North America died in its cage in an Ohio zoo. Apparently it was not just the unrestrained slaughter that brought this about. This bird needed the wilderness. It lived largely on the acorns and beechnuts of the hardwood forest, and when the forest was gone the pigeons went too. When Mr. Gerish brought the narrow-gauge railroad to the north woods he killed off the passenger pigeon.

What happened to the pigeons happened also to the grayling, a tasty game fish that once was abundant in the Au Sable River. This fish was so plentiful that a man who could not catch at least fifty in one day felt that he had been having atrocious luck. There is record of one party of fishermen that took eight thousand fish in a few days, leaving many of them to rot on the bank. One man and his son made a living for years by shipping grayling to a Chicago restaurant at twenty-five cents a pound; two other men in 1874 floated down the river and killed and salted down one hundred and twenty pounds of fish each day, selling them to lumber camp cooks. While the grayling was being caught at this rate the lumbermen did the rest. Their log drives, soil erosion caused by the destruction of forest cover, and the silt-laden high water from tributary creeks that were temporarily dammed so that logs could be floated out, ruined the grayling's spawning grounds. By 1910, or a little before then, the fish was gone. It was a wilderness fish, and pretty soon there was no more wilderness.

Destruction of the wilderness not only killed birds and fish; now and then it killed people as well, striking them down with the terrible weapon of fire—that weapon which the present generation has come to understand and to use and which may some day get seriously out of hand. Like all the other lumber-producing states, Michigan has its fearful memories of forest fires. The worst of them, ironically, came in places where most of the forest had already been cut down.

The lumbermen were not good at tidying up after themselves. When a crew had felled all the trees within reach and cut off the tops and branches so that the trunks could be sawed into logs and carried away, the debris was usually left lying where it fell. It lay there after the lumbermen moved on—mile after mile of it, sometimes—and the dead wood lost all of its moisture, the needles turned brown and grew brittle, and after a year or two or three the area became one vast, unignited menace, as danger-ous as an exposed powder magazine, waiting for one little acci-dent. Underneath it and all around it was the duff—dead needles and leaves from whole generations of wasteful wilder-ness growth—putting the earth itself in shape to go up in flames.

It did not take a complicated run of bad luck to produce a catastrophe. A hard drought in late summer and early fall would set the stage. Then there might be a spark from a wood-burning locomotive, or from a campfire or a settler's cabin chimney, a bonfire started by some farmer to get rid of the deadwood and prepare a field for planting, a glowing coal from a pipe care-lessly emptied along an old tote road—any of these could start a fire. Sometimes the fire would burn itself out. Sometimes it would not; or, if it seemed to, it would leave smoldering embers in the dead matted grass by a dry swamp, or in the topsoil itself, sending up a thin drift of smoke, ready to burst out in open flame if a high wind came along. People who lived in the lumber country learned to read the signs. Hot weather, no rain, aromatic scent of wood smoke haunting the air, faint haze along the skyline: these added up to danger. All that was needed now was a strong wind.

When the wind came the little invisible fires were whipped into vigorous life, and any blaze in the wreckage of cutoff tops and branches leaped up into a great conflagration. The flame was exultant and malignant, moving swiftly with a drumming roar that could be heard faraway like a sustained rumble of distant thunder. When the wind persisted the fire would reach out ahead with flaming tentacles to start new fires far in advance, so that men in the path of the blaze had less time to escape than they thought they would have. Men used to insist that the intense quick heat distilled flammable gases from the pine wood, so that the very air became explosive; and they said that now and then these would blow up as they sped downwind, setting all they touched ablaze—houses, barns, railroad trains, trees, cattle in the fields, the coat on a man's back. Whole villages were burned, and sometimes the people in them, trapped before they could get away or taken by flames from the air as they ran across a pasture or down a road.

A lumber town was terribly vulnerable. It was always surrounded by big stacks of lumber—seasoned pine, ready to burn at a touch. Often enough the streets were composed largely of sawdust, and there were whole mountains of sawdust by the mills. In the early days proper equipment for fighting fires was lacking; most sawmills kept a long row of barrels full of water on the roof, to be upended in case of danger. If a town did have a fire engine the machine was prized, and was kept painted and polished within an inch of its life. The city of Alpena had a famous engine with a roving commission; it was frequently put on a steamboat and sent up and down the Lake Huron shore to fight fires in towns that lacked equipment of their own.

Alpena bought this engine after a fire destroyed most of the city. This was in 1871, a drought year of terror and destruction

all across the state. A mighty forest fire swept down to the out-
skirts of the upper peninsula lumber center, Menominee, wiping
out whole towns in Wisconsin as it came, killing fifteen hundred
people. Manistee was largely destroyed, its lumberyards going
up in fire and smoke, schooners taking fire at the docks; a steamer
trying to take townspeople to safety out in Lake Michigan had
to ram a blazing wooden drawbridge three times before it could
break its way through. The state's capital city, Lansing, was
threatened by one fire, and Saginaw itself was damaged by another. Glen Haven and Holland, on Lake Michigan, were consumed; across the state there was a devastating fire in the Thumb,
where thousands of people were made homeless. Out on Lake
Michigan and Lake Huron shipmasters groped blindly through
a fog of smoke.

All in all, most memorable; an ominous footnote to the history
of the lumber country. Yet the rest of the country did not pay
much attention, because the fall of 1871 was the time of the
great Chicago fire, which took place just as the Menominee fire
was reaching its climax. Besides, a fire in a big city was a once-
in-a-lifetime affair, while the forest fires in Michigan came just
about every year. A brush-fire war may kill more people and
cost more money than a campaign from Normandy to the Rhine,
but somehow it does not quite compel the attention in the same
way. We can take loss and suffering in our stride as long as they
are not too concentrated.

Like practically all villages in the lumber country, our town
of Benzonia had its fire-scare. I was about eleven years old at
the time, and I had to admit afterward that it was not really
much of a scare, which is to say that the place was not actually
in danger. Still, it was real enough while it lasted; as witness the
fact that on a Sunday all of the able-bodied men stayed away
from church to go down the south road to fight the fire. (It took
something quite out of the ordinary to empty the church in that
town on Sunday.) For days the air had been hazy, with a smell
of wood smoke, and I remember that on this particular Sunday

the haze was so heavy that you could look straight at the sun, at midday, without blinking; the sun simply glowed a dull red, as if it was about to go out altogether. As the men went south to try to create firebreaks and beat out pesky little advance-guard flames, we small boys were sternly forbidden to go with them; probably the last thing the men wanted was to have to keep track of a flock of scatterbrained boys playing games on the edge of a forest fire. I was not especially anxious to go out there, anyway, and I think most of my chums felt the same way. We had heard too much about what forest fires could do.

Ours apparently was not one of the all-consuming fires, and by Monday they said it was under control. I do not now recall whether we got a healing rain or whether the fire just was not big in the first place, but the danger passed away and there was never a recurrence. Most of the lumbering in our immediate vicinity had been finished years earlier, and the cutting that was still going on was not extensive enough to create the endless piles of forest refuse that were responsible for the big conflagrations. Besides, the pine in our county was long gone, and while the dead branches and dried leaves of hardwood timber would make a hot fire they did not give it the explosive, incalculable quality fires had in the pineries.

One by one, all up and down the state, as the supply of timber ran out, lumber towns became familiar with the noise of the last whistle, which the sawmill people sounded when they were about to go out of business. A mill that had consumed all the logs it could get, and was to be dismantled and moved away or sold for scrap, would let the final head of steam in its boilers exhaust itself through the whistle. When the buzz saws and the edgers and the jolting gang saws and the clattering conveyors at last fell idle for good, the boss would pull the whistle cord, tie it down, and let the steam go up to join the clouds. One long, haunting blast—the same that had been rousing the townspeople and calling men to work for a generation or more—would go echoing across the plains, slowly losing its pitch and its volume as the pressure died, falling at last to a dispirited moan and at last fading out altogether . . . and that mill was out of action forever, and possibly the town along with it, and people would begin to wonder what they were going to do next. They had never had any asset but the wilderness, and when the wilderness died hard times were at hand.

The death of the wilderness sometimes had odd side effects, as in the case of the Kirtland warbler.

The Kirtland warbler is a trim little bird, just under six inches long from stem to stern, with dark gray back and wings and a pale yellow shirt front; a perky bird, distinguished from other warblers by his habit of flicking his tail about for no apparent cause and by his extreme choosiness in his selection of a place to live. He will breed, build nests and raise a family only in a place that is grown up with immature jack pines; once they get more than fifteen or eighteen feet high he concludes that the neighborhood is not suitable and gives up. Now jack pines come up, unbidden, in the burned-out pine country, so the Kirtland warbler established himself on a tract a few miles square somewhere in the valley of the Au Sable and there he lives—there, and there only, as far as anybody can find out; if you want to see him you have to come to central Michigan.

The trouble is that the jack pine forests in the burned-over country have been getting mature. The wilderness is returning, and as it returns it threatens to drive this particular wilderness creature out of existence. It appears that the Kirtland warbler could be saved only by a few carefully controlled forest fires, which would produce the kind of forest in which this slightly finicky bird can prosper. In view of the fact that the state of Michigan for more than half a century has been taking elaborate pains to keep forest fires from happening at all, this represents an odd turn in the road.

CHAPTER SEVEN

Cows on the Campus

The last of the logs were still drifting down the Boyne River when Father concluded that he had had enough. He had tried his hand at making money, and it had lasted just long enough to convince him that he was at a dead end—not because the money was hard to get, but because this was not in the least what he wanted to do. I did not know anything about such matters at the time, but later I understood that although he had been fairly successful—as far as anyone could be successful, selling shares in the future in a town whose inevitable decline was clearly visible even before the crest had been reached—he discovered quickly enough that he was woefully miscast, and I believe that down inside he felt mildly guilty for having so much as tried it. He carried with him, from his youth to the day of his death, the notion that man is born to a splendid debt—that he owes, to some force beyond the circling stars, the duty of spending himself to the uttermost for something beyond his own well-being. This conviction is a hard thing to live with; or perhaps it is a very easy thing, because its imperatives are at least distinct and living seems much more important than making a living; in any case, it rarely leaves a man in doubt about what he ought to do. So when the trustees of Benzonia Academy notified him that they would like to make him principal of that shaking, imperfect and probably doomed institution he accepted without hesitation. We moved back to Benzonia in the summer of 1906, and at the age of fifty Father began a new career: George R. Catton, head man of a shaky preparatory school.

New in a sense; if he became responsible for the survival, growth and development of this enterprise the task at least lay in the general field of education, and he had been in that field nearly all of his life. Yet it was a field in which he was almost fantastically unfitted to serve, as far as formal preparation was concerned, and he probably could have got into it nowhere on earth except in the frontier society of the Michigan lumber country at that particular stage in its development. Father was an educator, but technically he was almost wholly uneducated. He had never been so much as graduated from high school, and to the end of his days he was never enrolled in a college. He was a self-taught teacher, lifting himself by his own bootstraps, somehow managing to lift others along with him. He prepared young people to go to college; which is to say that he gave them the training, the broadened outlook and the habits of study they would need if they were to do college work. More than this, he made them want to go to college, and persuaded a surprising number of them that even a student without any financial resources whatever could go on and win a college degree if he tried hard enough. (Summertimes you could work and lay by a little money; at college you could earn your board and room, by waiting on table, tending furnaces or doing other odd jobs; once convince the college authorities that you were really in earnest, and they usually would find some way to smooth the path for you.) Perhaps that was the core of his teaching—the idea that you can be whatever you want if you really want it. All that matters is your choice of goal. Be careful what goal you choose, because some day you may reach it.

He fitted in perfectly at Benzonia Academy. At a time when the state as a whole was waging war on the visible surrounding wilderness this school saw itself as waging war on the wilderness of ignorance, whose tangled undergrowth was also visible out in the clearings the lumbermen were creating. The sense of mission was powerful. The forests were being destroyed for a purpose: so that men and women could have better lives after the forests had been removed. That the physical obstacles to achievement were being taken away was interesting but not particularly important. What mattered was to teach men and women that the obstacles to their mental and spiritual development could be destroyed. Man had control of his future, but that control did not in the least depend on improved machinery or mechanical progress. According to Holy Writ, the kingdom of Heaven lay within; a man who hoped to enter the kingdom had to blaze a trail through his own heart, and to do that was the whole point of human existence.

It sounds quaint and faraway now. To suppose that man's real antagonist is himself rather than his environment is to turn workaday standards upside down. We know how to conquer the environment—or at least we would, if it would just stay conquered, once beaten—but how do you defeat that inner antagonist? With education, transmitted by an uneducated man through a school which had not a tenth of the resources it needed? At this distance that seems an odd way to build the road to the future. Yet the desperate and dangerous chaos of today *is* the future toward which men seventy years ago were moving. Perhaps the road actually chosen was a trifle odd too.

I do not know much about Father's early life. His parents came to the United States from a farm in Yorkshire, England, a decade or more before the Civil War, and he was born on a farm near Constantine, Michigan, down near the Indiana border, in 1856. I can remember only one story about his childhood, a story so slight that it means nothing; as a nine-year-old he was working in a field one spring morning when a man on horseback came pelting along the road, reined up by the fence, and told him to run to the house at once and tell his father and mother that General Lee had surrendered the Army of Northern Virginia. Father ran in with the news, the horseman galloped off, and that is all there is to the story. Of the rest of his boyhood I know nothing

whatever, except that his home obviously was full of piety and held the improvement of man's mind and spirit in high regard. Apparently it was sheer poverty that kept Father from getting an education. What formal training he got seems to have come from the public school system of Constantine; I believe he had a little time in high school there, but he was not able to remain and finish the course. At an early age he was out on his own, earning a living . . . by teaching school.

He knew perfectly well, of course, that a schoolteacher, even in the informal grade schools of that day, needed more education than he had been able to get, so he set to work to educate himself. It must have been a laborious process. He bought a Latin grammar, and probably copies of Caesar and Cicero as well, and taught himself Latin; aided, possibly, by some rudiments picked up during his brief stay in high school. He studied English grammar and composition, and applied himself with especial enthusiasm to the study of history. Bit by bit he ground it out, led on in part by nothing more exalted than the need to keep at least one jump ahead of the students he was teaching, but driven also by the consuming desire to broaden his mental horizons and develop his powers. In the end, he succeeded. His speech, his outlook and his habits of thought were those of an educated man. He was an extremely good teacher—by the testimony of those who studied under him—and a competent school administrator, and in the end it developed that he was ideally suited for the tasks the academy offered him. But his earnest, persuasive, repeated advice to earnest students—go on to college even if you haven't a cent in your pockets, show them that you can do the work and make them take you—must have come from the heart.

However all of this may have been, by his early twenties Father was in a place called Kalkaska, which was then a busy sawmill town on the Grand Rapids and Indiana railroad. In Kalkaska, presently, he found himself wearing two hats; he was pastor of a small Methodist church and he was also superintendent of the village school system. (During this period some local bigwig was due to deliver a public lecture and was worried for fear nobody would attend. Father tried to reassure him. "I can promise you," he said, "that at least two people will be present—the Methodist minister and the superintendent of schools.") The Methodist connection he did not keep, and I suspect that it was slightly informal. Years later, while we were living in Benzonia, he was duly ordained as a Congregational minister, and I do not believe that the ins and outs of doctrinal differences between the various Protestant sects ever meant much to him. He needed to be active in the school and in the church, because he had a message to impart and he wanted either a rostrum or a pulpit, or both. After a number of years in Kalkaska he moved to Cadillac, where again he was a superintendent of schools, and late in the century he went to Benzonia to try his hand at teachers' training for the dying college. And finally, after his one venture into the business world, he took charge of the academy.

Looking back, I sometimes wonder that I never learned more about his early years; the full story would be interesting, if I had it, but I never asked him about it. He was a warm-hearted man, but somehow he was out of my reach; our relationship was slightly Biblical, and I was much in awe of him. I once mentioned this to one of my uncles, and he expressed surprise; my father, he said, was one of the friendliest, most approachable men he had ever known, and I remember that Mother once remarked that Father was an extremely easy man to live with. Certainly I remember our home as a place without tension, where there was a good deal of laughter. But there it was; there was some kind of cutoff.

Long after his death, when I asked men who had known him to tell me what sort of man he was, almost all of them began by saying that he had a quiet but highly alert sense of humor. One man told how he and Father once walked down a street in Grand Rapids and came up behind two women, one of whom was saying that she had never in her life seen a really bald man. At this moment Father and his friend swung out to walk past this pair.

Father said not a word, and looked neither right nor left, but as they got in front of the two he removed his derby hat and held it over his breast, in the manner of a good patriot saluting the flag, thereby exposing one of the shiniest bald heads in Christendom, all agleam in the afternoon sunlight. There were gasps and muffled sounds of laughter from the ladies, but Father paid no attention. He never talked about it afterward, but he had to listen many times while his friend told the story, and each time Father would chuckle quietly.

He played for chuckles rather than guffaws, and I think he usually meant to amuse himself rather than others. He savored small jokes, and he liked men who made him laugh when they did not mean to—like the acquaintance who sold a thriving small-town restaurant and retired to a lonely farm on the far side of Crystal Lake. Father asked him why he had done this when the restaurant was doing so well, and the man replied: "Mr. Catton, I just got tired of eternally cantering to the public." When Father traveled about our county his life was brightened by the roadside signs that had been painted to advertise a store in the neighboring town of Honor. The store was owned by a man named Case—brother to our local speedboat man—and he had hired a man to go about daubing the words "Try A. B. Case" in all suitable spots. Unfortunately the man was a Pennsylvania Dutchman who spelled words the way he pronounced them, and for years the fence rails and wayside boulders for miles around bore the legend: "Dry A. B. Case."

Father was easily amused. Now and then at the dinner table, after he had asked the Lord's blessing and had taken up carving knife and fork to serve, father would discover that someone had forgotten to put on any dinner plates. He would look at Mother, very serious, and say: "My dear, since I've been sick I find that I can't serve without plates." Once in a while when we set the table one of my brothers or I would intentionally leave the plates in the pantry just to evoke this remark. It never failed. I suppose it was pretty feeble, but it helped to lubricate things. Our village barber, John Whiteman, was divorced and remarried, and a young woman who taught at the academy told Father not long after her arrival that at some church social she had met two women each of whom was presented as Mrs. Whiteman: were they, she asked, related? Father took it in his stride. "Only by marriage," he replied.

There never was any malice in any of Father's reachings for a chuckle—his makeup contained not a trace of the practical joker—but once in a great while his impulse led him astray. A notable occasion came just after he became principal of the academy, when he met a member of the faculty named Clement Strang—a lanky, serious man of Father's own age and general degree of baldness, a Congregational minister who taught courses in science. This man entered Father's office, extended his hand, and said, "My name is Strang." This was an opening Father could not resist, and he inquired: "Any relation to old King Strang?" (Much as a man meeting a Mr. James might ask: "Any relation to Jesse James?") With vast dignity the man replied: "He was my father."

This was a poser, because King Strang had been one of the most bizarre, notorious characters in all the middle west. He was a Mormon, and when the murder of Joseph Smith in 1844 threatened to leave the sect hopelessly confused and fragmented Strang announced that a revelation from God showed that he, James J. Strang, had been appointed to be the new leader of the flock. Most of the people followed Brigham Young, who was equipped with a better revelation, but Strang collected a number of the faithful and led them up to Beaver Island, which offered sixty square miles of uninhabited wilderness in the northern part of Lake Michigan, twenty miles from the mainland. Here, on a little harbor, he founded the village of St. James. The people went to work to clear the woods, lay out farms, catch fish and build houses, and before long Strang proclaimed that this colony was the Kingdom of St. James and that he was its king. He got a metal crown and an elaborate robe—from some theatrical costumer, most likely—and had himself publicly crowned, and from then on he was King Strang.

He was the only crowned king in the American republic, and his elevation drew attention. So did his colony. By the early 1850s it contained fifteen hundred people, hard workers and obedient subjects, and between them and the Gentiles on the mainland something like a state of war developed. The early Mormons had had trouble with their neighbors in Missouri and in Illinois, and the story was the same in Michigan. All sorts of wild tales were told. It was alleged that King Strang's subjects frequently raided mainland settlements to despoil people of their goods, and mainlanders said that the Kingdom of St. James was no more than a nest of pirates. If a schooner went missing anywhere in upper Lake Michigan, people would say that Mormon pirates had seized it, sending vessel and crew to the bottom and carrying the loot to the island. There were also lip-smacking stories about licentious living. King Strang proclaimed the law of plural marriage, and he had four wives. One subject who refused to go along with this law was the first Mrs. Strang, who had married Strang under conditions of rigid monogamy before the kingdom was established; she retired to her home in Wisconsin and let the kingdom get along by itself.

King Strang was more than just a freak. He was an accomplished lawyer—once, when the charges of piracy were taken up by the authorities, he submitted to arrest, went to Detroit to stand trial, and triumphantly won acquittal for himself and his followers. He was also a canny politician. He got control of Emmett County, on the mainland, and had himself elected to the state legislature—the only legislator in America who was a monarch in private life. In addition he was a man of learning. He wrote an account of the flora and fauna of Beaver Island that was published by the Smithsonian Institution and that is still referred to by scholars. He imported a printing press and established a daily newspaper, and he built up a respectable library. All in all, a man of parts.

What might have happened to him if he had been able to live out a normal life span is beyond telling, but the man and his times were too stormy. Some of his subjects found his monarchial rule unbearable, and in 1856 a couple of them ambushed him and shot him. Mortally wounded, he clung to life for a number of weeks and had himself taken to Wisconsin, where his first wife cared for him until he died. On his death the island kingdom fell apart. Gentile mobs swarmed all over the place, sacking the village and driving the Mormons away, and today about the only traces of the religious dictatorship are a couple of Biblical place names like the Sea of Genesareth and Mount Pisgah.

Clement Strang made no attempt to conceal his ancestry, but he quietly insisted that one thing must be understood: he was King Strang's son by Strang's first wife. The point here was that this was a binding legal marriage under the prevailing law of the Gentile world whereas the later, plural marriages were not. As a pillar of the Congregational Church Mr. Strang may now and then have found that being King Strang's son was a cross to bear, but at least he was a legitimate son and he wanted people to know it.

Benzonia accepted him from the start, and if that conclave of orthodox believers found him sound he obviously had nothing of King Strang about him but his surname. He served on the academy faculty for a few years, and then either retired or found another field; I do not remember what did happen to him except that his son Thurlow Strang took root in Benzonia and lived there for the rest of his life. Thurlow Strang was an expert cabinet-maker, and when a few years ago I needed a desk and bookcases in the place where I work he built them for me. He died only recently.

One of Father's problems in the academy was the business of selecting the faculty. It usually consisted of four people besides Father, one man and three women, one of the women being a music teacher without other responsibilities. The academy tried manfully to give its students adequate preparation for college, and by and large it succeeded, but the faculty was spread pretty thin and finding people who could do the work properly was not easy. Pay scales were low, and living conditions were somewhat special. Benzonia was first and last a Christian community, working at it every day, and the teachers had to fit in, which is to say that they had to be people of blameless habits of life and speech, fully addicted to the evangelical doctrine. They also—for the first few years, at any rate—had to accept living quarters without central heating or inside plumbing, and in a primitive village the winters were somewhat oppressive. You had to mean it to serve on the academy faculty in those days.

The hardest job was to find a suitable man. There never was more than one, and at times (taking human frailties into account) there was only about half of one, but there was no help for it. The job just called for more talents than the average young college graduate had, and I can recall some who were pathetic misfits; earnest lads who tried hard but who simply did not have it. The man on the faculty had to serve as a sort of assistant principal, taking general charge of things when Father was away. He had to teach chemistry and physics—for some reason these subjects were considered beyond the range of the women teachers, although the girl students had to take them along with the boys. He also might have to teach mathematics, and take over Father's classes in history and English in Father's absence, and he was supposed to be largely responsible for discipline. In addition he was head of the athletic department; to put it more simply, he had to coach all of the athletic teams. There was a high rate of turnover in this job.

Handling the baseball team was easy. The academy operated on the principle, since adopted in the big leagues, that it does not matter much who runs a baseball team because everybody understands the game anyway, and that was no problem. Football was different. It was a brand-new game as far as our part of the state was concerned, and the academy had its first team in 1910. Nobody knew anything about the game. The young man who had to act as coach bought a copy of a book by Fielding Yost, then coach at the University of Michigan, and painstakingly studied it night after night in a valiant effort to find out what he and his charges were supposed to do. Luckily, most of the high schools in our area were no better off, so the games that took place were not distressingly one-sided. I should add that the academy had no money at all to spend on athletics, and every player had to provide his own uniform. There was a cobbler in town who could put cleats on an old pair of shoes for a modest price, and that was the one item of equipment everybody possessed.

Basketball came later. Here the big trouble was that there was not a gymnasium anywhere in northwestern Michigan, and in most towns the games were played in what was ordinarily a dance hall. These places had low ceilings and slippery floors, dressing rooms either did not exist or were pretty sketchy, and it was impossible for the players to take a shower after a game. Our academy team played its home games in Case's hall, on the second floor of the building that housed Charles Case's general store. The hall consisted of one oblong room with a stage at one end, and when any amateur theatricals were performed they took place here. The ceiling was high enough, and the floor offered suitable footing, but there was hardly any room for spectators; they had to sit on what was ordinarily the stage, which was not large, or stand single-file along the walls, and you could get only so many inside the place. This was too bad, because basketball was the one sport for which it was possible to charge admission, football and baseball being played on the unfenced campus where the most you could do was pass the hat and ask for contributions.

Improbable as it may seem, the various athletic programs were moderately successful—that is, the students seemed to enjoy them. A few years later we took pride in the fact that one of our graduates, enrolling in Carleton College, was a star on the Carleton football team that defeated the University of Chicago, which in that far-off time was a football powerhouse. This boy was named Charlie Joy, and he lived on a farm south of town; he was always nice to my three-year-old sister Barbara, and she developed an enormous crush on him and used to drop off to sleep chanting his name in a reverent singsong. In the First World War he enlisted in the army, and in 1918 he was killed in action in France.

The academy was co-educational, and for several years the girls had their own basketball team, playing against girls' teams from the surrounding high schools. The games were slow, almost lady-like; the floor was marked off into zones, with guards confined to one zone, forwards to another, and so on, and there was not much running about or body contact. The players wore middy blouses and voluminous bloomers, and these games would have had no spectator-appeal whatever except that those bloomers ended just below the knee, so that the girls' calves were exposed. This led the rougher masculine element lining the walls to make appreciative remarks, and eventually the academy abolished the girls' basketball team on the ground that the atmosphere was improper. As I recall it, it was.

To have girls as well as boys in the student body of a boarding school raised delicate problems. In the nature of things the students at this academy were at all costs to be protected from the world, physically and spiritually isolated from corruption; it was also necessary to protect them from each other, and eternal vigilance was applied. After all, the girls were in their early teens, virginally innocent and (by definition) somewhat frail; most of them had not been away from home before, and their parents had entrusted them to the academy with a pious confidence that they would eventually return with the innocence undisturbed and the frailty, if possible, replaced by strength. Precept and example could do much, but they also had to be watched.

In the main this was simple enough. The girls lived and took their meals in a central dormitory, and each day's schedule was carefully controlled. Barber Hall, which housed recitation rooms,

ACADEMY, BENZONIA, MICH.

study hall and library, was just a few steps away, and all hands were kept busy from breakfast time until three-thirty or four in the afternoon. With the worst will in the world, even the most imaginative girl was not likely to get into any trouble between four o'clock and supper time, and as far as I know no one ever did. (After all, Benzonia's resources were limited; until the last few years of the academy's life the town contained not so much as an ice cream parlor.) After supper there was a social hour for both sexes in a recreation room in the basement of the girls' dormitory, but it was under the direct eye of authority; there were no unlit corners, and although it was permissible to play the piano, dancing was strictly prohibited—except for the Virginia Reel, which did not count. Promptly at seven-thirty curfew sounded, with a few strokes on the big bell in Barber Hall, and for the next two hours everybody studied, usually in the study hall with some member of the faculty seated by the entrance. At nine-thirty the girls went back to their rooms, and lights had to be out by ten o'clock.

Once in a while there was some evening entertainment in town—a concert, a lecture, perhaps a basketball game—and a boy could take the girl of his choice to this function provided he first got permission from Miss Bertha Ellis, a sprightly little lady who taught Latin and English literature and who doubled as untitled but remarkably effective dean of women. Permission had to be obtained in advance; at the proper hour the boy presented himself at the dormitory, Miss Ellis summoned the girl, and the two set off. The understanding was that the boy would bring the girl back without delay, once the affair was over, and to violate this rule was to commit a capital crime—that is, both parties were liable to expulsion.

Saturdays were more relaxed. In the winter girls and boys might go coasting or skiing together—usually the former; I do not believe any of the girls owned skis—and on pleasant days group hikes were often in order. The theory here apparently was that there was safety in numbers, and although it was possible for a boy and girl to slip away from the others and snatch a few moments by themselves nothing much ever came of it. Climate was on the side of the authorities. During a great part of the school year winter weather prevailed, and a youth who could achieve any constructive misconduct with a girl in the deep woods in the middle of a Michigan winter needed to be an authentic Viking from the Arctic fjords. There were none of these around Benzonia.

It all sounds more restrictive than it actually was, and I do not recall that the students felt especially oppressed. Some of the girls objected mildly to the rule against dancing, and now and then one who found the regulations governing dating somewhat irksome would say, plaintively, "When I'm at home my mother *trusts* me," but there never was any real complaint. Mostly the youngsters took the controls as they found them.

The fact that dancing was outlawed reflected a slight cultural lag. Many of the academy girls came from homes where dancing was considered harmless enough, but Benzonia stuck to the pattern laid down at Oberlin, whose standards were austere. There was in town a woman who had been matron of a girls' rooming house at Oberlin back in the 1890s, and she told about a meeting of the Oberlin matrons with the dean of women. One matron asked if late in the evening, after all male visitors had left, it would not be all right to let the girls dance with each other. The urge to dance was natural, she said, some of the girls had a strong sense of rhythm, and only the dance offered an outlet for it; in a safely manless world, could not this be allowed?

The dean of women met it head-on. If (she said firmly) there was a girl who simply had to dance in order to express herself, let her do this: let her go to her room (in the absence of her roommate), lock the door, draw the shades, and then—all by herself—dance to her heart's content. That would be quite permissible; that, but nothing more. This attitude prevailed in our academy. Dancing might be innocent enough, under certain conditions, but it was a snare for the weak and the academy would have none of it.

Actually, all of this was a minor concern with Father. He was finally responsible, of course, for the maintenance of moral standards, just as he was responsible for seeing to it that the academy's furnaces had a supply of coal, but it never got much of his attention. His primary concern was to make the academy a genuine educational institution and to find the money to keep it in operation. Here he had more than enough to do and precious little to do it with.

During the last two years of its failing life, just before 1900, the dying college had made Father its acting president, and he had been horrified by what he then learned. The college had a preparatory department, and at least three fourths of its students were enrolled there, with only about a dozen doing what passed for college work. Attendance was hit-or-miss. Many students attended for a few months and then dropped out, and the authorities countenanced this on the ground that a young person who got only part of an education was better off than one who got none at all, but what it all meant was that Benzonia was neither a recognizable college nor a respectable preparatory school. To persuade people to send their sons and daughters to Benzonia in the first place was a never-ending struggle, and to raise enough money to keep the institution in operation was even worse. In one year as acting president of the college Father estimated that he traveled more than one thousand miles by horse and buggy, digging out prospective students with all the ardor of a present-day football coach proselyting young athletes, and appealing to small-town churches for funds. In that year, he said, he had delivered more than sixty "sermons, lectures and addresses," most of them within a twenty-five-mile radius of home. Total donations obtained amounted to $249.67: a small sum indeed, but welcome inasmuch as the total college income for the year, counting tuition, board, and money received from college-owned lands, came to no more than $1,769.

Physical plant was about as bad as it could be. Father remarked that the students lived in rooms with "curtainless windows and battered walls," and said that classroom blackboards, desks and chairs were worse than those in the average one-room rural schoolhouse. Townspeople pastured their cattle on the campus, and Father reported with some wrath that "we have more browsing, bellowing animals continually in sight of our windows, obstructing the path of lady students on their way to and from classes, than will be encountered in any country school district I know of." He urged the trustees either to build fences or to have the law on the owners of the livestock. All in all, things were at such a low ebb that a visiting stranger usually looked on the place "with a sort of kindly compassion or contempt."

Father's final recommendation to the trustees was that they forget all about trying to run a college and make Benzonia an academy, pure and simple. While they were at it, he said, they ought to insist on a high level of quality in the instruction, so that the state university and various liberal arts colleges would accept academy graduates as students without requiring them to take entrance examinations. And, as a final rider, he urged that the institution simply must pay its head man more than the $600-a-year salary that had been paid thus far.

His recommendation was accepted, and Father went off to try the insurance business. (After all of that house-to-house canvassing for students, calling on prospective life insurance purchasers must have seemed fairly simple.) Now, in the fall of 1906, he was installed as principal of the academy he had helped to bring into being, and his own recommendations made six years earlier outlined his program.

Money was the big problem. Father was on the road a good deal, and I am sure that in the next few years he delivered many more than the sixty "sermons, lectures and addresses" he had mentioned in his 1899 report. The response was encouraging. The Congregational churches he appealed to gave more to the academy than they had been willing to give to the college; they were already supporting Olivet College and could see little reason for supporting another one, especially as undistinguished a college as Benzonia, but a preparatory school was another matter. Slowly the academy's physical equipment was improved. The deplorable blackboards, desks and chairs were replaced, Barber Hall was renovated and enlarged, books were added to the library, the cows were at last kept from making free with the academic groves, and there was a slight improvement in the faculty's pay scale. Best of all, in 1909 the landmark building, East Hall, was destroyed by fire.

This looked like calamity at the time. It happened on a snowy January morning, and apparently the fire began through some malfunctioning in the central heating system that had been installed a few months earlier. (Until then each girl's room in this rickety dormitory had been heated by its own wood-burning stove, the fires being kindled and maintained by the girls themselves. This was an obvious fire hazard, and the new furnace was supposed to bring greater safety. Somehow it had not worked that way.) Fortunately, all of the inmates of the building got out alive, but the building and its inanimate contents burned up quickly. Built of white pine that had been seasoning *in situ* for more than half a century, East Hall made a grand bonfire.

I enjoyed it very much. During my childhood there had been two other fires in Benzonia, and because they took place early in the morning in winter weather and I was a small child I had not been allowed to go to see either of them, which seemed to me highly unjust. This fire I was in on personally from the beginning, and although the flames destroyed all of my toys and a collection of copies of *St. Nicholas Magazine* that Robert and I prized greatly, the whole affair was most stimulating. Next day, in school, I was called on to stand up before the third and fourth grades and describe my experiences. I was hero for a whole day, and I felt like the Psalmist who (no doubt in some similar circumstance) boasted, "my cup runneth over."

Lacking these stimuli, the academy's board of trustees felt less ecstatic, but they soon found that the fire was a disguised blessing. As soon as lodgings for the dispossessed girls had been found in private homes around town, the trustees began thinking about a new building. At a mass meeting no less than $2,200 was pledged—a surprisingly large sum, considering the town's limited resources—and in the next few weeks enough more was raised to make construction possible. By September the new building was finished, ready for use. It was formally named Mills Cottage, our family moved into the principal's quarters on the first floor, the girls moved into the dormitory rooms on the two floors above, and the new school year got under way. For the first time the academy had something resembling a modern plant.

For if Mills Cottage was neither large nor architecturally impressive it was at least up to date. It had its own water supply, heating plant and lighting system; there were bathrooms, steam heat, acetylene lights, with a modern kitchen and dining hall. Pipes laid in a trench below the frost level extended water, light and heat to Barber Hall, and the day of outdoor privies, kerosene lamps and wood-burning stoves was ended. Classrooms and study hall were kept warm and decently lighted, and the laboratory where chemistry and physics were studied had Bunsen burners and sinks with running water. For the first time the academy ceased to look like something a frontier society had put together from odds and ends.

All of this was not much to brag about, but it did look like progress and there was a general air of restrained optimism. Father continued his money-raising efforts, and a few years later he somehow got enough to finance a dormitory for boys. This was something of a makeshift—a rambling frame building on the main street, facing the campus, which had once served as a village inn and which, with extensive remodeling and the addition of a new wing, was fitted up so that it could house fifteen or twenty young men. (Except for a few boys whose families lived in Benzonia, this took care of the entire male student body.) This building was christened Bailey Cottage, and although it was nothing at all to look at nobody found fault with it. The academy now had three buildings, inside plumbing and no cows on campus. This was little enough to show for the dreams and the courage behind the original thrust into the deep woods—for the humiliation quietly endured by dedicated men who saw their best efforts rewarded by nothing better than the "kindly compassion" of the outside world—but for the first time in many years it began to look as if this institution could survive. In the back of his mind Father nursed the idea that the academy might some day build a gymnasium.

Yet to raise money and provide new buildings were never his primary concerns. They were urgently necessary, to be sure; Father had taken office in an emergency, which someone has defined as a time when several things need to be done and each one has to be done first; but above everything else it was vital to raise the academic level to the point where the institution would deserve to survive. The academy had to be accepted by the state university as a school that turned out students properly prepared to do college work, and the university had field investigators to look into such matters. One or another of these men began to visit the academy once a year to see what was being done.

These visits never bothered the students much, but they were all-important to Father. I remember being in a third-year class in Latin one morning when the university investigator dropped in. He faced the class, waggled the copy of Cicero's orations which we were using as a textbook, and quite at random called on me to construe a paragraph for him. By God's own grace I was prepared that day, and I managed to flounder my way through it acceptably; the man quizzed a few others on points of grammar, and one girl had a hard time in a discussion of the gerundive, although she got to the finish wire all right, and at last the man left the room and went to observe something else. (It occurs to me that after all of these years I have not the faintest idea what the gerundive may be, but by now it probably does not matter.) Anyway, the university man was satisfied, on that and other visits, and we became what I suppose would now be called an accredited preparatory school. An academy graduate would be accepted without an entrance examination at the state university;

also, it developed, at Oberlin, whose academic standards were as lofty as its moral standards. It seemed that Benzonia Academy had established itself.

For the moment; but the crisis was permanent, and the money problem was in fact beyond solution. In the long run the school must be supported by its own section of the state, and the lumber business was in utter collapse; this section of the state was hard put to stay alive, and the chance that it could sustain even a deserving preparatory school got worse every year. Father and the trustees tried desperately to raise an endowment fund so that the school could at least be sure of its existence from one year to the next. The goal they set was pathetically low: $50,000. They were never able to raise a respectable fraction of that sum. If it lived at all the academy must live on a hand-to-mouth basis.

The load Father carried must have been almost beyond endurance. Hat in hand, he had to go here, there and everywhere just to keep the school alive, and at the same time he had to be eternally active to make certain that its life was worth saving. How he lived through it I do not know, yet he never showed the slightest signs of strain. At home he was relaxed, meeting life's problems with gentle humor. He liked to read aloud, and when things were at their worst he took us through Stephen Leacock's *Nonsense Novels*. One spring he applied to himself an alibi offered by Harry, the village odd-job man. Harry supported himself by having his wife take in washing, which he collected and delivered in a hand cart, and he engaged to plow a bit of ground where Father wanted to plant a vegetable garden. He failed to keep this assignment, and when Father asked him why he had failed Harry explained: "Well, Mr. Catton, I've got so much to do and everything else." Father chuckled, and told us that he was in the same boat: he had so much to do and everything else.

Actually, Father had energies to spare, and along about 1912 he spent much time making speeches for the Anti-Saloon League, which was just starting a big campaign that eventually saw Michigan vote dry just ahead of the national prohibition amendment.

I think his activity here came from the strong, unwavering religious impulse that led him to work so hard as an educator. He hated alcohol just as he hated ignorance, seeing it as an obstacle on man's climb toward the heights, and what he hated he attacked with all his strength. He was never stern or bitter about it, however, and the cartoonists' caricature of the prohibitionist, popular during the 1920s, showing a grim, lantern-jawed fanatic with an eternally unsmiling slit of a mouth, never applied to him. He had a good deal of John Knox in him, but it was John Knox with a tolerant sense of fun.

CHAPTER EIGHT

Interlude with Music

The early teens are a hard time to live through, but not for the reason that is usually cited. The arrival of adolescence, with its physical changes and its abrupt disclosure that life has an unexpected dimension, is not so bad. It is unsettling, of course, to realize that half of the world belongs to an entirely different sex, and some of the entrancing possibilities that derive from this can dance and shimmer along the skyline in a rather disturbing way, but the adjustment is usually made without too much difficulty and the mystified expectancy that results is on the whole quite pleasant. The real trouble is that for a few years one is lost between boyhood and manhood. The present hardly exists, and there is no past; nothing but the future matters, and although it is so close that it dominates the mind it seems faraway. Until it actually arrives one is marking time, and it is possible to get bored doing it.

I entered the academy as a freshman in the fall of 1912. I had finished the seventh grade in our village school, and for some reason Father concluded that I ought to skip the eighth grade entirely and go into the academy without further delay. Whether he had a poor opinion of the kind of work our grade school was doing, or felt that it would be good for me to get on a slightly higher level and move at a more demanding pace, I do not know, but I made the move and I was delighted to do so. I felt that I was really growing up—my thirteenth birthday lay just ahead—and classroom work suddenly took on a new aspect. It was no longer just one of the unavoidable drudgeries of boyhood; it was a time of preparation, and I felt obliged to consider what I was going to do with my life. It was taken for granted that when I left the academy I would go on to college, but what was I going to do after that? It was stimulating to look so far ahead and to feel that I was about to make a decision that would affect my entire life.

You never know where the road is going to fork. That summer of 1912 Father read to us certain magazine articles by a political expert, Samuel G. Blythe, dealing with the Republican National Convention in Chicago, at which Theodore Roosevelt felt boxed in and moved out to run for the presidency as nominee of his own Bull Moose Party. Father was a consecrated Roosevelt man, and he read Blythe's analyses of the situation with a deep interest that rubbed off on me. Finishing one of these articles, Father remarked that these reporters certainly did get around, see interesting things and have interesting experiences, and apparently the remark took root in my mind. A year or two later I spent several hours a day, during the summer vacation, working for a retired minister who had a chicken farm on the edge of town, and during a pause in the work the old gentleman turned to me and asked: "What are you going to make of yourself when you grow up, Bruce?" As far as I can remember I had not consciously made any choice, but now that the question was asked I replied unhesitatingly: "I am going to be a journalist." I finally did, too—although I must say that that was the only time in my life that I ever applied the word "journalist" to myself. I have never known a newspaperman who used it. Anyway, I had made up my mind. Whether I would ever have gone in that direction if Father had not read those Samuel G. Blythe stories, and made the comment he did make, I have no idea. Maybe the moral is that fathers ought to be careful what they say to growing sons.

If I had made up my mind at such an early age I did not know it for quite a time. Indeed, there was a period—during which I must have been a trial to my elders—in which I imagined that I was going to be a violinist.

It was not as if I had any especial talent. I liked music, I had a sensitive ear, and the sounds that can be drawn from a violin stirred me deeply, so when I was asked if I would like to take violin lessons I said I would like it very much; but of the deep, instinctive, all-consuming response a born musician makes at such a time I had not a trace. I wanted to play the violin, but it was not something that I wanted more than I wanted anything else. The music world lost nothing of any consequence when, in the course of time, I let the dream die and went off in another direction.

Still, some sort of desire was present. Underneath everything else, I suppose, was the notion that a violinist was a romantic figure. I wanted to be a violinist in much the same way that I wanted to be a locomotive engineer, a cavalry officer or a star pitcher for the Detroit Tigers. I needed to see myself performing to the admiration of everyone, including myself, in some very public place. These other roles were clearly beyond my reach, but apparently the violinist goal was attainable—and after all a concert hall was just as fine a stage as a locomotive cab, a battlefield or a big league ball park. So for a number of years I nursed the idea that I was destined to be a musician. I never quite took the dream seriously, but it was a nice thing to play with. It gave me a fine role to enact in the theater of the imagination. I noticed also that some of the loveliest academy girls used to listen, all entranced, with a faraway look, when they heard the right kind of music.

The facilities for developing a virtuoso in Benzonia were limited. There was an estimable lady in town, a Mrs. Flanner, who gave violin and piano lessons, and I was entrusted to her care. She did her best with me, but I had not progressed much beyond the sawing-and-scraping stage when she moved away and my training lapsed. Then, just as my parents were saying that it was a shame I could not go on with my music, Mr. Bucholz came to town.

Mr. Bucholz was far and away the best violinist I had ever heard. The concert stage in the early 1900s did not lead musicians of even the third or fourth rank into our part of the state, and here was a man who, by our standards at least, was straight from the big time. He was not, to be sure, a soloist, as the word would be understood in Chicago or Boston or New York, but he was no backwoods fiddler either. He had played for years in the first violin section of the Minneapolis symphony, and now some freak of fate had brought him to earth in Thompsonville, the railroad junction town a dozen miles east of Benzonia. (I have often wondered how a man like that got to our county in the first place, and how he stood it there—for a professional musician it must have been like the heart of the Sahara—but I never did find out.) He came to Benzonia to give a concert, and for the first time I heard what my chosen instrument could do when the right man was using it; and afterward he let it be known that he would come over from Thompsonville every Saturday to give violin lessons. My parents immediately signed me in as a student.

My first meeting with him was an experience. He had taken over one of the classrooms in Barber Hall—it was a Saturday, so the building was not in use—and when I came in he was striding up and down, violin under his chin, performing what seemed to me the most dazzling pyrotechnics, just as you can see two dozen violinists do backstage in a symphony hall half an hour before concert time. He laid his violin down, shook hands, and invited me to produce my own violin. I did so, wondering how it was to be tuned because there was no piano; and I immediately learned that Mr. Bucholz needed no piano for this job. Once the instrument was in tune he ordered me to tuck it under my chin and play something.

I made no music that first day. It was given over to basic training: how to stand, how to hold the violin, how to get my left arm in position, how to grip the violin with my chin. Nothing that I did was right, and Mr. Bucholz obviously felt that I needed rebuilding from the ground up. He pointed out that you did not hold the violin with your left hand; you held it with your chin and shoulder, leaving the left hand free for more important tasks, and to prove it he put his own violin under his chin, dropped his hands to his sides, and ordered: "Now—take it away from me." I hesitated, because I understood that a violin was fragile, but he insisted and I grabbed the neck of the instrument and tugged. Nothing happened: he had it clamped in place, and I was much impressed. Then he spent a long time showing me how to apply that sort of grip to my own violin, and when I began to catch on he tried to get my left hand into the proper position. It seemed to me that he was going to dislocate my wrist, but he kept at it, explaining why things had to be done his way; and while he was at it he took my hand away from the instrument, studied it carefully, flexed my fingers, and then for the first time looked at me with approval.

"You are very fortunate," he said. "You have a monkey's hand."

The ordinary hand, Mr. Bucholz said, was not really designed for the violin, and before he could make music the violinist had to conquer his own anatomy, forcing his hand and wrist into an unnatural position. The monkey's hand was different—in its shape, in the way it was attached to the wrist, and in other ways which I do not remember—and it could be put into the proper stance without strain. The rare human being who had a hand like a monkey's had a profound advantage when he undertook to play the violin. He could do easily what the ordinary mortal could do only by constant effort.

I was tempted to ask if that meant that monkeys could be better violinists than people can be, but I refrained. Mr. Bucholz was much in earnest, and besides I was somewhat impressed with myself. I had an asset other people did not have. Perhaps I really was meant to be a violinist. My opinion of myself rose, although it did seem too bad that I owed it all to a monkey.

I took music lessons from Mr. Bucholz for perhaps six months. I say "took music lessons" rather than "studied," because that expression is more accurate. Mr. Bucholz grew disillusioned; the Lord had given me as fine a left hand as any violinist could want, and I did not rise to my responsibility. I wanted to be a violinist, but I did not want to do all of the hard work that was necessary. He caught on, and became somewhat bitter. Apparently he had thought, at first, that something could be done with me, but I was just another teen-age fiddler and I suppose he had seen more than enough of them. I will not forget our last meeting.

Mr. Bucholz was leaving, getting out of Benzie County and going somewhere out-of-state to resume his professional career. He told me this, and then ordered me to run through the exercises he had prescribed at our last lesson. Unfortunately I had not been practicing much. This thing and that had come in the way; as Harry the odd-job man would have said, I had had so much to do and everything else. This became self-evident in a short time and Mr. Bucholz shook his head and told me to put my violin away. He looked at me sternly, and when he spoke his German accent was mildly intensified. "You haff a monkey's hand," he said. Then his look became a glare, and he added harshly: "But you also haff a monkey's head!"

Well, that was that, and I went away. I never saw Mr. Bucholz again, but wherever he went and whatever he did I hope nice things happened to him.

All of this was more instructive than I realized. By the time I left Benzonia I realized that I was not going to be a musician, and in college I took a straight liberal arts course, preparing for the day when, as I told the chicken farmer, I would be a journalist; but for several years I clung to the old romantic image, telling myself that I was actually a thwarted violinist and that things would be so different if fate had only been kinder. Eventually, however, I came to see that all of this was nonsense; I abandoned the romantic image, and got along much better without it. I had not been thwarted at all, and fate had not been in the least unkind. Mr. Bucholz had opened the door for me and had discovered that that was not where I really wanted to go. Reflecting on my experience with him, I at last made the same discovery for myself.

It is hard to realize, at this distance, how thin our musical atmosphere was in those days. We never heard any serious music because none was performed in our area. It could not be; there was no one to perform it (except, rarely, for a displaced person like Mr. Bucholz) and no audience to support a performer if one did appear. Radio and television concerts did not exist. Recorded music was skimpy. A few people owned record-players; we spoke of these devices as talking machines, or simply as victrolas, turning a trade name into a common noun, and in those days their capacity was limited. Instrumental music did not record well, and the playing time of a record was so short that symphonies and concertos could not be presented in any case. You could get military bands playing marches, dance bands playing popular tunes, and a few genuine artists like Mischa Elman playing things like *Humoresque, Träumerei* and Beethoven's *Minuet in G.* That was about it—except for operatic music.

If the talking machine made violins thin and pianos lumpy, it did catch the human voice in most of its splendor. Grand opera was available, and the performers were such world-famous people as Caruso, Melba, Homer, Gluck and Schumann-Heink. Their music made the desert a little less bleak; yet these records were expensive, nobody had much money to spare, and a family that had as many as a dozen of these recordings was most exceptional. Indeed, few people had record-players to begin with, and where one did exist it usually did no more than provide background music for casual conversation. Some of the people in town thought that my mother put on airs because she would insist on having her guests listen to the sextette from *Lucia* rather than to *Gems of Victor Herbert.*

But for all of this, music played a part in our lives. If we could not get the outside world to bring its music to us we performed for ourselves. We lived in a realm of remote country villages, isolated as no place south of Baffin Land is isolated today, frozen in with our own strained resources, and we made the best of it. The best may not have been very good, but at least it was of our own making and it meant a good deal to us. Recorded operatic selections might leave us feeling uncomfortable, but we found music that would speak for us and did the best we could with it. Our town had its own orchestra, and this was a central fact.

Like the college that had cattle on its campus and no money in the bank, this orchestra was small, surviving under handicaps. As a matter of fact it represented the same thing the school and the town itself represented, a reaching-out by earth-bound people who wanted to lay their hands on the stars, and if the stars turned out to be unreachable—well, they always are. At least the effort was made. Perhaps obeying the impulse brings its own reward; perhaps we do wrong even to think about rewards, because maybe there are none and the sky is empty, with the black places between the stars going on out forever; and possibly what we try to do means more than what we actually accomplish. Anyway, whatever this orchestra meant, we had fun with it.

Most of the time it contained about a dozen instruments—three or four violins, cornet, French horn, flute, clarinet, cello, double bass, tuba, drums and piano. (The piano was important; it more or less held things together, and to an extent made up for the thinness of the instrumentation.) Most of the players were adults. The village dentist, for instance, played the French horn, two merchants provided the cornet and the tuba, a farmer from the north shore of Crystal Lake played the cello, and the clarinetist was a young businessman from Beulah. (For a couple of years the orchestra had two clarinetists, the other one being a red-headed young man from Alabama who was principal of the high school.) For some reason the violinists were always in their teens—I do not know what happened to violinists in our town when they grew up—and the pianist was usually a young woman. Conductors came and went; generally the role was filled by the academy's music teacher, but at times the orchestra got along without a conductor, operating on a basis of mutual consent. This worked a little better than you might suppose.

Naturally, as soon as I began to play the violin I wanted to be in the orchestra. For a long time this was out of the question, because my skills were limited, but eventually—I may have been about fourteen at the time—I was considered a fit recruit and I became a member of the second violin section. This consisted of two players, a lad of about my age and general level of competence, and me. Whether you played first violin (we had two firsts, at the time) or second depended almost entirely on your proficiency. The kind of music we played made only moderate demands on the abilities of the second violinists. Mostly we came in on the afterbeat, providing a rhythmic substructure to the melody as stated by the first violins, and much of the time I do not believe anyone heard us at all. I felt inferior, but it was a beginning. I vowed that some day I would become a first violinist.

Humble as my position might be, I was swollen with self-conscious pride; I suppose I felt like a Washington correspondent who has just been admitted to the Gridiron Club. From time to time the orchestra gave concerts, at which admission was charged, and it was highly satisfying to stroll down the aisle, violin case in hand, to ascend to the stage and take my appointed seat there, to open the case and make a business of extracting the violin, tuning it, adjusting the bow, and riffling casually through the scores on the music rack, and then to gaze about in a bored manner, turning now and then to make some remark to the player next to me. Then, finally, the big moment would come and the concert would get under way.

I cannot remember much about our repertoire. Some music publisher apparently made a specialty of getting out scores that were within the grasp of orchestras just like ours, and he seems to have got most of the small amounts of money our concerts raised. We had a number of overtures whose names I have long since forgotten and whose melodies I never heard anywhere else; we played the Blue Danube waltz, and an arrangement of excerpts from Gounod's *Faust,* and Weber's *Invitation to the Dance,* and once in a while we did the anvil chorus from *Il Trovatore,* although our twelve-piece ensemble made this sound a bit tinny. Whatever we played, we gave it everything we had, and no ceremonial function in Benzonia was complete without us. We played at high school and academy commencement exercises; if the local school children gathered their forces to put on a cantata we played for that; we performed each week at Sunday School song fests, and now and then we went to some neighboring town to lay on a concert. All in all we kept busy, and my self-esteem rose.

But a serpent was climbing my apple tree. I was trying to live up to two entirely different images and the strain became excessive. Not only was I looking appreciatively at the talented young violinist who was seen and admired by everyone; I was also picturing myself as the dashing man-about-town and I could never get this second image into focus. Admittedly, Benzonia was not quite the place to be man-about-town in—indeed, it offered no possibilities whatever in that respect—but my wants were simple. I was willing to settle for appearance. I just wanted to look like the dashing worldling I had imagined, and all I needed to do this was a sleek pompadour. If I had that I had everything. Unfortunately it proved to be unattainable.

I should explain that at that time the young man of spirit and urbanity wore his hair long on top and combed straight back without a part on either side. This was simple enough if the lay of the land on top of the head was adapted to it, but mine was not. Heaven knows I tried hard, soaking my hair in water and then combing, brushing and smoothing with my hands until it was the way I wanted, but it never lasted. After about five minutes my hair would begin to dry out, and then it promptly fell apart right down the middle, with one unkempt mop falling down over one eye and another falling down over the other eye. To part my hair at all was inadmissible, but to part it in the middle was absolutely unthinkable. I was forever running my hands over my head to set things right, and my work was forever coming undone a few minutes later. This was a heavy load to bear.

Probably I ought to have taken heart from something John the barber had said to me a few years before this obsession took hold of me. John was a dedicated socialist, and while he trimmed my hair he used to give long lectures on socialism. As I recall it, most of the evils of the world came from Rockefeller, who figured largely in these talks. Anyhow, one day John was working on my hair when he discovered that I had a double crown, which he said was a great rarity and something to be proud of, because it meant that I could part my hair on either the right side or the left side, at my choice.

"I tell you," he said, gesturing with his scissors, "Rockefeller with all his millions couldn't buy that."

What Rockefeller with all his millions actually did was buy a wig, but I did not know that at the time and could not speak of it. But John had given fair warning: I could part my hair on either side, and if I left it alone it would part itself down the middle, but some sort of part it was going to have no matter what my intent might be. The smooth, sleek, sophisticated pompadour I could not have.

I came to my senses, at last, after one of our orchestra concerts. We had gone to Frankfort to play, and my problem was at its worst. Frankfort was more like a city than Benzonia was—not much more, actually, because it also was a small town, but compared to Benzonia it was a metropolis—and here if anywhere I ought to look like a debonair youth who had risen far above his country-bumpkin origins. But circumstance was against me. As an earnest violinist of moderate capacity I was something of a head-jerker, and when I fiddled my way through my assignments I used much body English; and the constant head-wagging, of course, destroyed any chance that my sleek, slicked-down hair-do would stay in place. Things were especially bad that night. Luckily, as it then seemed, there were quite a few brief rests indicated in my score, and whenever one of these came, even if it lasted for no more than a couple of bars, I would lay my bow down and run my hand desperately over that triply accursed crop of hair. All in all, I had a busy evening.

When the concert ended I started out of the building, violin case under my arm, and I came up behind a couple of local people who were exchanging greetings. One of them asked the other how he had enjoyed the concert, and the man replied that he had hardly noticed it—"I was so fascinated watching that young violinist trying to get his hair straightened out that I didn't pay much attention to the music."

I was crushed, of course, and for the first time I realized that I was in a fix. There I was, the young musician who was on public display every time the orchestra performed, building up my ego by the fact that I was undoubtedly the center of admiring glances; and it had not entered my monkey's head that those same glances took in every detail of my frantic attempts to keep my hair in order. I gave up, with a regular Fort Donelson surrender, and next morning I combed my hair with a nice part on the left side and forgot about being a young man about town. It was a relief to me and unquestionably to many other people.

Two things helped me to recover. The first was the example set by Dean Pettitt, who never dreamed that he was being an example for anyone. Dean was two or three years older than I was. He lived in Benzonia, attended the academy, and—now that Mr. Bucholz was gone—was far and away the best violinist anywhere around. He would have been our orchestra's concertmaster if we had ever heard of that expression, and I admired him greatly. He sailed effortlessly through demanding flights of music that were entirely beyond my range, and he had no mannerisms whatever; no bobbing and weaving, no wagging of the head, no concern about the condition of his hair, no thought for anything except the job at hand. Striving to pattern myself after him, I began to see that if you were going to make music the thing that mattered was what people heard rather than what they saw. My determination to enlarge my own capacity as a musician dated from the moment I took Dean as a model. He struck me as a glamorous person altogether; a lost soul, most likely, because he smoked cigarets, and now and then he picked up a few dollars by playing for dances in Beulah, but these lapses from the Benzonia norm only made him more attractive. I should add that to smoke was to invite expulsion from the academy, but Dean lived at home and was able to indulge in this abandoned habit without the knowledge of the authorities.

Improving my own technique was not easy because for a time there was no violin teacher. I "took lessons," after a fashion, from one or another of the piano teachers who flitted through town, but these estimable ladies were not of much help. They could lay out various exercises for me and they could insist that I practice faithfully, but they could not play the violin and could not show me what I was doing wrong and how I should correct my faults. Then, at last, in my final year at the academy, along came Amy Foster.

Amy Foster was a good violinist and a competent pianist as well. She had just been graduated from the Oberlin Conservatory of Music and she knew how to teach as well as how to play. She took me apart and remodeled me, weeding out the bad habits I had acquired and, like Mr. Bucholz years earlier, going back to fundamentals. I began to see that good music, even for a solo instrument, is not necessarily something you want to whistle. I also learned that if you were going to perform in public you left music rack and score behind when you got up on the platform; you had memorized the numbers you were going to play, you had them all in your head, put there by incessant work, and you brought them out by concentrating on what you were doing with no thought for anything else. If, in midflight, you stopped to think, asking yourself: "Now, just what comes next? Am I playing the repeat on this section, or is this the first time through?"—if you did that you were lost and nobody could save you. It was necessary to make the music a part of you and then to produce it, and conscious thought apparently had nothing to do with it. It goes without saying that there was no room at all for thoughts of your visual image.

I made progress. I found myself, at last, a first violinist in the orchestra; indeed, when Dean Pettitt was absent now and then

I became *the* first violinist, and although a couple of years earlier this would have filled me with sinful pride all it gave me now was a feeling of responsibility. If I did not actually proceed far along the road to real musicianship I at least had stopped thinking what a fine figure I was cutting and saw only how much more I needed to learn. I worked at it, and the work was done more readily because I had conceived an intense personal regard for Miss Foster. She was pretty, warmhearted, vivacious; she was, to be sure, several years older than I, and she was also a member of the faculty, and she was as unattainable as the North Star, but from my end of the violin I adored her.

All of this, of course, meant nothing much. Our orchestra produced no musicians. It was not intended to. We played just because we enjoyed it. The music we played was mostly mediocre and our performance was fairly ragged, yet we got something out of it. We see the universe by what we have done; experience, as the poet said, is an arch through which we glimpse a world we never can enter. We did not build a large arch, but we did open one small window—an arrow slit perhaps in the heavy wall of the gray fortress that confines us all—and it was like an escape. We saw just a little of the outer landscape, the hazy fields, the tumbled blue on the skyline, the quiet glory in the air, the enchanted road leading off where we could never go, and this was better than not seeing anything at all. With faulty technique but with some dedication we made a primitive painting, putting bright colors on a scene that was never quite real in the first place. Without consciously trying to do anything of the kind we enriched our lives.

You never know when you are going to meet someone special. Amy Foster was someone special, and although she did not make a musician out of me—that task was beyond human achievement —she at least enabled me, for the rest of my life, to get a better understanding of the music other people made. I shall always be grateful to her. Another special person I met at about this time was Leon Gray, who showed up in the fall of 1914 as the

Man on the Faculty. Father had at last found a young man who fully measured up to his job.

Mr. Gray was not impressive to look at. He was lanky, soft-spoken, with a slow smile, a huge nose, and long ungainly arms, and he came up to Benzonia immediately after his graduation from Alma College. Nothing ever made him flap. It was said that a friend, wanting to learn if anything could really startle him, once fired a shotgun under his bed while he lay asleep. Mr. Gray came awake without a fuss, looked under the bed, and mildly asked the friend what on earth he thought he was doing. He had an indefinable ability to win respect and obedience from the slightly unruly young men who inhabited our boys' dormitory, and although he was not physically imposing he somehow overawed and quieted the village louts who used to try to disrupt academy games and frolics.

My best friend in the academy was a lad named Donald Gibb, and he was the star student in Mr. Gray's chemistry class. One day, reflecting on what he had learned, Donald realized that you could make an explosive by treating cotton batting with nitric acid (and for all I know with other things as well) and so he made some and arranged it in a booby trap over the door to the chemistry laboratory, with an electric firing device to set it off when the door was opened. (I should add that later on Donald enjoyed a most distinguished career with Dow Chemical.) The booby trap worked perfectly, going off with a satisfactory bang when Mr. Gray opened the door. Mr. Gray surveyed the scene, examined the evidence, and at once sent for Donald, to whom he delivered an earnest lecture on the folly of playing tricks that might hurt somebody. Donald put on an innocent air and wanted to know why he was being accused.

"That's easy," said Mr. Gray. "You're the only boy in the class who is smart enough to do this."

Leon Gray was the most remarkable Jack-of-all-trades I ever met. It seemed that he knew a little about everything; in addition, he could teach you how to do things he could not do himself. He was no athlete, but he coached our athletic teams better than anyone had ever done; he could play no musical instrument to any extent, but he quickly became conductor of the village orchestra, and he was a good one. If a class or a group wanted to put on a play, Mr. Gray was the director-producer, although he knew no more about the dramatic arts than the average A.B. from a fresh-water college. In his quiet way he had a great zest for living; where he was, things happened, and we got the idea that working with him or studying under him was fun. His most fantastic achievement undoubtedly was his creation of a brass band out of nothing at all.

This was an expedient, arising primarily (though somewhat indirectly) from the academy's lack of a gymnasium, and if that seems an unusual reason for organizing a band I can only say that that is the way it happened.

Our winter sport program consisted of the game of basketball. The hall where we had to play was unsatisfactory, its lack of dressing rooms and shower baths was an offense, and its imperfect facilities were inadequate for more than one team. For a long time Father had been wishing that they could forget about basketball altogether until that far-off day when the academy could have a real gymnasium. Yet this did not seem feasible. The winter term was long, and the boys were apt to feel somewhat snowbound; basketball at least was something to occupy their minds, even though only a few could actually play, and it was hard to say what might happen if this outside interest were removed.

When he talked this over with Mr. Gray, Father met instant agreement. Under the circumstances, basketball had to go. Finding a replacement activity, said Mr. Gray, was easy; they would organize an academy band. Practically every boy in school would take part, and the project would keep all hands so busy that they would forget about the lost basketball team. The idea sounded good to Father, although he was just a bit skeptical: who was going to teach all of these boys how to play? Mr. Gray said that he would, and that it would be simple enough. The project was approved at the top. We were going to have a band.

The difficulties were outlandish. Something like fifteen or twenty boys would be involved. Two of them (including me) knew how to play the violin, and two or three more could play the piano; nobody else could play anything at all, and most of the lads could not even read music. Not one of us had ever played any kind of wind instrument. Mr. Gray knew more than the rest of us, but not very much more; in a general way he knew how the instruments were played, but he himself could not properly play any of them. All of us, the teacher and the taught, were starting from scratch.

He began by calling us all together and telling us what we were going to do. Then he gave us a blackboard lecture on the length of sound waves and its relation to pitch. I believe he rigged up a piece of rope and twitched the free end so that ripples ran along to the end that was made fast at the wall, shortening the rope from time to time and inviting us to see how the ripples changed. He blatted a note on a cornet, pressed a key and blatted again, pointing out that pressing the key changed the length of the vibrating column of air and so produced a different note. The whole thing was several miles over our heads, but at the same time it somehow had the effect of making everything clear. We were entranced.

How he made up his mind which boy was to play which instrument is more than I can imagine. He worked it out by some rule of his own, making assignments in such a way that for all of its imperfections our band would at least have proper balance. In one way or another—by dint of various rigid economies, I suppose, for we were a penurious crowd—we got the instruments. One at a time, Mr. Gray sat down with each one of us and did what he could to show us what we had to do and how we were supposed to do it; in most cases he had to begin by teaching his pupil how to read music. He got some scores, the simplest marches and two-steps available, and most of the boys got what skill they ever got simply by playing their parts over and over.

Mr. Gray had no trouble getting us to practice, because we were full of enthusiasm and eager to learn. His real trouble came from keeping our separate practice sessions from completely disrupting the life of the academy and of the village. During the hours when practice was permissible—late afternoon and early evening—the boys' dormitory was a madhouse, with all kinds of unmelodious noises coming from every room. It was necessary to make a special rule governing the piccolo. I do not remember who played this infernal little device, but whoever he was took to it as if he had been born for it, and he had excellent lung power. When he was in full blast—and he picked the thing up with amazing aptitude—you could quite literally hear him all over town. It was ruled that he could practice only in one of the empty classrooms in Barber Hall, between the hours of four and six in the afternoon; this was somewhat removed from human dwelling places, and in its cavernous interior the shrill piping was slightly muffled. Somewhat later, when we had made enough progress to get together, tout ensemble, and try our hands at one of our set pieces, the piccolo was by far the most audible of all the instruments. I do not know if anyone ever composed a piccolo concerto—I would hope not, definitely—but some of our practice sessions must have sounded as if that was what was being attempted.

Against all the odds, we made progress. How it was done I do not know. I do not even recall the steps by which Mr. Gray taught me how to play the B-flat clarinet. I seem to remember studying a brief beginner's manual of some kind, and I think he had studied it before me because—as he confessed later—until he organized this band he had never so much as had a clarinet in his hands. That he taught any of us anything seems an outright miracle. But teach us he did, and by spring he was planning our first public performance.

For by spring we had a band. It was not, I must admit, a good band; it must have been just about the worst one in the history of the state of Michigan, and by contrast our village orchestra was a veritable Vienna Philharmonic. The mere fact that the band existed was remarkable; the astounding, improbable fact was not that it played well but that it played at all. In the fullness of time we gave our first concert.

I wish I could remember what we played, but I cannot and maybe it is just as well. We had seven or eight numbers, and we played them right up to the hilt. I don't think Mr. Gray actually throttled the piccolo player, but he managed to tone him down somehow and we got through the evening without arousing public protest. Indeed, the audience seemed to enjoy itself, and I know that we who played in the band had the time of our lives. There was just one unfortunate incident, and—as anyone familiar with my record in the world of music might have foretold—it involved me.

To flesh out our slightly skimpy program we had a few specialty numbers. (Of all unlikely things, one of these was a duet for cornet and clarinet; we got through it all right.) Along with everything else, Mr. Gray had put together a male quartet, in which I sang a well-intentioned baritone, and we had a repertoire of exactly two songs. We were to appear twice, once just after the opening number, and once just before the close. Our first song was something about "A Bower of Roses by Bendemeer's Stream." I have not the remotest idea what the other song was; whatever it was, it was the only other song we knew. Two appearances, two songs; it seemed adequate.

We got through "Bendemeer" in fine style, and the audience demanded an encore. We bowed graciously, thinking that would do it, but people kept on applauding. They wanted another song, and this had us up a tree; we knew only one other song, and we had to render that later, and what on earth were we to do? The idea that we might just give them another verse of "Bendemeer" never entered our heads, but at last inspiration descended on us. For our own amusement we had sung "Good-

Night Ladies" a few times, and we believed that we did it well. Mr. Gray had never drilled us in it, but that did not matter; it was a song and we knew how to sing it, so we fell into line facing the audience, hummed around until we got the pitch, and then sailed into it.

It was too much for everybody except us. This after all was just the second item on the program, the whole evening was ahead of us, and we were singing "Good-Night Ladies"; and after about two bars a gentle ripple of laughter started. It broadened, ripened, and grew great until it possessed everybody but the four earnest youths who were doing the singing. It was not derisive laughter. Everybody was as friendly as could be. But the performance struck everyone as extremely funny, and after years of reflection I can see why. It *was* funny. We were deeply hurt, of course, and it was a long time before we four could quite understand what everybody had been laughing about.

Anyway, the Benzonia Academy Band gave its first concert to a large and appreciative audience.

CHAPTER NINE

Under the Lilacs

We lived in Indian summer and mistook it for spring. Winter lay ahead just when we thought June was on the way. The school, the town and the people connected with both were coming to an end that seemed to be a beginning. They had been created by an era that was closing, and nothing like them would ever exist again because what had brought them forth was gone; yet twilight at the end of the day looks much as it does at the dawn unless you watch the shadows move, and for a while time stood still. The shadows were not coming down the slope. They would dissolve when the sun rose, and the future—when it appeared: there was no hurry about it—would wear a familiar image. What we were going to be was determined by what had gone before. We accepted the unbreakable continuity of the society that had produced us.

That continuity, although we did not realize it, was already breaking apart. We knew of course that changes were taking place. The forests were gone, and all around us the little towns were falling into a long decline. The farms that had appeared so hopefully on the hills and in the wide flat valleys were going the same way. One by one—indeed, ten by ten, if anyone had bothered to count—they were going back to brambles and sumac. The section that had found it worth while to support us was becoming less and less able to carry the load. School and town had been built to provide a light in the wilderness, but now the wilderness was gone. We understood that there would have to be some readjustments.

But we hardly doubted that the readjustments would be made. Much had been invested, worth nothing at a sheriff's sale, worth everything to the investors: hard work, sacrifice, courage, and the wavering dreams that make a barren life tolerable because they reach out to something better beyond the high ground ahead. It was not possible that all of these could be wasted. Somehow, some way, all that had been done would justify itself. The light that had been lit on our hilltop could not be allowed to go out just because the surrounding darkness was gone. It would still be needed to light a path for the feet of men not yet taught to lift their eyes to the sky. We never bothered to formulate this faith. We just had it.

We had been brought up to believe in progress, and we did not think of progress in material terms. Material progress was of course being made, and it was welcome; in 1913, for instance, some utility company built a power dam in the Betsie River and our town got electricity, even including a few street lights, whose dim glow (if you happened to be abroad on some lawful errand after other folk had gone to bed) simply intensified the immensity of the night. Some day, we believed, there would be a public water supply, and it was even possible to suppose that eventually the main street might be paved, although that was obviously a long way off. But these things were not especially important. Our school and our town existed in response to a moral imperative. It was up to us to produce better men, and nothing else mattered very much. We were extremely unsophisticated, and in a way we were aware of it, but it was natural enough because in the time that had brought us into being there was so much less to be sophisticated about.

Now the trouble with the outside world that controlled our fate was not that it had cut down all of its trees but that it was developing an entirely new attitude. It had created a desert and called it progress, and it was beginning to suspect that man's salvation might lie in his ability to adjust himself to the results of his own advanced technology. To produce better men was all very well, if you had time for it, but the road to blessedness would probably be found in the conquest of man's physical surroundings rather than in the conquest of his own inner nature. What he could do rather than what he could be was the important thing. That this approach might finally lead to the production of a barbarian who happens to be a skilled technician meant little; improve his technology enough and perhaps he is no longer a barbarian . . . or perhaps there will not be anybody to tell the difference.

To read all of this into the story of the decline and death of an institution as completely unimportant as our academy is perhaps to stretch things just a bit. Yet this academy, like the village to which it was cemented, was the embodiment of an idea held by the society that had created it, and it died because the idea was replaced by something else. For punctuation in the account of this change, consider the periodic appearance of Halley's Comet.

This comet appears once every seventy-six years, swinging in from outer space, blazing briefly across our familiar sky, and then going off again on its mysterious round; once a thing to frighten gods and men, reduced now to the ticking of some inscrutable celestial timepiece, and perhaps none the less frightening for all that. It showed up on schedule in 1910, and one clear evening most of the town gathered on a knoll in the campus to have a look at it. I was out there along with everybody else, and I must say that I was disappointed. I had heard so much about this comet, and I expected something spectacular; all I could see—and I saw that only after much effort, asking annoying questions the while—was a dull thing like a smudged star, motionless, its fabulous tail something to be taken on faith. It hardly seemed worth looking at.

Still, I was impressed by the way people talked about it. Seventy-five years must pass before it would reappear. The grown-ups, of course, knew they would never see it again, but we youngsters were told that we might be around for the next visit, and we were invited to reflect on the wonders and marvels that would take place in the world before that day came.

Wonders and marvels there assuredly have been, and the day has not yet come. The point is that the last time we saw the comet we looked ahead with confidence. God was in His Heaven, and man at least was in his right mind. We could dream any dreams we liked and they were bound to be good ones. The one thing we could not possibly foresee was that the next time the comet came around we might be so appalled by the things that had happened since the last visit that we would be afraid to look ahead to the next one. We have learned much about the comet's homeland in outer space, and about the depths and forces that lurk there, and we have also learned a few things about the dark spaces and unspeakable powers in man himself, and none of this knowledge has been reassuring. The clock goes tick . . . tock, measured, inexorable, and it frightens the children. What if they lay hands on the pendulum and stop it? It is just possible that some day they may do it.

For there is a strange malady that afflicts unlucky planets. They become infected by microbes known as men—the human race, to use the language of science.

No one knows how these microbes get started. The old belief that living things are generated spontaneously by inert matter is no longer respected, but when and how these organisms reach a planet remains a mystery. A great deal of speculation has been devoted to the subject but no firm conclusions have been reached. No matter: if the planet's luck is out the infection does take place and the malady has to run its course.

For a long time the progress of the malady is imperceptible, and it is hard to see that anything serious is wrong. There is some burrowing and gouging, the outer skin is marred here and there, pockmarks appear in places, and minor excrescences are created; but it all amounts to no more than a surface irritation, and there seems to be no cause for alarm. This semiactive stage, as it might be called, endures for a long time, yet it contains the elements of change; the proliferation and development of these microbes follow a pattern which is not yet wholly understood. They spread all across the surface of the planet, and they form dense clusters in certain spots, and all the while they consume more and more of the planet's substance; there seems to be some strange law, imperfectly studied, which makes their destructive or consumptive capacity increase at a rate progressively faster than their increase in numbers, although the latter increase is dismaying enough when considered by itself. Not yet fully examined is the strange impulse which seems to make a sharp rise in the numbers of the microbes—an increase in the density of human population, to lapse into the jargon—follow each rise in destructive power. That this impulse exists is obvious, but it requires more study than has yet been given it.

It needs to be examined with care, because it seems that at this stage of the malady the microbes undergo some fundamental change in their nature. An element that seems wholly illogical can be detected. The universal instinct for self-preservation begins to be overshadowed by an impulse for destruction. Men destroy one another in enormous numbers, but this is only natural because the survivors will have sole possession of the host body; much more ominous is the fact that they now seem bent on destroying the planet itself. Probably it would be wrong to assume that conscious thought is involved, and yet there does seem to be a change in (if the expression is permissible) the way these microbes regard their own life cycle. They break away from all of the old limits, as if there had been an actual change in objective. For the first time, to increase their powers seems to become an end in itself. It appears that the planet is in serious trouble.

For now appears the worst symptom of all, sure sign that the malady is approaching either its terminal stage or its moment of supreme crisis. The increased powers are exercised to the extreme limit, almost as if the microbes had ceased to care about the planet and were bent on infecting the universal life system that governs it. Men make themselves free of the sky, as if the barriers of time and space no longer meant anything. At the same time they learn how to crack the force that binds the infected planet's cells together, so that the globe lies in danger of going up in one stupendous flaming lifeless cloud, taking its microbes along with it. And finally, understanding just a little too much about the laws governing their own existence and development, they prepare to create life itself in their own laboratories, without benefit of trumpets or clouds of glory; becoming busy with test tubes and microscopes, they triumphantly get ready to remake themselves, disastrously, in their own image. And all the while, faster and faster, they consume or destroy the planet's own life sources—its growing things and its minerals, its soil and its air and its water—and the waste products arising from all of this lie upon the planet's flesh like an intolerable scurf.

Within limits the upshot is predictable. The planet may die outright, either in one burst of flame or by a final attrition of its vital forces, leaving it a spinning clinker in lifeless space. The microbes may, on the other hand, destroy themselves and leave the afflicted planet to recover as best it can. Or, conceivably, there may be another shift in the attitude of these bacilli, reducing the blind drive toward destruction and making them something the planet can continue to tolerate. There do not seem to be any other possibilities.

The clock goes on ticking. Halley's Comet will come back, probably caring hardly at all whether anybody will be around to see it. We saw it go away, from our little hilltop, and if we believed that there would be many changes before it returned we never doubted that at least they would be good. The comet might come from the realm of eternal darkness, but there was no danger that it would bring the night back with it. We believed in the triumph of light.

And there was an enchanted light on our landscape then. It

was Indian summer sunlight, stained by the shifting colors of dying leaves, haunted by the gentlest delusions, and in a way it was easy to see that an era was closing. Yet that was nothing to worry about; another era would follow, and it undoubtedly would be better. We were upheld by a faith that came from the very air we breathed. Mankind was at its springtime. We knew it, and we waited for Indian summer to bring out buds and blossoms.

It was easy to feel this way because Benzonia's concerns were small—small enough to fit into the deepest recesses of the human heart—and its history was uneventful. The individual might have his own pack of grief, suffering and shattered hopes to carry as he clambered up the long stairway, but the community as a whole knew contentment. A less worried place probably did not exist anywhere. We were isolated from the rest of the world, and the isolation was pleasant. The happenings that tug at the memory today were small happenings.

The town was essentially a crossroads settlement, with a cluster of wooden business buildings rising where the north-south road intersected the main road from west to east. There were three general stores, a meat market, a bank, a barber shop, a post office, a drug store and a blacksmith shop, and for a time there was a run-down hotel that hardly ever had any guests. The drug store resembled a modern drug store only in that you could get a prescription filled there; it had no soda fountain, it sold no candy, and its interior was so dusky that you had to grope your way to the counter. The barber shop, where I used to listen to lectures on socialism, contained a pool table, although I do not remember ever seeing anyone play on it. On the wall behind the pool table there was a sign, "If you can't pay, don't play," and for a long time I misread it and thought it said, "If you can't *pray* . . ." which struck me as a natural admonition in a God-fearing community.

The blacksmith shop was interesting, although the blacksmith did not like to have small boys hanging around. He was important to us, however, because if we found any bits of old iron he would buy them from us, and so he was an occasional source of pennies; we had no pocket money whatever, and to get two or three cents was to become rich. Money thus obtained was almost always spent on candy at Simon McDonald's general store. We felt that Mr. McDonald gave more for a penny than the other stores did, and he sold an odd confection of peanut butter coated with chocolate that came three-for-a-penny and was highly enjoyed. This store, by the way, was like the country store of tradition. Toward the rear there was an open space in front of the counter, with a wood-burning stove surrounded by chairs where men sat and smoked corncob pipes and discussed matters of state; I believe there was even a cracker barrel in connection.

Mr. McDonald, a remarkably genial, easygoing man, enjoyed the distinction of being just about the only Democrat in town. Ours was a devoutly Republican community, and when the village went for Theodore Roosevelt in the 1912 election we all felt mildly guilty about it. During the 1912 campaign all of us boys wore party campaign buttons pinned to our shirts, and the only Woodrow Wilson buttons I remember seeing were those worn by Mr. McDonald's two sons, Douglas and Dwight. They lived just across the road from us, and we were good friends, and I used to tease them about those buttons: why wear the emblems of a sure loser? They got even, with accrued interest, when the election returns came in; and some time next spring Mr. McDonald was duly appointed Benzonia's postmaster. Everybody agreed that this was no more than right; Mr. McDonald was universally liked, and the political spoils system was accepted without question. When he took office Mr. McDonald sold his store to his brother-in-law, Ernest Judson, another man who was highly regarded by everyone. He played the cornet in our village orchestra, and he was my Sunday School teacher; he used to take the class on a brief camping trip every summer, and my memories of him are all pleasant.

The McDonald-Judson store sold groceries and hardware, and

ain Street
Benzonia Mich

the services of a tinsmith were available here, so that if something went wrong with your downspouting or the cistern pump you could get it fixed. The store of E. T. Huntington, across the road, carried groceries and dry goods, and did not cater to the lounging element. This store smelled pleasantly of coffee, ground to order in a big coffee mill on the counter in the rear, whose crank handle was attached to a huge red wheel. (I suppose the other stores had similar machines, but somehow the only one I remember was this one.) He carried big bolts of various kinds of cloth, and I liked to watch him cut off lengths of it with his enormous pair of shears; I used to get the idea that it would be pleasant to be a merchant some day, grinding coffee and cutting off bits of cloth, and filling kerosene cans from a tank in a room at the back of the store.

Mr. Huntington was a friendly man, but he had an austere side. He was a pillar of the church, and worked at it. Now that I think of it, that term would apply to most of the grown-up males in town; our church had more pillars than the Parthenon. Anyway, one Sunday afternoon a January thaw followed by a sudden cold snap had coated an acre or so of the campus with dazzling glare ice, and my brother Robert went out there to play, taking a good run and then jumping onto the ice and gliding along without benefit of skates. Mr. Huntington happened to walk by, and he called Robert over and asked him, with a somewhat informal severity, whether Father knew that Robert was out here violating the Sabbath. Robert promptly slunk home, all abashed. As a matter of fact, Father would not have cared much if he had known, because he was a good deal less rigid than the other pillars, but Robert did not realize this at the time and he had been brought up to respect his elders.

I always liked being sent on an errand to the third general store, which was owned by Charles Case. This was the largest store of the lot; Mr. Case sold groceries, dry goods and hardware, all three, the interior was almost as dimly lighted as the drug store, and he also sold firearms. While he was filling an order

I would stand by the rack and admire the .22 rifles. I wanted one very much but Father did not approve of firearms and in any case there was no money to spare for such things. Once or twice I was allowed to handle one of these weapons. I liked to imagine that I owned one and lived in a cabin out in the country—it never occurred to me that our whole town was out in the country, by any rational standard—where I would live on the game I killed, rabbits and partridges chiefly as I pictured it. I did not then realize that killing a bounding rabbit with a .22 rifle is a feat for Old Leatherstocking himself.

North of the business district, if that is the name for it, were the academy grounds, and on all sides there were roads and lanes lined with residences. Residential lots tended to be large, most of them had their own vegetable gardens, and in a good many cases there was a small barn behind the house; not a barn as a farmer would understand the term, but a sort of shed big enough to shelter a horse or a cow, with room for a buggy, a tiny loft for hay, and a storeroom for harness, gardening tools, and odds and ends of equipment that were just a little too good to throw away. The gardens were important. We always had one, even when we lived in one of the academy buildings, and in summer our evening meal usually consisted of sweet corn and ripe tomatoes, with perhaps some applesauce and cake for dessert. I don't think I have ever tasted anything better in my life. Corn and tomatoes taken from the garden less than an hour before they appeared on the table had a flavor that today's city dweller cannot even imagine.

For several years we kept a cow, quartering it in somebody's back-yard barn in the village and taking it out to pasture in a lot on the edge of town. To Robert, and then to me, fell the task of caring for this beast, and it was a task I did not enjoy. I did not so much mind the actual milking, but leading the cow off to pasture in the morning, collecting it in the evening, and going through the ritual of cleaning the stable, getting hay in the manger, spreading straw for bedding and hoisting buckets of water for the cow to drink did not appeal to me in the least. I do recall one morning when I was taking this creature down a remote lane to its pasture. I had seen, somewhere, an improbable picture of a rosy-cheeked Dutch girl tending a cow, and she had posed prettily with one arm around the cow's neck; it had looked most picturesque, and so—nobody being anywhere about—I thought I would try it myself. The result was not good. My coat was covered with fine hairs, I smelled of cow all day long, and the beast stepped on my foot. We were on a lane that was ankle-deep in soft sand, or I would have had some broken bones. I never again tried to pose with a cow, and to this day I approve of cows only at a distance. It occurs to me that some of my worst moments have come when I was trying to strike an attitude.

The village bank occupied a two-story building of its own, around the corner from the store buildings, and the only thing I remember about it is a singular incident that utterly disrupted the Sunday morning church service one winter's day.

This happened after Mr. Mills had retired, when our pastor was the Reverend C. W. Dunn. He was a good minister, and a friendly, warmhearted sort to boot; when I was sixteen several of us young bloods liked to drop in at the parsonage Sunday evenings, to stand around the piano singing hymns and then to sit down and eat a panful of chocolate fudge, which indicates that Mr. Dunn had a way with young people. I probably ought to add that he also had two charming daughters. Anyway, I liked him, but he seems to have had a stern side where evildoers were concerned; a village historian not long ago wrote that he "had many of the personal attributes of an Old Testament prophet."

One Sunday morning Mr. Dunn was walking along the sidewalk on his way to church, and when he passed the bank he saw, fastened to the doorknob, a big bow of black silk, neatly tied, with dangling ends. The bank's manager was a quiet, scholarly man, Mr. Sprout, and as Mr. Dunn stared at the silken ribbon he recalled that Mrs. Sprout had been quite ill and he concluded at once that she had died. It should be explained that in that day the village undertaker's first act was to fasten a somber wreath or banner to the front door of a home where death had taken place, so that passers-by might know that an afflicted family dwelt there; the Sprouts did not live in the bank building, to be sure, but what would be more natural than for the undertaker to put his wreath there for the whole town to see? Mr. Dunn turned at the next corner and hurried to the Sprout home, to offer his condolences, blaming himself for not having kept in closer touch. He got to the house and rang the bell—and the door was opened by Mrs. Sprout herself, very much alive and most happy to greet the minister.

Mr. Dunn was of course delighted to know that she had not died, but he was also flabbergasted; when he tried to explain why he had come, he was profoundly embarrassed, and the session in the doorway was about as unpleasant an experience as he ever had. The Sprouts heard his story and shared in his feelings. They explained that the lady had recovered in the natural course of things, they knew nothing at all about the wreath on the bank door, and they had never dreamed . . . At last Mr. Dunn stumped off for church, convinced that he and they had been victims of some malicious practical joke. By the time he got to church the Old Testament prophet in him had become dominant and was growing stronger minute by minute.

The early part of the service went as usual—hymns, Scripture reading, offertory, prayer and so on. Then Mr. Dunn got squared away in the pulpit, prepared to announce his text, and deliver his sermon; but before the sermon he had a word to say, and when he spoke he was Jeremiah at his sternest. He delivered a brilliant impromptu lecture on the evils of practical joking, went on to describe just what had happened, and then excoriated parents who did not teach their children that pranks like this were base and wicked. He was in good voice, and he emptied the vials of his wrath in most impressive style. When he finished he had communicated his feeling of outrage to one and all, and many a good citizen was uneasily wondering just what Junior had been up to in the last twenty-four hours.

Then people became aware that a man was standing up in the middle of the congregation: Thomas Pettitt, a man of substance, dignified and upright, one of the pillars with which this church was so abundantly blessed. Mr. Pettitt was saying that he guessed all of this was really his fault. He had been astir early that day on some errand, and as he passed the bank he had seen, lying in the snow by the sidewalk, this piece of black silk—a lady's scarf, presumably lost the evening before. He had no idea who the owner might be, but the scarf looked valuable and he could not simply leave it in the snow, where the winter winds might blow it away; it had seemed best to tie it to the nearest doorknob, which happened to be the bank's, where the owner would unquestionably see it the next time she passed that way, and it had never entered his head that this was going to cause any trouble. He was very sorry, and he had meant everything for the best, and . . .

(Confirmation was at hand. The scarf belonged to a spinster of excellent repute; a lady of almost incredible chastity, much given to good works. She had indeed lost it the evening before, walking home from some social gathering in the home of friends, and on her way to church that morning she found it where Mr. Pettitt had fastened it, reclaimed it, and draped it once more about her shoulders. It seemed a pity that she had not recovered it before Mr. Dunn passed by, but she could hardly be blamed for that, and anyway the mystery had been solved. There had been no practical joke.)

By the time Mr. Pettit was finishing his remarks several people were chuckling quietly. Then, at last, the whole affair struck everybody as uproariously funny, and the entire congregation gave way to unrestrained laughter; the only time, I am sure, in the history of the Benzonia church, that a service was broken up by general merriment. Whether Mr. Dunn was able to go on and deliver his prepared sermon I do not remember. I should think he would hardly have been in the mood for it. He had had a very rough Sunday morning.

That he had assumed that some brainless lout had attempted a vicious practical joke was only natural, because our town, for all of its sanctity, had its full share of such characters—aimless young loafers with clumsy hands, big feet and slack mouths, ready to guffaw loudly at anybody else's misfortune. They came into their own on Halloween, an evening on which the adult population resignedly feared the worst. There was none of the harmless "tricks or treats" of the modern day. Children might drape themselves in sheets and prowl along the sidewalks, giggling mightily and carrying jack-o'-lanterns containing lighted candles; they felt that they had done their job when they held a jack-o'-lantern up before somebody's window, and were highly pleased if the accommodating grown-ups inside cried out in simulated fright. There were usually informal parties for the older children, with much bobbing for apples, followed by a general blowout on cider and doughnuts, all pleasant and innocent enough. The trouble came when the lads in their late teens and early twenties went out on the prowl.

The whole point of their activities was the notion that to inflict genuine trouble on someone was very funny. It was the height of humor, for instance, to tip over a backyard privy, and if the privy happened to be occupied at the time that only made the joke sharper. It was also funny to carry off a buggy or a wagon, remove the wheels on one side, thrust the axles through a fence, and then fasten the wheels on again; this meant a good half hour's hard work for the owner, and was of course most enjoyable. One night some of the lads went behind Case's store and laid hands on a road roller—a ponderous iron cylinder full of concrete, pulled along the road, in wintertime, by oxen to pack the snow down. (They never used snowplows, except small ones on sidewalks; snow on the road was desirable, so long as it was firm enough for sleighs and cutters, because no wheeled vehicles were used in the winter.) With much effort, the Halloweeners hauled this contraption to the head of an alley that ran downhill behind the stores and turned it loose; it crashed into a shed, wrecking it, and leaving the luckless owner with a fifty-dollar repair bill. This was a triumph . . . I have never had any trouble understanding the miseries which General Sherman's army inflicted on the people of Georgia in 1864; it simply turned its small-town rowdies loose. They had their Halloween in broad daylight with full government approval, and I am sure they enjoyed it.

It would be possible to make too much of this. Halloween was our only Saturnalia. Most of the annual observances on other dates left pleasant memories. The Fourth of July was a big day, although I must admit that I never enjoyed it quite as much as I pretended to; there was too much loud banging going on, and it always made me uneasy. Newspapers and magazines then were just beginning to campaign for what they called "a safe and sane Fourth," but they had not made much headway. All kinds of fireworks were on sale everywhere, from tiny firecrackers that made subdued little crack-crack noises up to the giant cannon crackers that went off with a shattering bang as if a farmer were dynamiting a stump; these must have been pretty dangerous, and there were plenty of tales about some boy in the next town who had lost an eye, or a hand, in a premature explosion, although I do not remember that anybody ever got hurt in Benzonia. I suppose there were patriotic exercises on the Fourth, but I never went to them; my appetite for orations and for readings of the Declaration of Independence was extremely moderate. In the afternoon we usually walked down to Beulah, where there might be boat races or a ball game, and where ice cream sodas could be bought if you had any money; and in the evening various citizens would set off Roman candles and skyrockets in their front yards. Altogether, the Fourth was a big day, although as I say it was too noisy for my taste.

It was a little too noisy, come to think of it, for our dog Bobby, also. Bobby was a timid creature who hated disturbances, and about the time the second cannon cracker went off she would hurry to the woodshed and go into hiding behind a pile of stove-wood, not to emerge until night restored the silence. I think Bobby had a complex of some sort and was burdened with a deep sense of inferiority.

Bobby was a mongrel, largely Collie in origin, and she had been the runt of the litter. She never attained more than about two thirds of the size proper for a dog of her ancestry, and she had been born with a tail that was bushy enough but was only about eight inches long. People used to ask us why we had had her tail docked and would look mildly skeptical when we explained that nature had done it for us. Bobby had been spayed when a puppy, and her outlook was that of a confirmed, embittered spinster. She had no use at all for the sniff-sniff maneuver by which a male dog tries to get acquainted with a stranger. When this was attempted she would wheel about, snarling angrily, and slash out with her teeth, meaning to inflict genuine harm. She never got into any fights this way. The other dog was always too amazed to make anything of it, and would go ambling off wondering what he had done that was wrong.

Bobby's greatest trial in life was the presence in our home of a big tomcat, Mottas. (My brother Thurber and I had given him that name; I do not remember how on earth we devised it, but it stuck.) Mottas shared the hearthrug with Bobby, whom he consistently ignored, and Bobby loathed him with a high and holy hatred; I used to see her looking at him with more venom in her eyes than I have ever seen anywhere else. My brothers and I quickly learned that if Bobby (who was somewhat choosy about her food) refused to eat her supper, we could get her to consume every bite of it simply by offering it to Mottas; she would eat it, obviously, to keep the detested cat from getting it. One time we got her to eat a bowl of baked potato skins by using this device. It occurs to me that we had some touch of the *schaden freude* that I so deplored in our Halloween rowdies.

Anyway, Bobby's big day came shortly after my small sister

acquired a Persian kitten. Mottas did not approve—he wanted to be the only cat in the household—and when he thought he was not being watched he would try to kill the kitten. We always detected him in time, but the situation was not good. Then, one spring afternoon, Thurber and I were out in the back yard, and Bobby was trotting about with us, and from the spirea bushes beside the house there came an agonized yowl: Mottas had the kitten down and was trying to bite through the back of its neck. Thurber and I yelled, and Mottas let go and stalked off, trying to look innocent. Bobby was watching closely, and one or the other of us, feeling that Mottas ought to be taught a lesson, called out: "Go get him, Bobby! Go get him!"

Bobby let out a whoop—there is no other word for it, really—and took off like a greyhound; Mottas, seeing what was up, took off likewise and went bounding across the back yard as if the gates of hell had opened just behind him, which from his point of view was exactly the case. Bobby pursued, three feet behind, unable to gain but not losing any ground either, barking exultantly while she ran, the released fury built up by months of repressed hatred all coming to the surface at once. If she had caught that cat she infallibly would have torn him into small fragments. (A healthy tomcat chased by a dog can usually settle matters by wheeling about and preparing to fight; the dog is giving chase largely from a sense of duty and, if a showdown comes, is well aware that the cat's claws can inflict painful injury. But this case was different. Bobby would gladly have lost an eye for the pleasure of murdering this particular cat, and Mottas understood perfectly.)

This chase was one of the most spirited events I have ever seen. Several times Mottas ran straight past convenient trees that offered chances for escape; he was pursued so hotly that he simply did not have time to stop and climb. At last he came to a shed that housed the entrance to the academy's heating and pumping plant. He made one wild leap that put him on its eaves, six feet off the ground, dug his claws in frantically, and scrambled to the peak of the shed's roof, from which point he glared apprehensively at his pursuer. Bobby, realizing that he was at last out of reach, trotted back and forth a few times, jeering derisively, and then came bounding back to Thurber and me, wagging her stub of a tail and glowing with irrespressible happiness. I do not think I have ever seen a living creature displaying so much bubbling, uncorked joy, unless it was (more than half a century later) Mr. Steve Blass of the Pittsburgh Pirates just after he won the final game of the world series of 1971.

All in all, it was clear that Mottas's day as a member of our household was ended, and my parents got rid of him. My recollection is that they presented him to one of the village merchants, and that Mottas took up the position of cat-in-residence in a grocery store. This was a good assignment for any cat; drowse all day, and spend the night roaming the darkened store catching mice, with a can of salmon or sardines now and then for reward. I trust that Mottas enjoyed life; I know Bobby was a much more well-adjusted dog after he left. She and the kitten got along well enough, on a live-and-let-live basis.

One of the pleasantest holidays of the year was Memorial Day, universally known then as Decoration Day because it was the day when you went out to the cemetery and decorated graves. This day of course belonged to the Civil War veterans, although as years passed it more and more became a day to put flowers on the grave of any loved one who had died, and when it came just about everyone in town went to the cemetery with a basket of lilacs. Lilacs grow like weeds in our part of the country, and most farmers planted a long row of lilacs as windbreaks around their houses; in town almost every house had lilacs in the yard, and in late May the scent of them lay on the breeze. To this day I never see lilac blossoms without remembering those Decoration Day observances of long ago.

The Civil War veterans were men set apart. On formal occasions they wore blue uniforms with brass buttons and black campaign hats, by the time I knew them most of them had long gray beards, and whatever they may have been as young men they had an unassuming natural dignity in old age. They were pillars, not so much of the church (although most of them were devout communicants) as of the community; the keepers of its patriotic traditions, the living embodiment, so to speak, of what it most deeply believed about the nation's greatness and high destiny.

They gave an especial flavor to the life of the village. Years ago they had marched thousands of miles to legendary battlefields, and although they had lived half a century since then in our quiet backwater all anyone ever thought of was that they had once gone to the ends of the earth and seen beyond the farthest horizon. There was something faintly pathetic about these lonely old men who lived so completely in the past that they had come to see the war of their youth as a kind of lost golden age, but as small boys we never saw the pathos. We looked at these men in blue, existing in pensioned security, honored and respected by all, moving past the mounded graves with their little flags and their heaps of lilacs, and we were in awe of them. Those terrible names out of the history books—Gettysburg, Shiloh, Stone's River, Cold Harbor—came alive through these men. They had *been* there . . . and now they stood by the G.A.R. monument in the cemetery and listened to the orations and the prayers and the patriotic songs, and to watch them was to be deeply moved.

The G.A.R., of course, was the Grand Army of the Republic, the veterans' organization of those days. The Benzonia local of this organization was officially the E. P. Case Post Number 372, and it had been named for Edward Payson Case, a Benzonia man who died in 1886, a year before the post was organized. He must have been quite a man; he had enlisted in 1864, in the artillery, and his unit had been sent to Cumberland Gap on garrison duty and had finished out the war there, never getting into combat. Almost to a man, our G.A.R. members had been in violent action during the war, and they never would have named the local post after a noncombat soldier if he had not been an impressive sort of person. The monument they built, sometime in the late 1880s or early 1890s, was completely homemade. It was a fat column of field stone and mortar, no more than four or five feet tall, capped by a round slab of rock that was just a little wider than the supporting column; it looks like an overgrown toadstool, and it would be funny if it were not so unmistakably the work of men who were determined to have a monument and built one with their own hands because they could not pay for a professional job. The spirit that built it redeems it; it stands today as the most eloquent, heart-warming Civil War memorial I ever saw.

I remember the G.A.R. men as a group, rather than as individuals, although a few do stand out. There was Elihu Linkletter, a retired minister when I knew him, who had lost his left arm in the Wilderness. I never looked at him without thinking (in bemused small-boy fashion) how proud he must be to carry this visible sign of his sacrifice for all to see. Mr. Linkletter was devoted to birds, and he waged unceasing war on red squirrels on the ground that they robbed birds' nests and ate fledglings. He used to tramp about with a .22 rifle, shooting every red squirrel he saw; he could use it one-handed and he was a remarkably good marksman with it. There was John Van Deman, who once told me how he had been wounded in some battle in West Virginia; like all the other veterans he pronounced "wounded" to rhyme with "sounded," which somehow made it more impressive. There was Lyman Judson, who had served in the cavalry under Phil Sheridan and who had been invalided out of the service when, his horse being shot out from under him, he had fallen heavily on the base of his spine so that he suffered thereafter from a weak back. Forty-five years later, in Benzonia, he slipped on the ice and again fell heavily on the base of his spine. In some unaccountable way this cured him, and for the rest of his life his back was as sound and as pain-free as anyone's. And there was Cassius Judson (no relation) who in 1916 went down to Manistee to see *The Birth of a Nation*. When he got back I asked him if he had not been impressed by the picture's portrayal of the battle of Atlanta. Mr. Judson, who had been in that battle personally, smiled faintly and said: "Well, it wasn't much like the real thing."

Then, finally, there was John Morrow, who had been an infantryman in an Ohio regiment and who had once exchanged words with General William T. Sherman himself. ("Exchanged" probably is not the word, because Sherman did all of the talking.) Anyway, during the Atlanta campaign Morrow and some comrades were out on patrol, and they came to a stream where there was a grassy bank with trees to cast a pleasant shade, and the day was mortally hot, and so they all stacked arms and stretched out for a breather. Just then Sherman and some of his staff rode up, and Sherman came over to find out what these soldiers were doing. When he found out, as Morrow remembered it, he "used language that would make a mule driver blush" and in no time the boys were back on patrol in the hot sun. They did not hold this against General Sherman, figuring that it was just part of the fortunes of war.

By the time I knew them these veterans were in their seventies, or very close to it, and a hale and hearty lot they were. There was one man, whose name I do not remember, who lived on a farm a few miles south of town. He had fought at Gettysburg, and in 1913 there was a big fiftieth anniversary celebration of that battle, with surviving veterans invited to attend. This old chap went to Gettysburg, enjoyed the three days' activities, and then came home by train, and when he finished the trip, at Beulah, he found that the friend who was to have met him with a buggy to drive him out to his farm had somehow failed to make it. Quite undaunted, the seventy-year-old veteran picked up his carpetbag and hiked the five miles home. He could see nothing remarkable in this, because he had had many worse hikes during the war.

In their final years the G.A.R. men quietly faded away. Their story had been told and retold, affectionate tolerance was beginning to take the place of respectful awe, and in Europe there was a new war that by its sheer incomprehensible magnitude seemed to dwarf that earlier war we knew so well. One by one the old men went up to that sun-swept hilltop to sleep beneath the lilacs, and as they departed we began to lose more than we knew we were losing. For these old soldiers, simply by existing, had unfailingly expressed the faith we lived by; not merely a faith learned in church, but something that shaped us as we grew up. We could hardly have put it into words, and it would not have occurred to us to try, but we oriented our lives to it and if disorientation lay ahead of us it would come very hard. It was a faith in the continuity of human experience, in the progress of the nation toward an ideal, in the ability of men to come triumphantly through any challenge. That faith lived, and we lived by it. Now it is under the lilacs.

CHAPTER TEN

At Halfway House

The school year began late in September, and it always seemed to me that then the town came to life. The youngsters returned from the distant outside world, and our own world was complete again. There were old friends to be greeted, and new faces to be learned; there were not many in either group, because the school after all was extremely small, but a pattern that seemed as timeless as the march of the seasons was resumed. The clanging of the academy bell, morning and evening, marked the familiar rhythm. It had always been like this—a decade and a half can be "always," to a teen-ager—and it would surely go on like this.

Yet there was an odd quality to that fall of 1915, when I began my final year in the academy. It was as if I stood aside, now and then, and watched the scene of which I was a part. The scene itself was permanent (as I supposed) but I myself was a transient, and suddenly I began to realize it. Boyhood was gone and youth itself would soon be over, and full manhood lay not far ahead. I was both impatient and reluctant. The eggshell was about to break, and although I wanted this to happen I was not sure that I was ready for it. It seemed important to get the last bit of flavor out of each moment, if only for the reason that nothing like this was ever going to happen again.

We had a backwoods poet in our town, and he used to scribble ragged free verse in little exercise books; now and then, with clumsy shyness, he would let people see them. The gods had given him nothing whatever except the impulse to write, what he set down was largely incomprehensible, and we used to smile in a superior way at some of his flights. The only lines I remember were a couple which amused me—a sixteen-year-old can be intolerably lofty, at times—and yet they seemed to apply to me just as if they made sense. They ran, as I recall them, as follows:

Life is of what we make it, in the years of which we live,
With the days and months as passing by.

Clear warning: my life was of what I was making it, and it seemed necessary to pause and appraise the product now and then.

What I saw was moderately satisfactory. With all of its deficiencies, the school had been giving me something. I was plunging into my fourth year of Latin, making heavy weather of it but learning something just the same. I had studied algebra, and plane geometry, and was engaged now in a life-or-death encounter with solid geometry, which I detested. I have never forgotten the lecture I got from Father when he learned that I had flunked a monthly test in that hideous subject; that a son of his should fail to pass a test through sheer failure to study hard enough—he undeniably had me, there—was more than he could bear, and he spoke with vigor. Except for the absence of profanity, I suppose his talk was much like the one General Sherman delivered to that loafing patrol in Georgia. The effect was salutary. I was forbidden to use my bicycle until I had made up the failed test, and I applied myself ardently. You could not do much with a bicycle in Benzonia because all of the roads out of town were of gravel or soft sand, wholly unsuited to bicycle riding; however, one could cruise along the sidewalks on the hilltop, and now and then one could induce one of the academy girls to ride on the handle bars, which was very pleasant indeed . . . Pleasant for me, that is; I suppose the girls must have been rather uncomfortable.

Along with the Latin and the mathematics, I had been given a fairly good grounding in ancient history. This was considered useful, because it helped to stitch together various events touched on in the Old Testament, but whoever taught it to me succeeded in making it interesting in its own right, and I liked it. Hannibal was a hero of mine, and so for some reason was Pericles. I liked the Babylonians and the Persians, but I had no more use for the Assyrians than the Children of Israel had, and I was not taken with the Romans—largely, I think, because Julius Caesar had written that dreadful chapter about bridging the Rhine. Also, as fourth-year Latin progressed, I found the pious Aeneas rather boring, and the antique Romans as a lot seemed stern and humorless, as indeed they still do.

There had been limitations, of course. The ancient world, as our textbooks had it, consisted entirely of the lands around the eastern Mediterranean. I had learned nothing whatever about India and China, and I never imagined that anything in Africa outside of Egypt was worth study. By odd chance, however, I did know something about ancient America. We were thoroughly drilled in American history, and somewhere along the line Father remarked that the academy library had Prescott's *Conquest of Mexico* and *Conquest of Peru,* and recommended that we look into them. I do not know whether anyone else followed his advice, but for some reason I did—living at close quarters with him, I had learned that when he urged you to read something you had better read it—and Prescott opened a magnificent vista. Nothing in the story of Egypt or Greece or Rome seemed half as fascinating as this account of the strange societies that had grown up on our side of the Atlantic. Those legendary people with their gleaming cities, their barbaric customs and their astonishing way of rising from unrelieved savagery to the very margin of civilization—the Aztecs and the Toltecs, the Mayans and the Incas—they obviously came straight out of enchanted fable, but they were wholly American. Mexico was a long way from Michigan, and Peru was even farther off, but they were in the New World and in a way they belonged to me. When I read Prescott's account of their downfall I was entirely on the side of the Indians.

I hated Cortés, and wished that the Aztecs had managed to wipe out his whole command on that memorable *Noche Triste,* and I thoroughly despised Francisco Pizarro—who, as a matter of fact, still seems one of the most repellent characters in history. I wanted to know more about these lost nations off to the south, and for a time I dreamed of becoming an archaeologist and digging in the ruins of Central America.

I was not able to learn much more than I knew when I finished reading Prescott. There was not, actually, at that time, very much in print, and none of it was within my reach. I have today a fairly good collection of books on the subject, and hardly any of them were written before 1920. Father did have a book called *Ancient America,* by someone whose name I have lost, and it had a few facts Prescott did not have, but even at the time I recognized it as a pedestrian job. (Come to think of it, Prescott would be a hard act to follow.) I read a third-rate novel, *The Fair God,* by General Lew Wallace, and I found it interesting but unrewarding; all the general knew about the Aztecs he got from Prescott, and I had read Prescott myself. At one stage I sat down to write a novel, basing it on the life and times of Nezahualcoyotl, King of Tezcoco. Fortunately, nothing ever came of this. I realized after a time that I was not up to a novel, and anyway how could you do a piece of fiction whose hero is named Nezahualcoyotl? Utterly impossible.

Somewhere, at about this time, I laid hands on a book about the mound builders, and my field of interest broadened. This book was written in the 1890s, or thereabouts, and it would be of no value at all today. It never touched on such matters as the Hopewell and Adena cultures which modern students have to know about, and it had been written long before the anthropologists had devised dignified scientific language to veil their mysteries from the vulgar. It accepted a theory that was popular at the time, when the wisest men knew nothing about the mound builders except that they built mounds: namely, that some more or less civilized people wandered into the American middle west one or two thousand years ago, built cities and monuments and developed various arts and crafts, flourished mightily for a time, and then wandered away to an unknown destination, driven off no doubt by predatory savages who coveted their riches. What I learned, in short, was sadly incomplete and mostly wrong, but that made no difference. It struck close to home because our part of Michigan was on the fringe of mound builder country. These mysterious people were next-door neighbors in space if not in time.

Furthermore, there was something about them. They had come into the wilderness as the advance guard of civilization and the wilderness had finally beaten them. (Possibly they had cut down their trees too fast?) They had had cities, I understood, and an elaborate social organization, with temples and myths and a body of learning which the wilderness folk did not have, and nothing at all remained except that the land was haunted by a dim memory. The temple fires went out and the temples turned into grassy knolls, nothing remained of their cities except earthen ridges in prairie and forest, and the people themselves had gone to another place, taking the remnants of their plans and their dreams with them.

That could happen, in other words. People could lose. Looking into the misty past for men who were no longer there could give one a different perspective on the present. Perhaps what we ourselves were doing would leave no more traces than those men had left—mounded earth, a wisp of unheeded prayer hanging on the wind, an indecipherable record of a lost effort swallowed by the forest. Shelley, whom I had recently met, knew all about this, for he had known Ozymandias, but I had not supposed this had any bearing on what we were doing in Michigan. Now I began to see it all in a different way.

This was chilling but it was also exciting. The absolute certainties embodied in a revealed religion and an unquestioned faith are walls raised for protection against the unutterable cold of interstellar night, but when they begin to collapse there is a sense of relief, as if it might be a privilege to roam off across the unending wastelands. I began to feel that I was indeed growing up. The spirit of the eternal sophomore descended on me, and I knew more than my fathers ever knew.

Part of the time, anyway. It is easy to take the tragic view (which I proudly supposed that I was doing) as long as you do not know what tragedy really means. Pessimism has a fine tart flavor when you know that everything is going to come out all right. When life is just beginning it is possible to grow romantic about the notion that when it ends all the stars will go out, because your unvoiced conviction is that you will nevertheless see them go out and will go on to explore the external darkness and find out what lies beyond it. My worldly wisdom was a pose, and somewhere down inside I knew it.

Still, there it was. The academy that existed in order to confirm young people in their inherited Christian faith had set me reading the English poets, and some of them told me things not found in the Bible. (Not in the parts I was familiar with, that is; the author of Ecclesiastes would have had a word for me if I had listened to him.) I had by now a fair acquaintance with Shelley, Keats, Wordsworth and Tennyson, and they had shown me things not always visible from our Benzonia hilltop. I had also read Swinburne, and Matthew Arnold's despairing hymn on Dover Beach, and that rhythmic perennial of the newly fledged skeptic, FitzGerald's version of Omar's *Rubaiyat;* and these were strong medicine for a lad who, at the age of nine, had successfully called on God to help him fill the woodbox. It seemed to me that some of the poets found beauty in a measured denial of all the things which, I had been told, gave life its meaning and its majesty, and although they did not exactly convince me they jarred me loose from some of my moorings. I don't suppose they have that kind of impact on anybody nowadays.

The academy also required me to study chemistry and physics. I found these difficult, but what I could understand seemed interesting. Leon Gray did his best to explain atoms and molecules, and while he did not actually take me far—he could not, because knowledge of such matters was rather limited then—he aroused my imagination. I began to understand that the material world was not necessarily what it seemed to be; that solid matter might not actually be solid after all, and that profound mysteries dwelt in the soil beneath my feet as well as in the stars above my head. In an odd way, this smattering of wisdom seemed to point in the same direction as the lore of the scriptures. It indicated that life is a miracle surrounded by incomprehensible marvels. I assured myself, pridefully, now and then, that I was losing my faith, which seemed to me to be a prodigious happening, but about all I was actually doing was transpose it to a different key.

This transposition did not bring as much of a jolt as I liked to imagine. I had been reared, of course, in a fixed fundamentalist creed, and yet the sharp corners had been sanded down quietly. My father was as devout a man as Benzonia possessed, but he was familiar with the higher criticism and he was not invariably literal in his interpretation of holy writ. I came to understand that the men who wrote the Bible wrapped eternal truth in high-flown figures of speech, and departed from strict objectivity in order to convey messages to men of limited understanding. It was no shock to me to realize that the whale probably did not swallow Jonah and that the sun had gone on swinging across the sky despite Joshua. It seemed possible to discard these fables and still accept the birth in the manger and the rolling away of the stone from the entrance to the tomb.

The process of entering the modern world, in other words, was not altogether painful. Yet there were problems. I was sailing close-hauled, against the wind, swinging constantly from one tack to the other, from the sunlit certainties of revealed religion to the uneasy twilight of defiant skepticism, and now and then it was a wrench. I had an especially hard time when I was sixteen and our church put on a solid week of revival services, complete with an imported evangelist, magic lantern, colorful slides to illustrate the more imposing parables, and passionate appeals to sinners to repent and come to the mercy seat. Why our town had such services I have never been able to understand, because there cannot have been a village in all the middle west that needed them less than we did. I know Father did not altogether approve, and the word was passed that academy students were not expected to attend. They could go if they wished, provided that they first got formal permission to be out after seven-thirty at night, but hardly anybody did it.

However, I went to all of the services. (I think this worried my parents a little, because they did not care much for the way this evangelist whipped up youthful emotions, but they did not say anything to me about it.) I had been worrying about my soul just then, and this seemed a good time to expose myself to the eternal verities. The result was not good. The speaker had the evangelist's trick of frightening people so that they would give up their sins, and inasmuch as he was an eloquent man he frightened me and made me eager to repent. Unfortunately, I had no impressive sins to repent. Benzonia just was not the place to lay in a stock of them and I had never enlarged on the few opportunities that seemed open. However, I had had doubts—still had them, and nursed them along with some pride, and to have doubts was to sin. The evangelist said so, unmistakably.

He had a story which (I came to understand much later) was part of the standard equipment carried by any proper evangelist. There was this girl, in a town like our own, and she sat in church and heard the minister say that any person who chose to live even for one day without making a clear profession of faith was taking a dreadful chance. Impishly, this girl took a hymn book, scribbled "I'll take the chance" in her unmistakable handwriting, and put the book back in the rack. That night—that very night, mark you—she went for a sleigh ride with friends, the horses ran away, the sleigh was upset, and the girl was killed. The evangelist did not need to add that she had certainly gone to hell.

Tough, beyond question; and, equally beyond question, contrived and phony. I was just bright enough to see that, and it made me furious with this glib, shallow man who demanded that I accept something monstrous. I had never felt that the faith in which I grew up was oppressive and crippling, but suddenly he made it seem so. For the moment I wanted no more of it.

The mood did not last long, of course; few moods do, at sixteen. The memory of that stupid man faded, eventually, like the shadow of a gruesome dream after one has struggled up out of sleep, and I returned to a more or less normal existence. I may have been groping hard for a new grasp on the fundamentals of the faith which I was trying so hard to lose; in any case I became most active in our church's Christian Endeavor society, which was a sort of teen-agers' prayer meeting, and sometime during the winter I was sent as our society's official delegate to a Christian Endeavor convention, or rally—I do not know what they did call it—at Traverse City. I realized that to be chosen thus was an honor, it was stimulating to spend an entire day and night away from home without parental guidance, and it was nice to meet so many other young people; among them, a pleasant young woman from our neighboring village of Thompsonville, who was the night telephone operator there and seemed most personable. I can remember just about nothing at all of what happened at the convention; indeed, the only clear picture I brought back was of the final afternoon when, the sessions having ended and there being two hours to spend before train time, this telephone operator and I slipped away and went to a vaudeville show. I suppose Traverse City at that time was on the bottom rung of the vaudeville circuit, but that made no difference; nothing in our County was on any rung at all, I had never seen vaudeville in my life, and the afternoon was memorable. We caught our train properly enough, the girl got off at Thompsonville, and I continued on to Benzonia, vastly pleased with life. And that was that.

Except for an incident that came two or three nights later. I should explain that our family had at last moved out of the principal's quarters in the girls' dormitory, and now we occupied

our own home, which was a great improvement all around, and on this evening we were just sitting down to supper when the telephone rang. My father went to answer it—the instrument was in the hall, outside the dining room door—and he returned in a moment, cast a speculative eye on me, and said that there was a long distance call for me.

Long distance calls were not common, in that time and place. I had never received one in my life, and never expected to; such calls commonly grew out of some dire emergency, like a death in the family, and that I should be receiving one was the wonder of the year. My parents were very human, and my younger brother and sister were even more so, and as I clumped out to the hall to take up the telephone I was much aware that everybody was going to be hanging in breathless suspense on every word I uttered. (Who on earth can be calling *him*? What in the world is this all about?) It did not occur to me to close the door before I picked up the receiver.

The caller, of course, was my friend in Thompsonville. She was on duty at the village switchboard, nothing whatever was going on, and it seemed to her to be the most natural thing in the world to insert a plug, flip a key and chat with this boy she had just met. So she began to chat. Had I got home all right? How was I feeling? Didn't I think the convention had been most interesting? Had she thanked me properly for taking her to the theater? And wasn't it funny when that man played the violin with a frying pan? (Yes, there had been an act in which that happened, but I can't go into it now.) This went on for some time. I fumbled for answers, well aware that every word I said was being absorbed by the dear ones in the next room; I do not think I have ever been so deeply embarrassed in my life, and my remarks grew more and more laconic. It dawned on the girl, at last, that something was wrong, and finally (may Heaven bless her) she said that it had been nice to know me, and rang off. She had learned ahead of her years, I suppose, that the effervescent, carefree male met at a convention tends to be self-conscious and reserved when tackled in the bosom of his family. I never saw or heard from her again, and I was sorry because she had been nice.

I got back to the dining room eventually. My parents undoubtedly were brim-full of questions which they forbore to ask, but my brother and sister had no forbearance at all and they asked many questions all in a moment. I answered them with what I hoped was chilling dignity, and at last managed to eat the meal of dust and ashes which had been set before me. I acquired that evening a dread of the telephone which has never entirely left me. I also learned that when explanations are in order, consciousness of total innocence in act and in intent does not help at all.

However, my final year in the academy was not entirely made up of flannel-mouthed evangelists and friendly telephone operators, nor did my worries about the state of my soul cast much of a shadow across my path. On the contrary, that year was one of sustained happiness; because even though I had doubts about my soul I had a firm belief in life, and there were times when the flavor of it was almost unendurably good. When I look back I get disconnected pictures of a time when the commonest events seemed to hint that simply to be alive was to be surrounded by transcendent miracles which could neither be explained nor ignored. Now and then the earth itself seems to speak, and although it uses a language not our own it is not wholly unintelligible. It implies that what we see when we look about us is only a shadow cast by the ultimate realities that lie beyond our vision. Life becomes exciting just because it is life, and simply to be alive is intoxicating. It is foolish to worry about the soul because it is one of those realities.

The most commonplace scene could be eloquent. One that I remember was something we called Arbor Day, celebrated in the spring when a suitably warm day came along. The idea was that the new grass on the flat plain of our east campus was being choked by the matted dead grass and leaves left there in the autumn and that the campus would not be green and pleasing unless this mat were removed. So on Arbor Day all classes were suspended at noon and the students were equipped with rakes and bushel baskets and set to work, raking the dead stuff out of the turf and collecting the debris in piles or in long ridges and then setting fire to them.

This was fun. Anything was better than being shut up in a classroom on a warm spring day, the work was easy, there was time for mild horseplay—for some reason it was fun to lie flat on one's back and see if one could balance a rake on the tip of the chin—and the smoke formed a thin haze that came down the April breeze so that the air smelled like autumn and spring combined. It was wonderful to be alive. A ripple of tiny flames would cross a stretch of lawn, leaving a black area in which green blades of grass stood out clearly as if each blade were happy to be released. Whether this really was good for the sod, or whether we just thought it was, I have no idea, but it was very good for us. The campus became part of the Elysian Field, the young people (all laughter and movement) became the golden girls and lads of far-off poetry, and suddenly it seemed that if we waited awhile there would be a revelation. The revelation never actually came, but it could be sensed, waiting just offstage.

For we lived then in a time of great expectations. We believed in ourselves and in the future, and we welcomed all of the omens that were good. We were not, to be sure, altogether half-witted. It is good to know that the world is not exactly what it seems to be, but to know this is to be dimly aware that it may be worse instead of better. These voices that spoke to us out of spring sunlight and the dawn of life could be lying, and a well-read person had to keep an ear open for confused echoes from the darkling plain. However, bookish knowledge did not necessarily mean much. We lived by our emotions rather than by our brains, and although we did not know where we were going we trusted the future. We lived for it, confident that when it came it would rub out all of the mistakes of the past. It was the one thing we really believed in. Mercifully, we could not know that when it finally came it would frighten us more than anything else on earth. We were at halfway house; the quarters were good, the grounds were pleasant, and there was a fine view of the surrounding country. What more could we want?

We had an acute sense of the impermanence of the present, and a haunting understanding that we were living for a time in a strange borderland between the real and the unreal, without enough knowledge of the country to tell one from the other. The daily routine, in study hall and classroom, was real enough, certainly; but so was the flood of moonlight that sometimes lay on the countryside at night, turning the plain gravel road south into a white highway that wound through enchanted meadows that would not be there at all when daylight returned. The reality of daily routine was going to vanish presently, and then it would be no more tangible than the neverland that bordered the moonlit roadway. Would memory be any more reliable than imagination? When both are forever out of reach, does what you once were count for more than what you once thought you might be? We live in dreams, and while we can we might as well make them pleasant ones.

Mostly they were. Yet there was something about our north country (or maybe it was something about me) that issued disquieting warnings now and then. There was the emptiness off to the north, thousands of miles of it, with the cold tang of the ice age in the air; to the south was the land of the mound builders, whose best efforts produced nothing more than unobtrusive scars on the earth; and all about us were the bleak acres of stumps, the dying towns and the desolate farms that were being given up, discards in a game where most of the players had lost. Now and again these things demanded thought.

There was for instance one January morning that winter when Lewis Stoneman and I went sailing on skates. I do not know whether anyone does that nowadays, but it was quite a thing at the time and we had read about it in some magazine. You took thin strips of wood and made an oblong frame, about four feet

long by three feet wide, added a couple of cross braces for stiffen-
ing and for handholds, and covered the frame with a piece of
discarded bed sheet cut to size. Then you went to the ice, put on
your skates, held the frame in front of you, and let the wind take
charge. I talked about this with Lewis, who was a student at the
academy and was for some reason known as Yutch, and it
sounded like fun. We built the frames in the basement of Father's
house, talked Mother into giving us a frayed old sheet, tacked
pieces of it to the wood, got our skates, and one Saturday went
down to Crystal Lake to see about it.

We were in luck. The lake had frozen late, that winter, and
although the countryside was covered with snow there was little
or none on the ice, which was smooth and clear as plate glass.
Skating conditions were perfect, the sun was bright, the bare ice
was like polished steel, and there was a brisk wind from the east
—which was fine, because we were at the eastern end of the lake
and the open ice stretched away to the west for more than eight
miles. We put on our skating shoes, knotted the laces of our
regular shoes together and hung them about our necks, got out
on the frozen lake, held the sails in front of us, and took off.

The wind was strong, blowing steadily and without gusts, and
it filled our sails and took us down the lake at what seemed a
fabulous speed. We had never moved so fast on skates before—
had not imagined that it was possible to move so fast—and it was
all completely effortless. All we had to do was stand erect, hold on
to our sails, and glide away; it was like being a hawk, soaring
above the length of a ridge on an updraft of air, and it felt more
like flying than anything that ever happened to me, later on in
life, in an airplane.

Neither one of us knew anything at all about sailing. To tack,
or even to go on a broad reach, was entirely beyond us; we had
to go where the wind blew us, and that was that, and now and
then I was uneasily aware that skating back against the wind, by
sheer leg power, was going to be hard. However, there would
be time enough to worry about that later. For the moment it was

enough to be carried by the wind. The whole world had been made for our enjoyment. The sky was unstained blue, with white clouds dropping shadows now and then to race along with us, the hills that rimmed the lake were white with snow, gray and blue with bare tree trunks, clear gold in places where the wind had blown the snow away from sandy bluffs, the sun was a friendly weight on our shoulders, the wind was blowing harder and we were going faster than ever, and there was hardly a sound anywhere. I do not believe I have ever felt more completely in tune with the universe than I felt that morning on Crystal Lake. It was friendly. All of its secrets were good.

Then, suddenly, came awakening. We had ridden the wind for six miles or more, and we were within about two miles of the western end of the lake; and we realized that not far ahead of us there was a broad stretch of sparkling, dazzling blue running from shore to shore, flecked with picturesque whitecaps—open water. It was beautiful, but it carried the threat of sudden death. The lake had not been entirely frozen, after all. Its west end was clear, and at the rate we were going we would reach the end of ice in a short time. The lake was a good hundred feet deep there, the water was about one degree warmer than the ice itself, and the nearest land—wholly uninhabited, in the dead of winter— was a mile away. Two boys dropped into that would never get out alive.

There was also a change in the ice beneath us. It was transparent, and the water below was black as a starless midnight; the ice had become thin, it was flexible, sagging a little under our weight, giving out ominous creakings and crackling sounds, and only the fact that we kept moving saved us from breaking through. It was high time, in short, for us to get off of that lake.

Yutch saw it at the same moment I did. We both pointed, and yelled, and then we made a ninety-degree turn to the left and headed for the southern shore. If we had known how to use our sails properly the wind would have taken us there, but we knew nothing about that. All we could think of was to skate for the shore with all speed, and those sails were just in the way. We dropped them incontinently, and we never saw them again, and we made a grotesque race for safety, half-skating and half-running. We came at last to the packed floe ice over the shallows, galloped clumsily across it, reached the snow-covered beach, and collapsed on a log to catch our breath and to talk in awed tones about our narrow escape.

We got home, eventually, somewhere along toward dusk. We at first thought we would skate back, but the wind was dead against us and skating into it seemed likely to be harder than walking along the shore; and besides we had had all of the lake we wanted for that day. We put on our other shoes and plodded cross-country through the snow, three miles to Frankfort, at which place, the afternoon train having left, we got a livery stable rig to take us to Benzonia. (I am not sure Father altogether appreciated having to pay the liveryman the required two dollars; he earned his dollars the hard way, and he never had many of them. However, he paid up without a whimper.) We got home in time for supper—we ate that evening at Mother's table, and not in the academy dining hall—and when we were warm and full and rested we found that we had a tale to tell, and told it, leaving my parents no doubt wondering just how much youthful exaggeration the tale contained. Actually, we had not so much as got our feet wet, and our escape had not been quite as narrow as we believed, but we had had an authentic glimpse over the rim and we did not like what we had seen; although, now that it was all over, it was fun to talk about it.

Yet the whole business cut a hard groove in my mind. I found after a while that I did not want to talk about it. I did not even want to think about it, but I could not help myself. What I had seen through the transparent bending ice seemed to be nothing less than the heart of darkness. It was not just my own death that had been down there; it was the ultimate horror, lying below all life, kept away by something so fragile that it could break at any moment. Everything we did or dreamed or hoped for had this just beneath it . . . One gets knotty thoughts, sometimes, at half-way house.

This seemed especially hard to digest because it came so soon after Christmas.

Christmas, without any question, was the greatest day of the year. It was not just that it was a time for receiving gifts, although Heaven knows that was enough in itself; the suspense of the last few days before Christmas was almost too much to bear, and the culminating moment when we walked into the living room on Christmas morning and saw the lighted tree with the packages underneath it was undiluted ecstasy. But aside from all of this—taking color from it, but springing from something deeper —was the implicit assurance that everything was going to be all right. This was a religious holiday and we never lost sight of the fact. The most sacred of all legends revealed itself then as the almost incredible truth, and all but literally we went about on tiptoe. On starry evenings during Christmas week groups of young people would go about town, stopping before various houses to sing Christmas carols, and as their harmonies floated off across the night we could see the town of Bethlehem not far away, and our snowy Michigan hills became one with the tawny slopes of Palestine. (Nothing infuriates me more, nowadays, than the way these carols have been reduced to department store commercials, nor am I assuaged when I am reminded that I ought to be glad that that monkey has been taken off my back. I cannot complain if people no longer think them holy, but I wish they would keep their feet off them.)

By the time I was sixteen the old excitement of Christmas gifts had of course worn somewhat thin, and I was ready to admit that the intense emotion centering about the tree in the living room was primarily something for small children, whose ranks I had left. Yet in some ways Christmas that year had an impact it had never had before. It seemed to come out of what I had always considered a routine observance: the Christmas Eve celebration in the village church.

Every year, on the night before Christmas, or sometimes on the last Sunday night before Christmas, the tallest balsam that could be got into the church was erected on the raised platform where the choir ordinarily sat, and it was covered with homemade decorations: looped chains made of colored paper, white popcorn threaded on long strings, tinsel stars, metal clips holding lighted candles, and so on. We had no electric lights for Christmas trees in those days; we simply used candles with open flames, burning within inches of drying evergreen needles, and the fire hazard must have been considerable. I should think a few houses would have burned down every year, but it never seemed to happen. Anyway, the church was filled with people. It was imperfectly lighted, and its interior seemed immense, larger than life, dominated by the great tree that reached up to the shadows just beneath the rafters, its tiny flames all twinkling. Just to be in the place was to partake of a mystery. The services were extremely simple. There were carols, prayers, readings of the gospel story of the first Christmas, a few quiet remarks by the minister, distribution of candy canes and molasses-and-popcorn balls to the small children, and a final hymn: and when the wheezy organ (pumped vigorously by a sweating young man behind a screen) sounded off with "Joy to the World," and the doors opened to let us out into the winter night, it was as if we heard the sound of far-off trumpets.

Walking home afterward was what did it. It was cold and there was plenty of snow, which creaked under our feet as we went along the road, and the silent air seemed to be echoing with the carols we had sung; and overhead, infinitely remote yet for all of that very near and comforting, there was the endless host of golden stars whose clear flames denied the darkness. The message was unmistakable. Life was leading us—somewhere, somehow, miraculously—to a transfiguration.

It stayed with me. I felt that I had had a glimpse behind the veil. I had seen the ultimate truth, and that truth was good; or so, at any rate, it seemed to me at the time. But while this remembered vision still lingered I had gone on that wind-borne cruise along the Crystal Lake ice, and at the far end of it I had seen something altogether different. Under the ice lay a flat denial of everything I had seen beyond the stars on Christmas Eve. I had had two visions, of the horror and of the transfiguration, and they seemed equally authentic. What did I do now?

I turned for comfort to that gnarled, gifted and somewhat purblind seer Thomas Carlyle, and he did not help much. He spoke of the everlasting nay and of the everlasting yea, but he implied that you worked your way out of one and into the other —which was all very well, except that I had them both at the same time. They spoke with equal force. I could not accept one and discard the other. They went together; forget both or live with both. Since they were, as I then believed, unforgettable, it seemed to me that I had to adjust myself to them.

I realized, finally, that these contrasting visions were not actually at war with each other; they were simply the two sides of the same coin. Life's dimensions are infinite. It reaches from the abyss to the heights, and it touches the truth at each extreme. It stretches between terror and hope, and given the terms on which it is lived it cannot do anything else. The worst and the best visions are true, and the ultimate truth that embraces both is fantastically beyond comprehension. Life is a flame burning in water, shining on a sea that has no shore, and far overhead there are other flames which we call stars.

CHAPTER ELEVEN

Requiem for the Homemade

More than half a century had passed since he left the army, and the Drummer Boy of the Rappahannock was getting on into his mid-sixties. He was spry enough, trim and erect in the blue uniform of the Grand Army of the Republic, with the double row of brass buttons marching down the coat, badges on the left lapel, black campaign hat on top of a gray head; and although he was undeniably getting old he did his valiant best to seem ageless, as if he always carried his boyhood with him. He was, as you might say, a professional Civil War veteran, and for years he had made his living—whose base, to be sure, was the regular check from the government pension office—by reminding other veterans of the great days that used to be. He had a set line of patter, memorized and carefully rehearsed; he had a partner, also a veteran in old soldier's blue, who fed him his lines and acted as master of ceremonies; he had a few songs that had stood the test of years of peacetime campaigning; and, most important of all, he had his drum, on which he was more or less a virtuoso.

The Drummer Boy, in short, was a commercial entertainer whose circuit was strictly limited to the G.A.R. posts of the middle west. Over the years I suppose a number of performers played this circuit. They never could have survived in the regular theater, because the entertainment they offered was highly specialized, and pretty thin stuff to boot; they needed a preconditioned audience, and they could find that only among the old soldiers. A Grand Army post that booked a performance by one of these artists would sell tickets to the general public, but the purchasers were almost always close friends or relatives, fully prepared to like any program the old soldiers liked. Also working in the performer's favor was the fact that he had little competition. There were no movies in the smaller towns and villages, and no regular theaters either, and most of the time the citizen in search of entertainment simply had no place to go. The average audience was prepared to make allowances.

The Drummer Boy was engaged to appear before the Benzonia G.A.R. post sometime early in 1916. His primary function, aside from bringing a few dollars into the post's treasury, was to make old memories vivid for men to whom nothing but memories mattered any more, and he did this smoothly enough. He beat the long roll, and rattled off some of the shorter calls by which orders were occasionally transmitted, and he solemnly beat out "Taps," the formalized arrangement of slowly tapped-out strokes on the drumhead that ordered quiet and lights out in camp in the days before a bugle call did the job more melodiously. He and his partner ran through their regular line of jokes, anecdotes and reminiscences, and they came at last to the big set piece of the performance—the reproduction, on a taut drumhead, by a drummer boy grown gray with years, of the mighty sound and tumult of a Civil War battle.

The Drummer Boy's partner announced this number, telling us to imagine a line of soldiers prowling forward across fields and woods in the dim light of early morning. First, he said, we would hear single musket shots, as skirmishers made contact; then, here and there, there would be clusters of shots, as squads and platoons went into action. Later there would be volley firing, where whole regiments and brigades became involved, and the volley firing would soon give way to intense file firing, in which every infantryman loaded and fired as rapidly as he could without further orders. All of this would be accompanied by bursts of artillery fire, piece by piece at first as the guns tapped experimentally at enemy positions, then fire by batteries rising to sustained gunfire all along the line, with unbroken musketry running along as treble over this booming bass . . . the whole rising to a climax that seemed likely to lift the roof off of Case's Hall.

All of this kept the Drummer Boy of the Rappahannock extremely busy. Whatever its other merits may have been, this performance was impressive as an exercise in sheer acrobatics. My impression is that the Drummer Boy's partner brought out a drum of his own and pitched in to help; he must have done so, because all of the noise that exploded across the auditorium could not have come from just one drum. However that may have been, the battle reached its peak and then rolled on to victory, the enemy presumably driven off in rout, and at last the racket subsided, coming down finally to scattered sniping by rear-guard parties—then silence. The battle was over, and so was the performance, and we applauded vigorously and went home, vastly edified.

I would not have missed it for anything; and yet that evening did something to my attitude toward our home-grown Civil War veterans. Instead of looking heroic, larger than life-size, giants from the magical mist of an age of greatness, they suddenly looked pathetic. I think this was because of the way the Drummer Boy's partner introduced the battle scene. Remember, this was taking place in 1916, and the war in Europe had been going on for the better part of two years, and so this master of ceremonies had adapted his patter to present-day conditions. He did not tell us that we were going to listen to the sounds of a Civil War battle; in a noble effort to come up to date the old chap assured us that we would hear the sounds of battle as they were currently being heard on the Western Front, in France—and that was the pinprick that exploded the toy balloon.

We may have been living in an isolated backwater but we did read the daily papers and the weekly and monthly magazines, and we knew that this was no battle from the Western Front. In the war that was going on in 1916 there were no skirmishers prowling out across empty fields, looking for invisible enemies,

and the batteries in today's war did not pick up their parts one gun at a time, firing tentatively until the fight beat itself into shape. This was a war of barbed wire, a war that was all taped and measured, confined within rigid limits but at the same time taken beyond all conceivable limits; its stuttering machine guns swept every field and hillside from Switzerland to the English Channel, its artillery barrages might go on for days at a time, and when its gunners spoke of "drum fire" they meant something that was beyond either the experience or the comprehension of drummer boys from Virginia's river valleys. Two drums in a rural town hall might effectively create the illusion of an imaginary battle from the age of fable, but Verdun was beyond them. It became clear, suddenly, that our gallant old Civil War veterans had simply been left behind by time. They had been part of the present for half a century, but now they unmistakably belonged to the past. For the first time in my life I felt sorry for them. Pity diminished them, and they did not look quite the same after that.

And to see them in a new light was to see everything else in a new light, because they and what they stood for were basic to what I supposed to be the immutable order of things. Unintentionally but effectively, the Drummer Boy forced me to see that the world was changing. This of course should have been evident to anyone who grew up in the despoiled lumber country, where permanence was subject to revision or indeed to outright cancellation every few years, but the most obvious of lessons sometimes comes hard. To understand that the conditions under which life is lived must change is simple enough, but the terms on which it is lived ought to be unchanging; so said all the law and all the prophets. The trouble now was not so much the fact that the world was changing as the cold hint that the world was going to exact terms unlike anything I had imagined. Its whole scale of values had quietly been transformed.

I had been growing up with the notion that life's problems, although often difficult, were at bottom simple. To confront them took courage, ideals, high principles and unwavering faith. The

heroes of the 1860s had these qualities; the crisis of their day
had been met and passed, and a permanent gain had been made
—which proved that the world was becoming progressively
better because the advance of man rested on a simple exercise of
a few ancient virtues. This was one of life's certainties, as revealed
on a Michigan hilltop in the early years of this century. But if
today's crisis had to be met in an entirely different way than the
earlier one, all certainty was gone.

And it seemed clear that it was being met differently.

War does one thing pitilessly: it holds up, before the eyes of
the society that is waging it, the essential reality on which that
society is based. It is a cruel mirror, apparently as distorted as the
mirrors in an amusement park, actually (on the long cold glance)
not distorted at all. And what it showed in 1916, for that and sub-
sequent generations, was that the race had entrusted itself to a
new belief. Its highest faith now was in the machine rather than
in the spirit; in the mechanical devices man's brain could invent
rather than in the illimitable miracle that originally set that brain
free to speculate, to plan, to dream and to hope. The only reality
worth mentioning is the one that can be seen, touched, tinkered
with, improved—or, at times, exploded. Get into the machine
you have made and ride wherever it takes you. There is no other
road to salvation; or to damnation either, if that makes any
difference.

This harsh gospel, to be sure, was not really new. Even my
noble Civil War heroes, valiant though they undoubtedly were,
had relied heavily on the advantage they got from their country's
prodigious industrial plant. It could make the things they needed
for fighting—from locomotives to canteens, from gunboats to
carbines—faster than war could destroy them; much, much faster
than anything the Southern Confederacy could do. The whole
point of Sherman's march to the sea was that it involved unrestrained waste and destruction. To destroy was good; indeed, it
was the price of progress. The state of Michigan had been (as

they said) developed by man's ability to turn forests into stacks of sawn boards faster than nature could produce the forests in the first place. It had never seemed necessary to worry about what all of this meant, but somehow the dismal failure of the Drummer Boy's attempt to transpose 1864 into 1916 had been disturbing and it seemed to call for thought.

A prep school senior is not well equipped to follow such a line of thought to its proper conclusion, and anyway things are clearer now than they were then. About all I got out of it at the time was a general feeling that something was wrong somewhere, as if the rules of the game had been changed without due notice. Dimly taking grotesque shape somewhere in the background, not yet really recognizable, was the one dismaying fact that governs our progress across the Sinai desert of the modern world; we have set all our other qualities aside and have entrusted ourselves entirely to our mechanical ingenuity. Proud that we have escaped from age-old superstition, we have condemned ourselves to live in a world of our own creation, a world which we fondly believe has no mysteries. We are made helpless by our own omnipotence.

The richest fruits of this began to be visible in the First World War, which shows perfectly what happens in a technician's world. Obviously, if your enemy stands in your path (as in wartime he does) you want to destroy him, and if you are going to do that it is well to be thorough and business-like, not to say scientific, about it. Instead of going at him with bare hands, clubs and stone knives you bring up the most ingenious and intricate destructive instruments your scientists, and inventors can provide, and the only guideline to follow here is the idea that if you can just bring to bear on your enemy more of these things than he can bring to bear on you, you are going to win. All of this, of course, has to be done without restraint; if it is good to drop a ton of high explosive on your enemy, it is ever so much better to drop a thousand tons on him, and better still to multiply that by a factor of at least one hundred. In the end, if all goes well, you obliterate your opponents and all that remains is to go in and pick up the pieces. You are absolutely certain to win provided you just wheel up enough machinery.

The first trouble with this is that your enemy is wheeling up machinery as fast as you are; and the second trouble, which is much graver, is that this adds up to making war without doing any thinking about it—a sure road to disaster. The one thing that is clear now about the 1914 war is that mankind's intelligence was in a coma. The brains that devised, ordered and persisted in such offensives as those at Verdun, on the Somme, along the Chemin des Dames and in front of Passchendaele were not, properly speaking, brains at all. There was a certain amount of activity by the central nervous system, of course, and the purely mechanical problems involved in getting men and machines up to the point of action and removing the debris afterward—such debris as could be identified and picked up for salvage, that is—were handled quite smoothly, in the main. But to say that human intelligence was actively involved in these matters is to talk obvious nonsense. The men who directed that war succeeded only in turning it into something nobody could win. They wrecked their own countries, made Europe practically uninhabitable for decades, and left the world doomed to fight another disastrous war simply to get out from under the wreckage left by the first one. Human stupidity has had no greater triumph.

The full extent of this colossal mismanagement was not, of course, visible at the time. It was years before people would see what an incredible mess had been made of things. At the time we could only confess that what was going on resembled nothing that had ever happened before; we comforted ourselves with the faith that something good would somehow come out of it all and that somebody somewhere must know what ought to be done. (That sentence contains four of those miserable uncertainty-words—something, somehow, somebody and somewhere—and on due reflection I think I will leave them there. We *were* uncertain, and the uncertainty was not confined to a preparatory school campus in northern Michigan, either.)

What was really bothering us was a point that might have been clear enough if we had known how to identify it. The world had simply gone awhoring after false gods. Having committed itself to them it had to go where they took it, and this was bound to lead to confusion, because of all the gods man has ever worshipped the most completely inscrutable are the ones that stand behind the altars in the age of applied technologies. They give man the illusion that he at last controls his own destiny; he becomes able to reshape his physical surroundings as he sees fit; he discovers that at last he can produce more than enough of everything to go around, and unhappily he fails to see that among the things of which he can produce a blessed abundance are intolerable woes. What protected man in the old days was his awareness that there were things he just could not do. That awareness is gone, and if in its departure it took with it the last barrier on the road to the bottomless pit we shall probably find out about that in due time. Man knows now that if he tries hard enough he can do anything he wants to do—fly through the air, leave the planet altogether, create life out of sea foam and sand (well, those aren't exactly the ingredients, but they are near enough) and unlock the power that holds the eternal mountains above the plain. By the unformulated tenets of his new religion, what he can do he must do. The one impossibility now is to turn back, or to go at half speed. This machine (to repeat) operates only at full speed. Unfortunately, it cannot be steered.

So man can do anything if he tries hard enough, and to try hard enough is not simply to furrow the brow and flex the muscles but to make unlimited use of every resource at hand. Moderation becomes impossible, and if it were possible it would be regarded as sinful. The new theology has borrowed, without credit, one of the fundamental planks in the old religion: despite his disclaimers, man stands at the center of the universe. It was made for him to use, and the best and wisest men are those who use it most lavishly. They destroy pine forests, and dig copper from beneath the cold northern lakes, and run the open pits across the iron ranges, impoverishing themselves at the same time they are enriching themselves: creating wealth, in short, by the act of destroying it, which is one of the most baffling mysteries of the new gospel.

Possibly it all began with Christopher Columbus, although he meant nobody any harm; because some such faith as the one we now have was implicit in the discovery of the new world. Or, if you want to spin it out a little finer, it began not so much with the discovery as with the fact that the discovery was made by a European. Up to that moment the European lived in a closed community, ignoring the fact that Africa was large and that Asia was larger and that he knew very little about either. His horizons might be remote, but despite the efforts of men like Marco Polo and Henry the Navigator they seemed to be fixed. His universe was finite. There was room for a limited number of people, and a limited number of ideas. Men who worked their hardest could produce food and clothing and tools and shelter for an equally limited number, and that was supposed to be all there was to it. Regardless of what might happen some day in the paradise beyond the sunset, on earth life consisted of an unending struggle to make not-quite-enough go around among increasing numbers. It may well be true that men believed so steadfastly in a better life beyond the skies because the chance of getting one on earth seemed so poor.

Then suddenly the lid blew off, and man began to suspect that the world contained a flowing, dripping abundance of everything. The shiploads of gold and silver that went to Europe from the mines of Mexico and Peru hardly counted, because you cannot do much with gold and silver but turn them into money; Europe did that, spent the money feverishly, and almost wrecked itself in the process. What really mattered was that for the first time there seemed to be room for everybody, and enough for everybody to eat, and enough of all of the things that are needed when men set out to make and build. The world lost its horizons, and as fast as new ones were found it began to seem that they were not fixed tightly against the curve of the earth; approach them, and you could see clear sky beyond. Apparently the world lay at the heart of an infinite universe, and man set out to make it so.

In an infinite universe plans have infinite scope, and they demand an infinite response. Man's desires expand as his world expands, and the urge to make those desires effective becomes restless, savage, irresistible. It is by no means wholly by accident that the foundations for the technological revolution were laid in the aftermath of the discovery that there was a new world. If the ocean rolls all the way to the Fortunate Isles you need something better than a wind-blown galleon to get there, and sooner or later you find out how to make something that will get you there faster. If, en route to the Fortunate Isles, you find the richest of continents thinly inhabited by a weak and unenlightened people you are going to push those people out of the way or trample them underfoot and take those riches for yourself; and if the earth is devastated and injustice is committed as you do this it does not matter. For the new situation sets you thinking beyond your means. There is no stimulus for the dreamer like the knowledge that every dream may sooner or later come true.

What was going on in the world in the second decade of this century seemed at times like a nightmare-come-true. About all that could be seen with certainty was the immediate concern, the war, and all that could be seen of that, in turn, was that it was bigger and more dreadful and less manageable than any war ever dreamed of. Yet the war lay on the surface, and the way it was being waged meant more than the destruction it was causing. For here was dismaying proof that the terms on which man was coping with the terrible problem of being man, naked under a remote sky, were changing almost beyond comprehension.

Man's reach always tends to exceed his grasp; now it was exceeding his understanding as well. War was simply the proving ground in which the extended reach and stronger grasp were being tested.

In 1916, of course, not all of the returns were in, and it took another war a generation later to make things clear. We see now, face to face, what was seen then only through a darkened glass; for a revealing illustration take an incident from the Drummer Boy's own war and carry it down to date.

In the summer of 1863 the United States army was trying to hammer its way into Charleston, South Carolina. It was unable to do this, and so someone got the idea that if Charleston could not be captured it might at least be destroyed; it was the cradle of secession and the stronghold of an aloof and aristocratic slavocracy, and to knock it down stone by stone would be a good thing. So with vast effort the army engineers built a battery deep in a quaking swamp, inland from the Morris Island beach and more than four miles south of Charleston, and in it they put an eight-inch Parrott rifle along with a supply of two-hundred pound shells filled with a new incendiary composition. They nicknamed this weapon the Swamp Angel, and when everything was ready the gunners hoisted the Parrott's muzzle for extreme elevation, put in an overcharge of powder, sighted the weapon just to the left of the steeple of St. Michael's Church (which was the only part of Charleston they could see) and opened fire.

The effort had been prodigious and the intent was vicious enough for anybody—it was impossible for the gun to hit anything but homes—but the equipment had not been perfected. The fire bombs did not work well, and although they did cause a certain amount of pain and destruction the bombardment could have gone on all year without bringing Charleston to surrender or destruction; and in any case the Parrott gun burst after thirty-five shots and the Swamp Angel ceased to be. A flat failure, in other words, by no means worth the effort.

But the idea that a city that could not actually be taken might be destroyed at long range fascinated military thinkers, and in the First World War it was tried again. This time the Germans got a special gun from Krupp, with a range of seventy miles or such a matter; nicknamed Big Bertha, in clumsy barrack-square tribute to the wife of the head of the tribe of Krupp. This gun was established miles away from Paris, hidden far behind the German line, and in due time it opened a bombardment just as the Swamp Angel had done.

The results were no better. More people were killed, more buildings were destroyed and probably more indignation was aroused, but Paris was not wiped out and the war was not won, and again it seemed that much ingenuity and hard work had been spent for no useful purpose. But the idea remained attractive, and in the next war the Germans brought out the buzz bombs, which were much more intricate, expensive and effective than anything the earlier generations had been able to create. They knocked down whole city blocks in London and might conceivably have done what their makers wanted them to do except that time ran out; the launching sites were either bombed out or captured before these formidable weapons could have their full effect, and London survived with few wounds that could not eventually be healed.

Fourth act, now, and America's turn again. This time the ancient problem was fully solved. One atomic bomb was tucked away in one airplane, and—on orders transmitted from half the world away—was dropped on the Japanese city of Hiroshima. Hiroshima to all intents and purposes was blotted out, along with many thousands of Hiroshima's inhabitants, most of whom died before they even knew anybody was shooting at them. In 1863, complete failure; in 1945, complete success. The proving ground had delivered its final report: man's reach no longer exceeded his grasp.

Now the significant thing here is not the calamitous nature of the new peril that was introduced into the world, but the progression by which the job was done. The idea took shape in the 1860s, but try as they would men could not manage it; scientific knowledge and technical competence then simply were not adequate. (The callousness of spirit and malevolence of heart that made men want such a weapon in the first place were there all along and needed no development, but that is another story.) In less than a century, using instruments, technical processes and ways of thought that no one in the 1860s had so much as dreamed of, man had broken through all of the old restrictions.

In that period of time man had in fact entered a new world, by virtue of a discovery totally unlike that of Columbus yet hauntingly related to it. (He showed that the world has dimensions far greater than had been supposed; now we are learning that the same thing is true of man himself.) It was not just mastery of the secret of nuclear fission that opened this new world; that was no more than the Watling's Island of this voyage. The real discovery was that man had, in himself or available to his hands, powers straight from the realm of myth and fable. Joshua flattened the city of Jericho without touching it; modern man, scoffing at credulous folk who could believe in any such tale, found himself doing precisely the same thing at Hiroshima. He had laid his hands on the power to work miracles, and no one could say what was going to come of it. Obviously, all of the old limits were gone. The situation called for an entirely new kind of faith—faith carried to an extreme, born originally of skepticism carried to an extreme.

The ancient texts spoke of the faith that can remove mountains. That faith no longer exists. In its place there is the faith —perhaps it is not so much a faith as a dazed awareness—that the mountains can indeed be removed, by unaided man rather than by an unseen power beyond the stars, if removing them seems to be worth while. Returning from a trip to the moon, an astronaut remarked soberly: "Now we can go anywhere." He was correct, and that is why this generation is so confused. It is trying to adjust itself to something that is beyond its understanding.

Like the Indians whom we dispossessed, we find ourselves obliged to live far beyond our means culturally, and there are times when it looks as if it would be too much for us.

It was too much in the 1860s, that legendary era whose nearness was symbolized by the drummer boy beating the long roll before the gray veterans in the village hall. In the 1860s the leaders of the cotton belt made one of the most prodigious miscalculations in recorded history. On the eve of the era of applied technologies, in which more and more work is done with fewer people and less effort, they made war to preserve the day of chattel slavery—the era of gang labor, with its reliance on the same use of human muscles that built the pyramids. The lost cause was lost before it started to fight. Inability to see what is going on in the world can be costly.

Unfortunately this inability seems to afflict everybody.

The Ottawa brave who made a living by trapping beaver and exchanging the pelts for hardware and dry goods was utterly baffled when both beaver and the market for pelts vanished; now he had to make a living by means which seemed certain to destroy the basis on which he lived. Baffled similarly was the military man, who won success by constantly improving his weapons only to discover that when he had at last perfected them he could not use them without destroying the society that had produced him. And the generation we knew, one of whose most modest, microscopic and endearing achievements was the creation of a tiny hilltop academy that was trying to prepare us to understand and to cope with the modern world—how was it faring? It was a generation that lived by applying a steadily increasing knowledge and ingenuity to the exploitation of the earth's boundless store of resources; and it was reaching the gates of the age of gold only to discover that the boundless store of resources was beginning to run out and that the consequent demands on knowledge and ingenuity were increasing by geometric progression, approaching the level at which they would be intolerable.

Our generation spoke to us through our academy, and although the mouthpiece was narrow and the voice was of limited range we did get a useful message. We were taught to look to the future; and although that teaching can easily lead to the simpleton's faith that eternal progress is the law of life, bearing its fruit as automatically as apple trees in a well-cared-for orchard, it is at the same time an excellent orientation for people bewildered because their times have gone out of date. For the tendency in such a condition is to become a prisoner of the past. Realizing that things can not again be as once they were, and feeling that something precious has been taken away, we are all too likely to conclude that the golden age lies somewhere behind us. The people who lived in it may not have known that it was a golden age, but we discover it for them and string out long tales, sad and beautiful in sunset red and gold, about the ease and peace that once lay upon the earth. We center our hopes on something that is long gone; knowing that the future cannot be as rich and rewarding as the irrecoverable past we let it take shape of itself. The land of night must be marvelous; it contains the best the race can ever have.

Regarding the past so fondly we are unable to get it in proper focus, and we see virtues that were not there. Like all the rest of the world, Michigan a generation or so ago was a much simpler place than it is now, and as today's complexities grow too intricate to understand we look back on the lost simplicity and credit it with qualities it did not really have. Thus we note that from the beginning the state has been shaped and conditioned by that shining waterway in blue and gold, the chain of the Great Lakes. From the red man's bark canoe to the seven-hundred-foot steel ore carrier, vessels of one sort or another have carried men and their cargoes along this highway, and life in our state has always depended to a large extent on the use that is made of the lakes. Now it seems perfectly apparent, looking back, that fifty or one hundred years ago these lakes offered the lone individual opportunities which are not offered to him today. The field of independent enterprise, as we say, was wider than it is today.

Thus: toward the end of the last century there was a man over on the Wisconsin shore who was owner, captain, cook and entire crew of a small schooner, with which he made his living. He sailed out of Milwaukee, cruised up the lake to a pebbly beach he knew of, anchored close in shore, went over the side waist deep in water, and, by hand, loaded his craft with round stones. When he had a full cargo he sailed back to Milwaukee, tied up at a city dock, and sold these rocks for cobblestones. It is recorded that he could make a round trip about once every fortnight, and that a cargo of cobblestones brought him twenty dollars. When bad weather kept him in port he hired out as a stevedore on the docks. During the four or five months when winter closed the port (except for a few steam-driven icebreakers) he of course could not operate at all, and how he lived is not stated; but live he did, year after year, on a toilsome one-man operation the like of which would be quite impossible today.

He was not the only small operator. Not long ago a student examined records of the old Life Saving Service, predecessor of the Coast Guard, to draw up a fairly comprehensive list of shipwrecks on the Great Lakes, and he ran across instances of commercial craft not much bigger than present-day pleasure boats. Here are a few samples:

Schooner *F. Fitch,* thirteen tons, lost off Point Betsie in 1898 with a cargo of fruit worth $200. Value of the schooner is given as $300.

Schooner *I. May Brown,* twenty tons, lost in 1895 off Michigan City with a cargo of gravel worth $40; value of schooner is given as $400.

Sloop *John Edward,* eleven tons, lost off Saugatuck in 1876 with a cargo of vinegar; no valuation for vessel or cargo is listed.

Schooner *May Cornell,* eight tons, sank off Grand Point Sable in 1894 with a cargo of shingles worth $70. The schooner apparently was worth $300.

Schooner *O. Shaw,* forty tons, lost off Calumet Harbor in

1904 with a $75 cargo of sawdust. The value of the schooner is given as $250.

. . . It would be possible to extend the list, but this makes a representative sample. These, bear in mind, were just the vessels that got into the records by being wrecked, whether with or without loss of life. Obviously, for every one of these small schooners that foundered there were many others that voyaged safely and uneventfully from one port to another, bearing cargoes of modest value and making, presumably, a modest living for their owners. The average craft of this size, no doubt, was operated by the owner, who might be assisted by a son, a brother or a hired hand; certainly none of these ventures could have been robust enough to support much of a crew.

In any case, it is hard to look back on that era without feeling that it offered more freedom for the lone individual, more incentive, more reward for the independent person who was not afraid to work hard and risk much, than today's efficiently organized, highly mechanized economy has to give. This may not have been the golden age, but in a time of giant corporations and sprawling conglomerates it at least looks like a fragment of the golden age.

Until you stop to think about it.

That Wisconsin sailor who traded in cobblestones may indeed have been a free spirit who had not yet been crowded out by the truck and the diesel engine, but he must have been leading a dog's life just the same. He was technically independent, but he was nevertheless exploited within an inch of his life. Reflect a moment on the back-breaking work and the acute physical discomfort involved in that career; reflect also on the fact that out of the forty dollars that made a good month's income he had to support his schooner and lay aside enough money to take him through the winter; before you get through you are bound to conclude that if society no longer offers a man a chance to live that way society has not deprived us of anything worth keeping. No sailing craft is going to earn anything better than a pittance, hauling such cargoes the length of Lake Michigan; what is the freight rate on forty dollars' worth of gravel, or on seventy dollars' worth of shingles, or on seventy-five dollars' worth of sawdust? The owners and crews of these vessels were pinned down at the level of hopeless poverty. They were men beset, and the independence they enjoyed was a fraud which looks attractive only when seen from a distance.

There is no sense, in other words, in being bemused by the backward glance. The world we have lost might be a nice place to visit but we would not want to live there. The present may be disturbing and the future may be in the highest degree ominous, but nobody gains anything by seeing in the irrecoverable past a charm and a comfort which it did not have. We do not actually remember a better world. Our chances of building a good future may be poor, but they vanish altogether if we keep facing in the wrong direction.

It was an odd time to be going to school, that year 1916, especially when the school was as pathetically archaic as Benzonia Academy. The debris left by the nineteenth century had not yet been cleared away, and the educational process we were subjected to was part of it; as the years just ahead were to prove, the school could not live in the twentieth century, because— like the little schooners sailing offstage on the big lake—it was what we call a homemade institution. The drummer boy who beat out a requiem for the faded army that was all of his world was beating one also for this academy and the men who had made it and the thin heroic faith they lived by. It was a time of coming-to-an-end.

Yet it was a good time to be going to school, even so, and the promises inherent in life's challenge seemed far bigger than the tragedies it had already created. We who were students then carried a bigger responsibility than we could realize. We stood at the meeting place of two eras, a lost fragment of time in which no works of man's hands could endure. If anything was to survive it would be the faith, the hope and the vision that men had developed, the things that were not altogether homemade but that at their best contained some quality that would live. If these survived they would do so in us and in others like us. It is a pity we did not realize this at the time. We might have taken more pains.

CHAPTER TWELVE

Night Train

It all happened many years ago, and distance puts a deceptive haze on things remembered. As I look back on my final year in the academy I seem to recall the brief spring of 1916 as a time when life was extremely pleasant and singularly uneventful. The cataract might lie just ahead, but at the moment the river was lazy, without eddies or ripples. Europe was a long way off, and the echoes from its war reached us faintly, unreal and haunting, like the cries Canada geese make when they circle over Crystal Lake in the autumn, lining up the order of flight for their southbound squadrons. It was undeniable, of course, that soon we would leave our little campus and go to whatever was waiting for us in the outside world, but that knowledge simply added a vibrant expectancy to life. Everything imaginable was going to happen tomorrow, but right at the moment nothing was happening; if the time of waiting was almost over its final moments had an uncommon flavor. Although we knew that we ought to think long and hard about what we were going to do, once the spring ripened into Commencement Week and then sent us off into unguided summer, most of the time we were undisturbed. The present moment was like a six-measure rest that had been inserted into the score just as the composition was supposed to be coming to its climax.

Naturally, when I try to recall that time I remember hardly anything specific. I remember the spring sunlight lying on the campus, and the academy buildings taking on dignity and looking as if they were going to be there forever—which, alas, they were not; I remember the band practice, and the orchestra practice, and the long, aimless walks we took on Sundays, tramping off the last vestiges of childhood, seeing things for the last time without realizing that it was the last time, unaware that once you leave youth behind you see everything with different eyes and thereby make the world itself different. We would go across country to the power dam on the Betsie River, or along the shore of Crystal Lake to the outlet; and sometimes we went down the long hill to Beulah and then crossed the low ground to go up Eden Hill, a big shoulder of land that defined the horizon to the east . . . Eden Hill and Beulah Land, named by godly settlers for the Paradise where the human race got into the world and the Paradise it will enter when it goes out; or so people believed, although we lived then in the present and asked for no Paradise beyond what we had then and there.

From the summit of Eden Hill you could look far to the north and west, across the Platte Lakes to the limitless blue plain of Lake Michigan, with Sleeping Bear crouched, watchful, in the distance and the Manitou Islands on the skyline. Beyond the green weeded country to the east, hidden by the rolling easy ridges, was the lumber town of Honor, and if we felt like making a really long walk out of it we could go on over to Honor, walk around the mill and its piled logs—they were still carving up some last allotment of first-growth wood, although most of the county's mills were stilled—and then we could tramp the long miles home by way of Champion's Hill. This was a plateau which had been named half a century earlier by some Civil War veterans who made farms there; they had served in Sherman's corps in the Vicksburg campaign and something about the shape of this land reminded them of a great battlefield in that campaign and so they had put this Mississippi name in the heart of Northern Michigan as a reminder of what they had seen and done. And we youngsters walked across it, all unthinking, on our way home to Sunday night supper.

Spring is a short haul in our part of Michigan, and we were kept fairly busy once the snow was gone making preparation for the exercises that would attend our graduation, which would be a big moment. For all that it was so small, Benzonia Academy crowded Commencement Week as full of events as the State University itself; and the graduating class was so small—just eleven of us, when fully mustered—that everybody had something to do. Which reminds me that by ancient custom, running back fully five years, the graduating class was supposed to present a play as the final event of its academic life. Our class elected to do something called *Peg o' My Heart,* and of course nobody in the class had a vestige of acting ability, but somehow we got through the thing alive.

I remember practically nothing about the performance except that I was the leading man and, as such, was called upon by the script to kiss the leading woman, who was a most attractive classmate, just as the final curtain came down. Miss Ellis, who was directing the performance, made it clear that it would not be necessary or even permissible actually to kiss the girl; I could lay my hands gently upon her shoulders and incline my head slowly, and the curtain then would descend rapidly and action could be broken off with no casualties. I do recall that when the great night came and this portentous moment arrived we discarded Miss Ellis's instructions completely. I walked the girl home afterward so bedazzled by all that had happened that I was unable to muster the nerve to try to kiss her again. I think this puzzled her slightly, although I do not believe that she felt that she had missed anything much. Now that I think of it, she was the only member of the class I ever did kiss, it took what amounted to a convulsion of nature to bring that about, and there was no repeat performance. I suppose I was born for other things.

Fittingly enough, the class play was presented after all of the actors and actresses had ceased to be students at the academy. We were graduates, possessed of diplomas, the formal commence-

ment exercises having taken place that morning, and technically we were out in the world on our own. I suppose I never would have kissed the leading lady if I had not realized that as a graduate I was no longer bound by Miss Ellis's instructions forbidding bodily contact. The commencement exercises had been painfully dignified, and whatever they may have meant to the audience I myself felt that they had been most impressive. When I finally left the church, holding my rolled-up diploma like a field marshal's baton, I was full of high resolves and conscious rectitude, and I looked upon life from a loftier plane than I have ever occupied since.

This was partly because of the occasion itself and partly because of the commencement address, which was delivered by a retired minister from Chicago, a fine old gentleman who said all of the things required of a commencement orator without lapsing into banality or insulting anyone's intelligence. I remember that at one point he drew from his pocket a little metal tube, held it up for all to see, and explained that it had an eyepiece at one end and at the other a tiny needle with a radioactive tip; look through the eyepiece and you could see this needle giving off the tiniest sparks, which flashed and went out like shooting stars caught in a telescope from the land Gulliver had visited. They were (he said) like the atoms which science believed were forever circling and wheeling in the most solid rocks and pieces of metal—the moral of which was that the world was much more miraculous and wonderful than most folk supposed. A whole solar system could be locked up in a curling wisp of fog; we trod on the Milky Way whenever we sauntered along a path in the campus; and if man's knowledge of the atoms was limited as yet (said the speaker), it was constantly being extended and he predicted that we would know a great deal more about this exciting topic by the time we were as old as he was.

This was all most impressive, and I recall the mood that possessed me as an odd blend of exaltation and humility; I knew so much, and I knew so little, and the world which I was about to enter did seem to be exceedingly complicated and unknowable. But above everything else it looked exciting. My time at the railway junction was ending, the morning limited was coming in and I was about to get aboard, and although I had no idea where it was finally going to take me I at least knew that it was heading toward change. The big adventure was beginning, even though I started it, I must admit, by walking down the hill to Beulah and going to work as a waiter-on-tables in the summer hotel there.

If I was marching forth to high adventure then, I had to begin by marking time. I was going to go to college; that had been determined long ago, and by virtue of a little money saved, more money borrowed, and arrangements to work for board and room once college was reached, everything was all set. But I could not go to college until the middle of September and this was only the middle of June, to spend the summer in idleness was inadmissible, and inasmuch as the job at the hotel would permit me to sleep at home while the hotel provided me with three meals every day I could save almost every penny the waiter's job would bring in. So—down the hill, into the kitchen, on with the white coat and apron, and this is how you carry a loaded tray through a crowded dining room without dropping things on people's heads.

It all was most anticlimactic, no doubt, but it did not exactly seem so at the time. I was beginning to be independent, and although the independence was more apparent than real I was at least out of the house from dawn until dusk. If you have never been in control of any fragment of your life, to gain control even over a small part of it can be a heady experience; and to start off on the mile walk at daybreak, swinging down the hill before the town was awake, admiring Crystal Lake and the hills around it as the early light touched them, breathing the air that, essentially, had come drifting all the way down from northern Canada without once touching anything that would defile it, and to reflect while you were doing this that your boyhood at last was over and that every stride was carrying you nearer to man's estate—well, this was a moving and rewarding experience, even if it was totally undramatic. Life does not always need to be spectacular in order to be exciting.

We worked fairly hard. We were supposed to check in at six in the morning, and although there was a slack hour or two in mid-morning and two or three hours that could be taken off in the afternoon we were not through for the day until eight at night, and when the dining room was full—as it usually was, in the middle of the summer—we were busy. However, it could have been much worse. There was a sort of dormitory, back of the hotel, for such waiters as did not live at home, and in the afternoon we could all go in there, change to bathing suits, and then walk down the lawn to Crystal Lake and take a swim, which was enough to make up for any sort of drudgery. Now and then, on the beach, we would encounter young women who were guests at the hotel, and we could lounge and chat with them, and accompany them into the water, just as if we were not waiters at all. There was one afternoon, when another boy and I were having a pleasant conversation with a somewhat dazzling blond number, who wore what we considered a revealing bathing suit and who had quite a bit to reveal. (By modern standards, of course, her suit was prissy as could be, but in 1916 much was concealed from the vulgar gaze.) At any rate, while we were basking in this girl's company my friend Donald Gibb appeared.

Donald lived in Beulah, where his father owned a drug store, and Donald did not wait on table at the hotel; he was a good man with a camera, he made and sold picture postcards and he operated a little photo developing and printing agency. His time, on summer afternoons, was pretty much his own, and he was able to afford his own canoe; and now he came paddling up in this gleaming green craft, waved airily to the other boy and me, and asked the girl if she would care to go for a canoe ride. It looked like a good deal to her and she got into the boat and was wafted away, while my pal and I went splashing into the lake hoping that the canoe would sink, which it did not do. When we came out of the water and were heading back to our quarters, we were hailed by a man who, idling with a cigar on the hotel veranda, had witnessed the whole thing.

"You're a fine pair, you are," he said, "letting that boy cut you out like that. He just came up and took your girl away. Why didn't you turn his canoe over for him?"

We had to confess that we did not know just why we had not done something of the kind. It occurs to me, as I look back, that in that year 1916 my approach (if it can be called that) to the opposite sex was sadly lacking in the aggressive spirit.

As a matter of fact girls did not claim much of our attention that summer . . . We had no time for them, except for those afternoon recess periods, and we usually spent that time swimming, followed by a quick visit to Terpining's pavilion for ice cream, without bothering to see who was available on the beach. Actually we worked steadily, seven days a week, and the pay scale began and ended with a weekly wage of five dollars. We were allowed to keep all tips, which helped, but our guests were not at all lavish in that respect and many of them left no tips at all, so we did not make very much money.

However, we did not really expect to. If we could lay by a few dollars during the summer we were just that much ahead of the game; and besides, at that time and place the going wage for adult labor, unskilled or semiskilled, was fifteen cents an hour. A man who put in a ten-hour day on a six-day week thus had a take-home pay, for the week, of nine dollars, on which he had to support his family if he had one. Prices of course were much lower than they are now, but they were never low enough to make that kind of pay scale anything but bad. The men who worked for such wages were getting angry and their anger was becoming visible, even to me. I learned that summer, to my bewilderment, that even our own Benzie County—a bucolic section of the unstained Michigan countryside if ever there was one —had developed a number of outright Socialists, and although

I occasionally read about Socialists I had not expected actually to
see any, especially not this close to home. (They were much in
the minority, of course, but their numbers were fairly impressive
when the county's limited population was taken into account.)
Men could be seen reading Eugene Deb's *Appeal to Reason*
openly; men who lounged on their doorsteps in sweaty under-
shirts, gnawing at the stems of corncob pipes, not at all the sort
of men who went to our church every Sunday to listen to Mr.
Mills. Stranger still, one of the brightest of our Benzonia young
men, just graduated from (I think) Olivet College, came home
and announced that he was a Socialist, and he traveled about the
county giving lectures, always addressing his hearers as "Comrades." This was all right, in a way, because "comrades" was a
word hallowed by usage among our Civil War veterans, and
everybody liked this young man and respected his integrity; yet
it was disturbing to have avowed Socialists right in our midst,
and nobody seemed to know what to make of it. To my mind
Socialists were bewhiskered immigrants, normally to be found
only in places like the slums of Chicago, and Socialism was
wrongheaded, destructive and probably downright ungodly.

Father would assuredly have enlightened me if I had told him
about my state of mind. He was no Socialist, but he knew what
these men were angry about and he thought they were right to
be angry; in point of fact he was angry too, not because he himself had to work for a genteel-poverty income but because he
believed that greed, oppression and injustice (visible now and
then even in the idyllic forests of Michigan) were threatening to
destroy everything that America stood for. Whether he realized
it or not, he was looking for a broader field than the principal's
office at Benzonia Academy offered him. He had abundant
energy, he could write and speak with eloquence, and he had
an eye that could see, and he wanted to use those qualities for
something more significant than providing artificial respiration
for an undersized school that almost certainly would not survive
him. I did not at the time realize that he was going through

anything like this. In my self-centered adolescent way I regarded all adults as fixed stars in the sky of my own particular universe, and it simply did not occur to me that Father might be anxious to get out of one orbit and into another. I probably would have learned something, about his own state of mind and about the society we were living in, if I had asked him about these home-grown Socialists, but I did not do it—partly because I was not perceptive enough to realize that he would have a rewarding answer for me, and partly because he was abstracted that summer, all caught up in politics.

Father was a dedicated Theodore Roosevelt man, a card-carrying member of the Bull Moose Party. He had campaigned for Roosevelt, on the village and county level, in 1912, and in 1916 he had been elected a delegate to the national convention of the Progressive Party, and down to Chicago he went, to see the great leader in person and get inspiration for the approaching presidential election.

What he got, of course, was profound disillusionment. Like hundreds of other delegates, he had keyed himself up (in Roosevelt's own words) to stand at Armageddon and to battle for the Lord, and these were words he could rise to because he was both a devout Roosevelt man and a good Biblical scholar. But the emotional build-up led to nothing but a let-down. Roosevelt was not going to run for president after all, the Progressive Party had served its purpose and would be dismantled; instead of standing at Armageddon, rallying to a banner held high in a clanging wind, they were to go home quietly, vote for Charles Evans Hughes, and resume their places in the Republican Party which they had spent four years learning to distrust. Father never said much about it, but I am convinced that in the fall of 1916, for the only time in his life, he voted the Democratic ticket. Woodrow Wilson—precise, professorial, full of hard passions but apparently having no zest for living—might seem an unlikely heir for the Bull Moose legacy but he got a lot of Bull Moose votes that fall.

Father brought back from Chicago deep emotions that should have been discharged there and were not, and I think this helped to pull him out of the job he had trained himself for. From the classroom and the pulpit he had fought against ignorance, and against that combination of self-indulgence, ill will and stupidity that people of his generation called sin, and now it was time to do something else. He had not gone into the Progressive Party just because Roosevelt's mighty personality had overwhelmed him; he had been headed in that direction for a long time. I suppose he could be called a Populist, although I do not think he would have applied that term to himself, and anyway by this time it has become too vague to mean much; it is applied nowadays to practically anyone who flourished after 1885, lived west of the Alleghenies, and stood somewhat to the left of Grover Cleveland. An idea of the direction his thoughts had been taking is provided by a Fourth of July speech which he made in some small town in Michigan in either 1906 or 1907. The manuscript of this speech survives, and although it gives neither the place nor the exact date of delivery it is worth a glance as an example of the sort of thing a thoughtful man could have on his mind early in the present century.

The speech began conventionally enough by paying tribute to the heroes of 1776 and making proper mention of Lexington, Concord, Saratoga and Yorktown, but it did not go on to let the eagle scream in the traditional Fourth of July manner. It remarked that we look back on the past in order to find courage and inspiration to face the immediate future and that the Revolutionary War was fought to defend a declaration of principles which became "the rallying cry for the oppressed of every land." The battles of that war were the battles of all mankind, and the spirit that led men in '76 would yet be "the vital, potent force that shall astonish and overthrow domestic greed as completely as it once did a foreign tyrant."

Our task now, Father went on, was to achieve internal reform by means of the ballot, and this "always calls for virtues superior to those demanded in contests that are settled by the sword." The challenge was larger than the one faced in 1776, because "this business of the overthrow of greed is absolutely the greatest problem that ever confronted any people."

He did not leave "greed" as a vague generality that could mean as much or as little as anyone chose. To the best of his ability he spelled it out; in the manner, to be sure, of the early 1900s rather than the 1970s. He was talking about monopoly, about the "spirit of selfish individualism" which inspired monopoly, about the unreachable corporations which practiced "a great system of extortion," drove prices up under cover of a fraudulent protective tariff, kept wages down by importing whole shiploads of Europe's "pauper labor" against whose handiwork the tariff was supposed to be an essential bulwark, and used the vast powers of finance to exert an increasing control over the law, the press and the school in such a way as to make reform almost impossible.

"Whenever a man is found wise enough and brave enough to denounce these arch-conspirators against the people's liberties," he continued, "they accuse him of assailing the sacred rights of property and of being in league with anarchy." This outcry rallied the "honest respectable element" in every community—the frugal farmer, worker, merchant and professional man who had worked hard to save a competence for a rainy day—and in the end led them to defend "the very vultures that are gorging upon their vitals."

To overthrow these monopolists was an issue demanding immediate action, even though the task was "of such stupendous proportions as to appall those who would undertake it." We needed all the courage and inspiration our heroic past could give us—that mighty heritage of remembered bravery and determination that would in the end prove to be "our most valuable and tangible asset."

This of course was the jargon of old-line Populism, a shotgun charge aimed at the forces whom Roosevelt himself could only denounce as malefactors of great wealth, but there are two things to be said about it. First of all, this was not the spread-eagle Fourth of July bombast with which glib speakers of that era prodded at receptive rural patriotism; and beyond that it was an odd way for a small-town schoolmaster to be talking. The man who put that speech together, and then stood in the bandstand of a village park and delivered it before a sun-baked audience that was there half out of curiosity and half out of a sense of duty, was a man with something on his mind and with a determination to have his say about it. Obviously he believed that he saw something taking America by the throat and threatening to choke out, if not its life, at least its life-giving spirit.

Feeling so, he believed that to break this grip would be of service to all mankind. He had his full share of that profound conviction which lies so close to the headwaters of the American spirit: the conviction that if in the end the world is saved from disaster the saving will be done in America and by Americans. As a people whose ideas about the cosmos have at least in part an Old Testament base, we have a deep suspicion that we are the chosen people. We may not actually be the ones specifically mentioned in Scripture, but we feel that we are fairly close; maybe Providence made a supplementary choice somewhere along the way. (After all, no less a man than Abraham Lincoln, trying to nerve his countrymen for the shock of civil war, spoke of them as the *almost* chosen people.) This feeling is in fact one of the most powerful forces in American life, and now and then it leads to interesting happenings. It frequently makes us hard to live with, and it bewilders a great many people—including, often enough, ourselves. For every so often it impels us to take drastic action, and a subconscious belief in mission is not always accompanied by the sense to make a sound choice of the sort of action that is required. Sometimes we act with wisdom and at other times we do not. The same impulse that led us to destroy Hitler's obscenely contrived Nibelungen Reich, composed in equal parts of the fantasies of Teutonic chivalry and grisly shapes from the far side of midnight, led us a few years later into southeast Asia where we made obscene contrivances of our own.

But whether we act wisely or foolishly, we always feel that what we do is important to the whole wide world and not just to ourselves, and the responsibility runs all the way down to the conscience of the individual. We are mindful of the text which, telling the chosen ones that they were the salt of the earth, asked what the world would do if the salt ceased to be salty. A man who feels so will make no small decisions. Thus it happens that the elderly principal of an unimportant school in one of the remote parts of the earth, reflecting that time was short and anxious to make good use of the thin years that remained to him, might conclude that he owed to mankind a larger debt than he had yet tried to pay. What he did might mean nothing to anybody in particular, but by what he was and what he believed he would do it as if the fate of the world depended on it. By the end of the summer of 1916, I am sure, Father had made up his mind to leave the academy.

Of all of this I at that time knew nothing. I was thinking about myself, and about the great things that lay ahead of me; the place that had been all the world was about to become nothing more than a receding milestone, growing ever smaller with increasing distance but not actually changing. The institution that had shaped me (and in a sense it was simply an extension of my own home) would remain just as it always had been: always, that is, for the last ten or twelve years. Changes that took place would happen to me, not to what I left behind. My background was immutable, and when I finally went off to Oberlin I felt no need to take a fond backward glance.

A college freshman was as far from maturity then as he is today, but it did seem to me that I was just about grown up. Boyhood certainly was ended. Youth indeed remained, to be squandered as blithely as if it came from an inexhaustible store, but the mere fact that I could be prodigal of it if I wished made a difference. I felt that by getting to college, exchanging a small campus for a large one, I was being set free.

It seems odd, now, that I felt that way so deeply. Some forty years later I was briefly in fairly close touch with Oberlin, and the students were complaining bitterly that they had no freedom. The college felt responsible for the young people on its campus, and it tried to stand *in loco parentis,* possibly in a somewhat heavy-handed way. The students felt that this was stultifying and against nature, they would have none of it, and after a certain amount of effervescence they had their way and freedom reigned. The regime against which they rebelled was far milder than the one that prevailed when I was a student, but in the fall of 1916 I found the freedom of student life almost intoxicating. I suppose it is all in what you are used to. I had no way to measure the college system except by comparing it with what I had known at Benzonia, but that was enough; by that comparison, the situation at Oberlin bordered delightfully on anarchy.

That of course is absurd; we *were* in a strait jacket at that college; there were innumerable laws against all known forms of misconduct, and they were enforced with ferocious rigor. Fraternities, for instance, were outlawed; and in that same fall of 1916, just before the college year opened, it was learned that practically the entire Oberlin football squad had formed, and gave allegiance to, a secret fraternity. The entire football squad, accordingly, was thrown out of college without further ado, and a pickup team that was hastily organized with untaught volunteers, who went nobly forth to slaughter for the honor of the school, took a fearful beating every Saturday of the season; I believe Ohio State, which was just then emerging to big league status, beat Oberlin by 128 to nothing. And all of this happened to a college which, up to that hour, had always prided itself on the fine record its football teams made!

The college authorities, in other words, meant what they said, and they could be grim. And yet (to repeat) I was at least away from home, and I felt that I had freedom. One autumn evening, greatly daring, I went with another boy to the nearby city of Elyria, walked uncertainly into a saloon, and drank a glass of beer, after which we slunk out, full of the consciousness of guilt and high adventure, boarded an interurban and went hastily back to Oberlin. Never have I committed a sin that was as pleasurable and as exciting.

All of this, to be sure, is beside the point. Benzonia Academy was my fixed point of reference, and everything that happened to me was to be compared with what had happened in Benzonia. This put an unusual gloss on commonplace adventures, now and then, so that the innocent trip to Elyria seemed like a weekend lost around Sodom and Gomorrah; but it did no harm, and I had a deep affection for the place which, in a way, had seemed so repressive. The academy would always be there, and someday I would return, probably as a famous foreign correspondent on furlough, and tell the impressionable young people graphic tales about gathering the news in places like Paris and London.

The one thing I did not dream of at that time was that the academy was not going to wait for me. My own class of 1916 was second from the last class ever to be graduated there. At the end of the 1917 school year Father resigned his post, and one year later, in the summer of 1918, the academy closed its doors forever. Barber Hall was torn down a few years later; it was a fire hazard, a place subject to being broken into by rowdies, and a building of no conceivable use. The boys' dormitory, which had been a rambling collection of gable ends stuck together almost at haphazard, was cut to pieces and the pieces were taken away to make dwelling places. And the girls' dormitory, on the first floor of which our family had lived for several years, was turned into a village community house. It survives to this day, a most serviceable old building, looking rather hollow-eyed because its upper floors are boarded up and present blank, uncurtained windows to the public gaze. It has been in existence for well over half a century, and less than a decade of its life was devoted to the function for which its builders intended it. Nothing less dramatic than this building's story, and nothing less important than the death of the academy which had built it, could easily be imagined. But I keep thinking about both.

A graduate of the academy, meeting Father in the fall of 1918, asked him why the academy had disintegrated. Father replied that any small, undernourished institution of that sort was simply the reflection of one man's activity: when the man ceased to be active the institution ceased to exist. Whether he was consciously adapting Emerson's remark that an institution is the lengthened shadow of one man or worked the thought out for himself I do not know, but he had the right explanation. Benzonia Academy, founded by dedicated men to light an educational lamp in a wilderness which, left to itself, would remain in darkness, had outlived the condition that called it into being. The wilderness had been destroyed and the academy had become an anachronism. Once it existed because a state needed it and a community willed it; in the end, no longer really essential, it existed because one man willed it. When America went to war in the spring of 1917 he focused his will on another objective. It took the academy just a year to die.

A new era was beginning, and if the academy had not quite prepared us to understand it the same can be said of every other school on earth. No one was prepared, anywhere, and the deeper we get into this new era the more baffling it becomes. All that seems clear is that the mind of man now is obliged to adjust itself (without loss of time, and under penalty of death) to the greatest revolution in human history; a revolution, not in the relations of class with class and society with society, but in the nature of man's idea of the universe and of his place in it. We have won a fight that we ought to have lost; which is to say that we pretty largely control the world we live in, and its levers are in our hands even though we have no idea what to do with them. We can go anywhere and do anything, and because the fabulous machine we have created can neither be reversed, put in neutral or turned aside we have to go and do to the utmost limit, which is as likely as not to be our own destruction. Not since he came down out of trees and lost his tail has man been compelled to make such an adjustment in his ways of thinking. The breaking of horizons that took place in the Renaissance was a false dawn in comparison. He is headed now, infallibly, for the infinite . . . in either direction.

The academy in fact had done as well as it could, and if it left with some of its students the idea that what they do here should be done with an eye on its eternal consequences—well, a man going out into the twentieth century could be given worse advice.

When America went to war Father saw the war through Woodrow Wilson's eyes and heard the summons in Wilson's voice; if Theodore Roosevelt, in the showdown, had failed to call him to Armageddon, Wilson sounded the call and Father responded. He left the academy to support the cause as a free lance, believing that his eloquence and his knowledge of world history ought to be of service. His knowledge of world history was limited and may have led him at times to unsound judgments; but men in a position to know far more than he knew did no better with what they knew, and all in all he did a good, serviceable job. He wrote analytical articles for various Michigan newspapers, and he set up a series of lectures explaining the causes and the meaning of the war and traveled up and down the state delivering them to a considerable variety of audiences. These talks seem to have gone over well in the high schools—an enthusiastic educator in Saginaw wrote that they "should be presented in every high school in the United States"—and a former academy student, finding himself early in 1918 wearing khaki with other trainees at Camp Custer, was marched with his battalion into the mess hall one day to listen while Mr. Catton explained the true significance of the war. He had one lecture on "spiritual conscription" designed for church groups, explaining how Christians could sustain the young men who were being taken into the army; and in a notebook wherein he jotted down points to be made in his talks he scribbled this sentence: "The one inevitably oncoming thing, in politics, industry, commerce, education and religion, is *Democracy*."

All of this, of course, was a venture that had no tomorrow. He had cut loose from his job and had in fact destroyed the base on on which the job had rested, and once the war was over nobody was going to want articles or speeches about why we fought and why we had to win. Furthermore, he was sixty-two years old, and his prospects in a postwar job market were not good. Presumably he was well aware of this, and privately, where no one could hear him, he did a little whistling for his courage's sake. In his notebook there is a yellowed newspaper clipping, worn by much handling: a poem entitled "At Sixty-Two," which apparently he had read many times. One stanza gives the tone of it:

> *Just sixty-two? Then trim thy light*
> *And get thy jewels all reset;*
> *'Tis past meridian, but still bright,*
> *And lacks some hours of sunset yet.*
> *At sixty-two*
> *Be strong and true,*
> *Scour off thy rust and shine anew.*

Excellent words, but it did not lack as many hours of sunset as might have been thought. For a long time Father had suffered an abdominal pain, with certain distressing symptoms, which he did his best to ignore. But sometime early in 1919 the matter reached a point where it could be ignored no longer, nor could it be concealed. He confided, at last, in a doctor, and learned (as I suppose he had expected to learn) that he had cancer, and that although an operation would presently be performed it was not likely to do much good. His number, in other words, was up, and now there was nothing to do but get his affairs in order, compose his mind, and wait for the end.

. . . Old age, as I said before, is like youth in this one respect: it finds one waiting at the railroad junction for a train that is never going to come back; and whether the arrival and possible destination of this train is awaited with the high hopes that youth entertains when it waits for its own train depends, no doubt, on the individual. I think Father had hopes.

But you know how it can be, waiting at the junction for the night train. You have seen all of the sights, and it is a little too dark to see any more even if you did miss some, and the waiting room is uncomfortable and the time of waiting is dreary, long-drawn, with a wind from the cold north whipping curls of fog past the green lamps on the switch stands. Finally, far away yet not so far really, the train can be heard; the doctor (or station agent) hears it first, but finally you hear it yourself and you go to the platform to get on. And there is the headlight, shining far down the track, glinting off the steel rails that, like all parallel lines, will meet in infinity, which is after all where this train is going. And there by the steps of the sleeping car is the Pullman conductor, checking off his list. He has your reservation, and he tells you that your berth is all ready for you. And then, he adds the final assurance as you go down the aisle to the curtained bed: "I'll call you in plenty of time in the morning."

. . . in the morning.

ACKNOWLEDGMENTS & BOOK LIST

Even a book as personal to the writer as this one could hardly be produced without help. In the course of preparing and writing this book, I found that I needed to call on a number of people—for documents, for photographs and newspaper clippings, for the reminiscences that would assist my own imperfect memory, sometimes simply for a chance to talk about the faraway times which we once shared and which were not recorded anywhere. Among those who were particularly helpful, and to whom my sincere thanks are extended, are the following:

Mrs. Flora Pettitt, Helen and Robert Catton, Leonard Case, Mrs. Fern Wheeler and Roy Tower, all of Benzonia, Michigan.

Alberta and Donald Gibb, of Honor, Michigan, and Vero Beach, Florida.

Al Barnes, of Traverse City, Michigan.

Dr. Ione Catton, of Claremont, California.

Dorothy B. Hensel of Frankfort, Michigan, curator of the Benzie Area Historical Museum.

Catherine Stebbins of Frankfort, who wrote *Here I Shall Finish My Voyage*, an extremely scholarly study of the final days of Father Marquette. Miss Stebbins argues—convincingly, it seems to me—that he died and was buried at the mouth of the Betsie River, where Frankfort is now.

Harriet Kilbourn, president emeritus of the Little Traverse Regional Historical Society; Philip Marco, president of the Society, and Merton Carter, the Society's museum display chairman; all of Petoskey, Michigan. They were most helpful with material bearing on early days in the Petoskey area. Miss Kilbourn steered me away from a grievous error of fact which I was about to commit in my discussion of the lumber era, and Mr. Carter gave me a copy of his paper, "Shame on the Shore," a detailed account of the way in which a canny real estate operation separated members of the Cheboygan Band of Indians from their land.

Two very close friends who had a good deal to do with the inception of this book are unfortunately no longer here to receive expressions of gratitude. I can only remark that I owe much to the late Edna Case and the late Lynn Pettitt, both of Benzonia.

A book of personal reminiscences can hardly have a formal bibliography, but it does seem advisable to append a list of books and pamphlets which I found useful for material that did not come within the range of my own observation. I wish to acknowledge my indebtedness to them, and also to remark that the list might be useful to any reader who wants fuller information on various points that I have discussed briefly. I found the books enjoyable as well as helpful, and I believe others will feel the same way about them. The list is as follows:

Al Barnes: *Vinegar Pie and Other Tales of the Grand Traverse Region*. Detroit, 1959.

Andrew J. Blackbird: *History of the Ottawa and Chippewa Indians of Michigan*. Ypsilanti, Mich., 1887; reprint by the Little Traverse Regional Historical Society.

William Boulton: *Complete History of Alpena County, Michigan*. Alpena, Mich., 1876.

Dana Thomas Bowen: *Shipwrecks of the Lakes*. Daytona Beach, Fla., 1952.

Raymond D. Burroughs: *Peninsular Country*. Grand Rapids, Mich., 1965.

W. L. Case: *The Tragedy of Crystal Lake*. Beulah, Mich., 1962.

Elsket Barstow Chaney: *The Story of Portage*. Onekama, Mich., 1960.

Julia Terry Dickinson: *The Story of Leelanau.* Omena, Mich. 1951.

Willis Frederick Dunbar: *All Aboard! A History of Railroads in Michigan.* Grand Rapids, Mich., 1969.

James E. Fitting: *The Archaeology of Michigan.* New York, 1970.

John W. Fitzmaurice: *The Shanty Boy, or, Life in a Lumber Camp.* Cheboygan, Mich., 1889.

Arthur C. and Lucy F. Frederickson: *Ships and Shipwrecks in Door County,* Vols. I and II. Sturgeon Bay, Wis., 1961, 1963. The Fredericksons have also written first-rate brief histories of the Ann Arbor and Chesapeake & Ohio lines of car ferries.

Emerson F. Greenman: *The Indians of Michigan.* Lansing, Mich., 1961.

Frances Caswell Hanna: *Sand, Sawdust and Sawlegs; Lumber Days in Ludington.* Ludington, Mich., 1955.

Irene M. Hargreaves and Harold M. Froehl: *The Story of Logging the White Pine in the Saginaw Valley.* Bay City, Mich., 1964.

Harlan Hatcher and Erich A. Walter: *A Pictorial History of the Great Lakes.* New York, 1963.

Karl E. Heden: *Directory of Shipwrecks of the Great Lakes.* Boston, 1966. I found this book most useful, not least for its disclosure that many cargo-carrying schooners of the old days were small enough for one-man or two-man operation.

George W. Hilton: *The Great Lakes Car Ferries.* Berkeley, Calif., 1962.

William D. Hulbert: *White Pine Days on the Taquamenon.* Lansing, Mich., 1949.

Ferris E. Lewis: *Michigan Yesterday and Today.* Hillsdale, Mich., 1956.

Edmund M. Littell: *100 Years in Leelanau.* Leland, Mich., 1965.

Russell McKee: *Great Lakes Country.* New York, 1966.

George S. May: *Pictorial History of Michigan.* 2 vols. Grand Rapids, Mich., 1967.

Rolland H. Maybee: *Michigan's White Pine Era, 1840–1900.* Lansing, Mich., 1960.

The Old Au Sable. Grand Rapids, Mich., 1963.
…monly graceful, well-written book. I relied on it
…1 my discussion of the destruction of the grayling along
…er.

…Ratigan: *Great Lakes Shipwrecks and Survivors*. Grand
…pids, Mich., 1960.

…m Gerald Rector: *Log Transportation in the Lake States
Lumber Industry*. Glendale, Calif., 1953.

…ewis C. Reimann: *Between the Iron and the Pine*. Ann Arbor,
Mich., 1951. *When Pine Was King*. Ann Arbor, Mich., 1952.

Curran N. Russell and Donna Degan Baer: *The Lumberman's Legacy*. Manistee, Mich., 1954.

Catherine L. Stebbins: *Here I Shall Finish My Voyage*. Omena,
Mich., 1960.

William W. Warren: *History of the Ojibway Nation*. Minneapolis,
1957.

Mentor L. Williams, ed.: *Narrative Journal of Travels*, by Henry R.
Schoolcraft. East Lansing, Mich., 1953.